Edward Jewett

The Two-Wine Theory

Edward Jewett

The Two-Wine Theory

ISBN/EAN: 9783337324339

Printed in Europe, USA, Canada, Australia, Japan

Cover: Foto ©Thomas Meinert / pixelio.de

More available books at **www.hansebooks.com**

THE TWO-WINE THEORY

DISCUSSED BY

TWO HUNDRED AND EIGHTY-SIX CLERGYMEN

ON THE BASIS OF

"COMMUNION WINE."

BY

Rev. EDWARD H. JEWETT, S. T. D.

WITH A REVIEW.

———— ♦ ‹ ————

NEW YORK:

E. STEIGER & CO., 25 PARK PLACE.

1888.

CONTENTS.

	PAGE.
Preface,	v. to vii.
Statement and Review of Correspondence,	3 to 8
Review of Opponents' Letters,	9 to 15
LETTER OF DR. H. CROSBY to E. H. JEWETT,	18
CORRESPONDENCE,	19 to 108

CORRESPONDENTS CONTROVERTING THE TWO-WINE THEORY:—

	PAGE
H. C. Potter, Cardinal Gibbons, W. A. Smith,	19
D. K. Kohler,	20
G. H. Smith, L. W. Beattie, Bishop Dwenger, A. Oliver,	21
A. C. Kendrick, A. Ulmann, J. W. Malcolm, J. B. Taylor,	22
James H. Hoadley, Albert Wood, Henry Mottet, J. C. Boyd,	23
Paul Van Dyke, Thos. K. Beecher, Stephen Kealy,	24
D. McLane Reves, Chas H. Smith, L. A. Lambert, J. M. MacKenna, J. W. Shackelford,	25
T. P. Savin, Pascal P. Kidder, Myron Adams, Samuel P. Halsey, S. H. Jagger,	26
W. H. Harrison, I. K. Brownson, Wm. G. N. Lewis, D. M. Fackler,	27
C. W. Camp, A. F. Hewitt, Henry S. Jacobs,	28
Thos. B. McLeod, L. P. Cummings, E. P. Marvin, E. C. Lawrence,	29
F. T. Hoover, W. Ormiston. Elias Child, J. C. Grimmell,	30
Jas. L. Meagher, George Fairlee,	31
S. Burnham, Edwin F. Hard, O. C. Pope, James W. Hillman, J. T. Smith,	32
C. P. A. Burnett, Hermann Raegener, Isaac O. Best, Paul Quattlander,	33
Charles E. Robinson, Robt. B. Clark, James Aug. Healy,	34
George Hardy, R. B. Fairbairn. Fintan Mundwiler, Arthur Sloan, Conrad D'Oench, C. P. Sheldon,	35
Michael Clune, G. P. Gow, N. W. Benedict, W. H. Luckenbach,	36
P. F. K., Conrad Emil Lindberg, A. B. Hart, W. D. Wilson,	37
Herbert G. Lord, L. J. D., Wm. N. Cleveland,	38
Herman C. Riggs, George W. Lay, Warren W. Walsh,	39
James Bassett, C. C. Tiffany, Geo. B. Spalding,	40
C. A. Walworth, Geo. H. Nicholls, F. M. Gray,	41
D. Torrey, C. H. Van Winkle, Chas. Wood,	42
Walter North, J. A. Spencer, Spencer L. Hillier,	43
O. F. Ebert, H. R. Lockwood, Frank Rogers Morse, W. C. Doane, Amos Skeele,	45
E. M. Pecke, C. H. Parkhurst, Signature illegible, Dr. Edward Hipelius, Reese F. Alsop,	46
Clarence Buel, Theo. A. Eaton, Geo. F. Nelson, Anson P. Atterbury, Samuel Miller, Isaac O. Rankin,	47
Anson G. Chester, Theo. B. Roth, E. J. Babcock, F. D. Huntington, Talbot W. Chambers,	48
Adolph Schabehorn, Henry B. Cornwell, L. S. Mitchell,	49
Hamilton B. Holmes, M. Van Rensselaer, Charles E. Lindsley, Reuben W. Howes, Jr.,	50
J. B. Reimensnyder, William J. McCord, Randell C. Hall, Isaac Maguire, D. Parker Morgan,	51
Halsey Moore, D. D., Julius Ehrhart, James Mulchahey, E. H. Cleveland,	52
Lewis H. Morey, Edward B. Brady, James M. Whaton, G. B. Foster,	53
Samuel Dodd, William Waith, Sam'l Buel,	54
James Otis Lincoln, Geo. R. Vandewater. John Anketell, A.M., W. W. Lord,	55
James W. Ashton,	56
J. R. Kendrick, Ira S. Dodd, Charles Seymour, T. S. Drowne, J. E. Johnson,	57
Wm. Allen Fisk, Fred. J. Pohl, Henry M. Sanders,	58

PAGE.

Bishop Schereschewsky, Wayland Spaulding, Wm. D'Orville Doty, W. Stirling, 59
C. Leb. Wisswaesser, Joseph Gamble, W. J. MacDowell, - - - - - 60
Geo. B. Hopson, T. A. Nelson, F. S. Bradner, Sam'l M. Akerly, - - - - 61
Benj. L. Herr, G. V. Leichel, J. Spaulding. - - - - - - - 62
P. F. McSweeny, - - - - - - - - - - - - - 63
A. H. Seeley, W. T. Gibson, - - - - - - - - - - - 64
Henry H. Stebbins, Charles M. Belden, Geo. H. McKnight, H. B. Fry, - - 65
Nathaniel Schmidt, John Tatlock, E. J. Morris, T. R. G. Peck, - - - - 66
E. A. Huntington, R. D. Sinclair, - - - - - - - - - - 67
Charles M. Tyler, J. H. Trussell, Benj. W. Dwight, C. E. Hiscox, - - - 68
J. Nicum, Samuel H. Virgin, G. F. Krotel, T. A. Leggett, - - - - - 69
P. Schmitt, John Minor, A. P. Brush, F. R. Holt, - - - - - - 70
William V. Tunnell, W. C. Smith, H. M. Wyman, I. Elmendorf, E. E. Thomas, - 71
Horace Fraser, Jesse F. Forbet, C. S. Harrower, - - - - - - - 73
A. S. Fish, John Abbot French, Frank Russell, - - - - - - - 74
Geo. H. Goodsell, A. R. Hewitt, J. N. Morris, L. R. Webber, - - - - 75
E. T. Hiscox, Arthur C. Kimber, John W. Kramer, Wm. H. Sybrandt, - - 76
Chas. H. Curtis, I. S. Pettengill, J. Newton Stanger, G. Harwood Pattison, - - 77
James Zilliox, D.D., D. F. Bonner, Summerfield E. Snively, L. R. Webber, - - 78
Fenwick M. Cookson, Issac Brayton, E. C. Hull, Thomas A. Becker, Bishop of
   Savannah, Ga., Charles S. Olinsted, Beverly R. Betts, - - - - - 79
Dr. L. Wintner, L. B. Rogers, D. Murdock, J. F. Elder, - - - - - 80
Wm. S. Hubbell, J. A. Saxton, Arthur H. Allen, - - - - - - - 81
W. C. P. Rhoades, T. J. Conant, John H. Edwards, - - - - - - 82
John T. Wilds, J. Ford Sutton, J. S. Bacon, Benjamin Parsons, - - - 83
Daniel C. Tyler, Russell A. Olin, R. F. McMichael, T. L. Randolph, John C. Ager, 84
Henry Wilson, Joseph R. Kerr, - - - - - - - - - - 85
Jas. H. Kidder, H. H. Allen, J. N. Marvin, Chas. J. Jones, - - - - 86
H. P. S. Bogue, Richard C. Morse, James B. Finch, - - - - - - 87
O. F. Ebert, - - - - - - - - - - - - - 88
James B. Finch, - - - - - - - - - - - - 88–90
W. C. Rabe, C. E. Keller, E. H. Goodwin, F. Granger, Hamilton W. Pierson, - 91
A. P. Bissell, - - - - - - - - - - - - - 92
Geo. C. Yeisley, Theron R. Green, Douglas Putnam Birnie, - - - - 93
W. J. McDowell, - - - - - - - - - - - - 93–95
H. T. Love, - - - - - - - - - - - - - 96
O. F. Ebert, Rollin A. Sawyer, John Williams, - - - - - - - 97
George F. Seymour, Benjamin H. Paddock, E. E. Beardsley, - - - - 98
Extract from the *Pacific Churchman*, - - - - - - 98, 99

CORRESPONDENTS SUSTAINING THE TWO-WINE THEORY:—

P. M. Rightmyer, A. S. Cowles, - - - - - - - - - 100
Thos. A. Sanson, James Stuart Ainslie, J. L. Burrows, - - - - - 101
Henry Ward, S. Nelson, H. H. Shelland, - - - - - - - 102
D. H. Hannaburgh, J. H. Ecob, - - - - - - - - - 103
Geo. H. Horne, George P. Noble, - - - - - - - - - 104
George D. Horton, J. C. Long, - - - - - - - - - 105
H. Pohlmann, Wilbur F. Crafts, Epher Whitaker, - - - - - - 106
C. H. Traver, J. W. Whitfield, C. R. Green, - - - - - - - 107
Geo. H. Horne, J. L. Burrows, LL.D., - - - - - - - 108

Note to Letter No. 4, 1st series, - - - - - - - 109
Appendix A : Declaration of House of Bishops, - - - 111
Appendix B: "Communion Wine," - - - - 113 to 174
Appendix C: Additional letters received after Correspondence had
   been electrotyped, - - - - - - - - - 175, 176

PREFACE.

IF some future Disraeli should undertake to write an account of the literary curiosities which have appeared during the present century, he will find abundance of material for a leading article in what has been written and published in support of the generic or two-wine theory. The literature thus produced is curious—indeed, *unique*—on account of the gigantic assumptions and blunderings, misunderstandings and misinterpretings, sanctimonious misjudgings, and acrimonious accusings of opponents contained in it, as well as for the amount of time wasted, and the sums of money spent in propagating a delusion. It is certain to be known through coming generations as the leading *craze* of the nineteenth century.

When, and by whom, the theory originated, is a matter of some doubt; but its birthplace was in the United States, and the time, about fifty years ago. Attractive as a novelty, and offering, as was supposed, a powerful support to the cause of teetotalism, it called out the interest and vigorous advocacy of many, both learned and unlearned. And, as is usual in such cases, there was a jumping at conclusions, before the matter had been carefully examined on all sides. Ancient literature was ransacked, and everything possible was gathered up that had any apparent bearing on the subject. By zeal outrunning discretion, passages were torn from their connections and pressed into the service, whether they had any legitimate bearing upon it or not—thus setting at defiance, as the result has shown, every principle of literary truth and honesty. For well-nigh half a century, the press has teemed with volumes of pretentious learning, such as " The Temperance Bible Commentary "; Kerr's " Wines: Scriptural and Ecclesiastical "; and Samson's " Divine Law as to Wines "—all published, or republished, by the National Temperance Society, and accompanied by a host of pamphlets, booklets, and leaflets, remarkable only for their parrot-like repetitions of what others had said before them. And the delusion still continues, although greatly checked in important quarters; while the work of disseminating pitiable falsehood goes on, stimulated by ignorance and fanaticism, under the patronage of that society. We have ourselves, within the past three years, bought works over its counters, which, for stupidity, dishonesty, and mendacity, are not only a curiosity, but a disgrace to the intelligence and moral honesty of the present generation.

Time, however, works its revenges. Careful examination by scholars has resulted in revealing the utter baselessness and worthlessness of the arguments and authorities brought forward in support of the generic theory. And this is the case all round the circle. The leading scholars of all denominations unite in rejecting it. In marked instances, quotations from classic authors, which have been held up triumphantly as evidence in its favor, are found, upon honest examination, to give most reliable help in confuting it. This is especially the case with the claim that the Greeks and Romans preserved *must* unfermented for use as a beverage; and, by implication, that the Jews did the same. That they preserved *must* for culinary and medicinal uses, is an undoubted fact. But that it was preserved for use as a beverage is an assumption which is contradicted by other facts. (See App. B, pp. 136, 137, 168.) As additional evidence, we refer to Pliny, lib. xxiii. cap. 18, where he speaks of its use for domestic and medicinal purposes, but makes no allusion whatever to it as a beverage. In fact, he states in the same chapter, that it is useless for the stomach, "*Mustum omne stomacho inutile.*"

Why, moreover, so total a silence as there is, with regard to any such use, in the literature of four thousand years, both sacred and profane, previous to the present century? Supposing *must* to have been thus used, it is utterly inexplicable that no Hebrew prophet, heathen moralist, or Christian father ever alludes to it, or recommends it as a safeguard against intemperance. Men like Clement, Tertullian, Jerome, Chrysostom, when denouncing drunkenness, never advise that if people must drink, to drink the "good man's wine"--the pure, unfermented juice of the grape. To give one instance by way of illustration: The last-mentioned, when dwelling upon the words "use a little wine," 1 Tim. v. 23, writes: "Not only against heretics, but also against the more simple of our brethren (this place is useful), who, when they see some behave improperly through drunkenness, instead of blaming them, revile the fruit given by God, saying, let there be no wine. Let us say to them, let there be no drunkenness; for wine is a work of God, but drunkenness is a work of the devil." Now here, certainly, was a splendid chance to contrast a safe with an unsafe wine. And such instances might easily be multiplied by thousands. If Chrysostom knew of a wine that would not intoxicate, *why does he give no sign of such knowledge?* Instead of that, he points to the abuse of an intoxicating wine, which he says is a "work of God." In a word, the oracles, when consulted, are dumb. This profound and universal silence, taken in connection with the facts already mentioned (App. B, pp. 169–173), has forced the conviction upon reflecting minds, and which is endorsed by common sense, that the whole thing is a delusion.

It is needless, however, to go on "slaying the slain." The theory is DEAD in the estimation of scholars worthy of the name. We have recently had in our hands nearly twenty letters, from Hebrew and Greek scholars and professors in our Eastern universities and theological seminaries—men like Drs. Schaff, Briggs, etc.,—in which they all repudiate it. We do not hesitate to express the conviction that not one first-class Hebrew or Greek professor can be found in the United States who would support it over his own signature.

E. H. J.

STATEMENT AND REVIEW.

IN the early part of the present summer the attention of the Rev. Dr. Crosby was called to the accompanying pamphlet on "Communion Wine," and having examined it, he made arrangements, without any knowledge on the part of the undersigned, to procure an edition of 5,000 copies for distribution. Of this number, 4,200 were sent to clergymen of all denominations within the State of New York, and to all the bishops, and such like dignitaries of the principal denominations in the United States, accompanied with the following circular:

116 East 19th St., New York, May 15, 1888.

REVEREND AND DEAR SIR :—Will you be kind enough to read Dr. Jewett's pamphlet herewith sent, and give (in your local press or by letter to me) your opinion as to its merits on the question of two wines ?

I ask this favor, not for private curiosity, but for the general good.

Yours, with respect,

HOWARD CROSBY.

In reply, two hundred and eighty-six letters have been received. Of these, two hundred and sixty-four are in favor of the views and arguments contained in the pamphlet,* and twenty-two are opposed to them. Besides these, thirty have been received containing statements that the writers had no opinion to express on the subject. Among the first-mentioned, there are quite a number, in which the writers, while fully agreeing with the views and statements presented, yet, for prudential and charitable reasons, deem it to be the best course to abstain from all fermented liquors, both in sacramental usage and as a rule of daily life.

Now, while we do, and must, respect men who conscientiously practice self-denial for another's good, and while we unhesitatingly acknowledge ourselves bound by the same Christian rule, under impelling circumstances—of which our own con-

---

* See Appendix B.

science can be the only judge,—we are not prepared to go to the same length with them. Feeling deeply the evils of drunkenness, and the woes which spring from it, and placing ourselves second to none in earnest desire and endeavor for their removal, we distrust the methods thus resorted to for that end. We claim no infallibility for ourselves, neither are we prepared to concede infallibility to those who differ from us. Let every one, as in God's sight, be fully persuaded in his own mind. And in what we may now say, our prayer is that it may be said for the advancement of truth, and in the spirit of Christian love.

The grounds of difference are both philological and moral.

1. The popular use of the word *temperance*. When used, as it now commonly is, in the sense of *total abstinence*, we regard it as a misnomer, and as a stumbling-block in the way of rightly understanding God's Word. Perversion of terms inevitably leads to perversion in conceptions and ideas of things; while a clear, cleanly cut definition is always a help in the apprehension of truth. The existing perversion of this word, with its accompanying perversion of scriptural idea, furnishes a pertinent illustration of this. As used by the Apostle, the word temperance, ἐγκράτεια, means continence, self-control, restraint in using, or enjoying; and in his statement, 1 Cor. ix. 25, that the athlete who strives for the mastery is "temperate in ALL THINGS," his thought is, that he exercises control over all his appetites and passions. He places himself under discipline, so that neither by overeating nor drinking, or by overindulgence in any pleasure, he should become unable to strive successfully. Temperance was thus understood by Christians in all ages, until modern sophistries darkened reason, and confounded things essentially distinct. A man can put aside ἐγκράτεια, temperance, in eating, in money-getting, in the enjoyment of any carnal pleasure, as well as in drinking. But where there is no use whatever of a lawful thing, there can be no temperance connected with it. The claim is made that the word also implies total abstinence, and we cheerfully grant the claim *when it refers to unlawful things*—not otherwise. In 1 Cor. vii. 9, St. Paul wrote, "If they have not continency, let them marry," where the verbal form, ἐγκρατεύονται, is used in the sense of re-

fraining from unlawful gratification. But he there shows, that what under forbidden relations is unlawful, under permitted ones is the reverse. And here the popular *petitio principii* comes in, viz.: All alcoholic liquors are evil, *per se*, and injurious. *Ergo*, they must be placed in the same category of unlawful things—with fornication, adultery, etc. !

Teetotalism is NOT temperance in its true apostolic sense, although popularly confounded with it, to the injury of truth and public morality. It is a pleasing delusion that it is so, but it is a delusion none the less. And when it prompts to the assumption, as is sometimes the case, that it is the mark of a higher life—that it evinces a more advanced spirituality of Christian conception and endeavor, than is attained by others, we withstand it to the face, as pure pharisaism. Total abstinence may, in certain circumstances, be most commendable self-denial, and an imperative duty; it may be an absolute necessity to moral safety; or it may be unreasoning fanaticism and designing hypocrisy. Whatever it may be, however, it is *never* Christian temperance. And the example set is not that of men who can use the things of this world without abusing them. It would be better to call things by their right names. Conceptions of truth and duty would be clearer, and Christian people would understand what it is they are doing.

The term "unfermented wine" is, in like manner, a perversion of language, and hence a stumbling-block to myriads. Like the popular use of the word temperance, it is a novelty, and carries an absurdity in its face—embodying, as it does, a *contradictio in adjecto.* The ancient writers, as we have shown (App. B, p. 137), discriminated very carefully between *must* and *wine*. In fact, there is no possibility of misunderstanding Pliny's thought, if his words are honestly dealt with. The *semper mustum—always must—*of which he writes, was so called for the simple reason that it was NEVER ANYTHING ELSE BUT MUST. The fermentation whereby *must* becomes *wine* was prevented, and therefore it never became wine. And in perfect accord with him are the other writers who treat upon the subject. Varro, for example, speaks (Lib. I. cap. 65) of *must* being put into the *dolium* (the large vessel in which the fermentation took place), that it might become wine—"*mustum conditur in dolium, ut habemus vinum * * * ut sit vinum factum.*"

We do not deny that unfermented grape juice may, in a loose and popular sense, be called "new wine," as sweet wort may be called "new ale or beer," and freshly pressed apple juice be called "new, or sweet cider." Such use of words is common in all languages. The mind simply goes forward to the perfected article without stopping at any intermediate stage. For example, the housewife speaks of churning her butter, and baking her bread, when in reality she does neither the one nor the other. She churns her *cream* that it may become butter, and bakes her *dough* that it may become bread. So, in like manner, the vintner may speak of pressing out his wine, when in reality he only has the *must* pressed out that it may become wine. And it would be no more silly to maintain that *cream* is actually butter before it is churned, and *dough* bread before it is baked, than it is to insist that *must* is actually wine before it is fermented. It is this proleptic usage which has furnished teetotal authors and orators with the greater part of their citations in proof that one thing is something else, *i. e.*, that *must* is *wine*. If word meanings here also were rigidly observed, there would be a clearing up of conception and understanding with regard to things identical, and things different; while many, doubtless, would refrain from using, as one element of the Sacrament, a substance supposed to be what *in reality it is* NOT.

2. The practice of using a different element from that originally appointed, for the reasons usually assigned, presents a moral aspect for consideration. It furnishes, as viewed from our standpoint, an instance of human self-will setting aside a positive injunction—*Do this*—and comes perilously near the assumption of a wisdom and regard for human weakness and necessity superior to those manifested by our Lord Himself. If the danger is as real as is claimed, was He unaware of it? Is it greater now than during the apostolic age? Let St. Paul's rebuke to the Corinthian Church answer the question. While each age and generation furnishes its own special temptations and dangers, in the main, notwithstanding occasional vacillations and backsettings,

there has been a progress upward in Christian temperance from the beginning. The assumption that all advance in sobriety is due to the influence of total abstinence ideas is false; for there is abundant evidence to show that Gospel leaven was leavening the whole lump, in this respect as in others, long before any teetotal platform had been erected, or any so-called temperance address delivered. Logically, they only who entertain humanitarian views of our Lord, can consistently occupy such ground as this. To suppose that by the use of wine He "set a trap of the devil," to use the shocking language of one of the following adverse writers, carries with it the implication that He did not foresee the danger, or that He was indifferent to it—either of which is an impious reflection upon His boundless wisdom and love.

That in extreme cases there may be danger of arousing a dormant appetite, we may admit; but never when the danger is felt, and the right means are taken to prevent it. In one of the following adverse letters, the writer, after stating that the custom in his congregation is to use unfermented wine, mentions as a fact, that in the Presbyterian congregation, where wine is used, a number of reformed drunkards had relapsed, and that it was a matter of common occurrence. How much of this flows from the working of a disordered imagination, or the prompting of sectarian bitterness, we are not prepared to say. As thus pressed, however, the argument evinces a sad display of Pelagian distrust in the efficacy of Divine grace. When St. Paul felt the pricking of his fleshly thorn, whatever it may have been, and prayed for its removal, his request was not granted. The thorn was there for discipline—for developing and strengthening character. But grace was given to bear its rankling. So may it be with every true follower of our Lord, at all times and under all circumstances. We do not believe that any communicant worthy to go to the Lord's table, no matter what his past life may have been, who is awake to his necessities, and seeks the promised sustaining grace, will fall. To admit the contrary, would involve the further admission, that one of God's weak children had been exposed to a temptation by our merciful and loving Lord, which he was unable to bear—that he who was against him was greater than He who was with him.

We regard the underlying spirit and principle, moreover, as detrimental to robust virtue and godliness. God's moral government (and equally so, membership in Christ's kingdom) calls for the formation of character through the exercise of the reason, conscience, and will; and this can be accomplished only as oppositions and temptations are met, wrestled with, and by grace overcome. The hermit, fleeing as for his life to the concealment and security of a desert cave, is not a high type of man. Virtue which has to be thus padded and protected is but a tender weakling—but a delicate hot-house plant, utterly unable to cope with the frosts and storms of out-door life. Christian athletes, in all ages, have been of a different mind, and of a different practice.

> "They climbed the steep ascent of heaven,
> Through peril, toil, and pain."

Yea, and humbly would we make the accompanying petition our own—

> "O God! to us may grace be given,
> To follow in their train!"

But, if a man is morally and spiritually weak, and despairs of the sufficiency of Divine grace to help him in overcoming temptation, then let him, by all means, flee from it. We have read the Bible wrong, however, all our days, if that is the highest form of Christian character and conduct. To be "in the world," and yet "not of the world"—to be exposed to and pressed upon by its cares, pleasures, and enticements, and yet to "keep the garments always white,"—corresponds, in our judgment, far more accurately with our Lord's ideal of what his followers should be, and do. To flee from temptation may be moral prudence; but to meet it, and by Divine grace to overcome it, is Christian triumph.

REVIEW OF OPPONENTS' LETTERS.

THESE letters, twenty-two in all, are remarkable productions. They are remarkable, not so much for what they contain, as for the utter lack of what, under the circumstances, they might have been expected to contain. In not one of them is there even an attempt at scholarly argument, in refutation of a single fact as stated in the pamphlet. Self-assertion, personality, and, in one or two marked instances, impertinence—one "weeps" freely—there is plenty of, but no seeming desire to weigh evidence, or balance probabilities. One has "glanced through the pamphlet"; another has looked far enough to "get the drift of it"; and a third has "not time nor space to go into its merits or demerits"; while all have evidently approached the subject with hostile feelings, and a determination not to have previously formed notions disturbed. In the main, all agree in a settled, unreasoning opposition, and are totally unapproachable by argument. The position assumed is that of men who say: "We have gone up into the loft and drawn the ladder up after us; the shutters are closed; the door is bolted and barred; there is no opening by which you can possibly come to us." Under such circumstances, argument, reason, truth, are powerless. In fact, it evinces a feminine, rather than a masculine, habit of mind, and reminds us of Lucetta, in Shakspeare's "Two Gentlemen of Verona":—

> "I have no other but a woman's reason ;
> I think him so, *because* I think him so."

In submitting the following comments, we shall confine ourselves to such points as may appear to demand notice. To take up every little objection would be unprofitable and wearisome.

One writer expresses surprise, and inability to tell why the pamphlet was written. For his information, we will say that it was written, in part at least, to counteract, in so far as possible, a modern form of Manicheism, which, under the garb of zeal for God, by its fanaticism, sanctimoniousness, confounding of things which are distinct, is deceiving the unwary and doing incalculable harm. Is the writer not aware how much censoriousness, misjudging of motives, criticising of conduct—even that of our Lord, verging on blasphemy—there has been, both spoken and printed, during the past half-century? Does he not know how virulent and persistent have been the attacks which some have made upon faithful, Christian men, because they have declined to ride the two-wine hobby, and to permit their conceptions of duty and moral conformity to be arranged after their pattern? The rabid spirit manifested by the writer of letter No. 2, in this series, furnishes a pertinent illustration of what is meant. He affirms as his belief, "that it is blasphemous to charge the Lord Jesus Christ with making, recommending to others, and Himself drinking, intoxicating wines or liquors." Now, if this be true, the whole Church of Christ, until the first half of the present century, when the two-wine delusion was invented in behalf of teetotalism, has been guilty of blasphemy; for not one of the writers during that period, who has voiced the general sentiment, has ever imagined that the wine made and drunk by our Lord was not wine in the ordinary sense of the word. Even so now, those of us who believe, and teach, that the miracle performed at Cana of Galilee was not a mere juggler's trick; and that He spake the literal truth when He said that He came eating and drinking the bread and wine from which John the Baptist abstained, are blasphemers! But this is very mild compared with much that might be adduced. The Rev. Dr. Moore, in a note to one of his masterly articles, quotes the following dreadful language from a lecture by Dr. Fowler, published by the National Temperance Society : " Jesus Christ is put on trial as a drinking man; for the alcoholic view of wine makes it necessary to say that Jesus is on the side of wine-drinkers. It puts Him on trial again, not for His life, but for infinitely more than life—for honor and virtue and integrity and character, and for all that is of value in His religion." He quotes also from the same lecture as it appeared in full in the New York *Christian Advocate*, the still more dreadful language, that if Jesus Christ drank alcoholic wine, He must be "put on trial, not as a sot, but as a moderate drinker, who, according to the law of human nature, with so many million illustrations, was possibly saved from becoming an example for sots by being crucified in early manhood." In view of this, we ask of both friends and adversaries, Was there not a cause?

In letter No. 1, the writer compares the " advocates of the one-wine theory" with the "advocates of slavery before the war," and intimates that the one has no more ground of authority in Scripture than the other. We have met with this argument before, and, to say the least of it, it is a fallacy. In order that an argument may be valid in such a case, there must be some ground of analogy between the things compared. But there is nothing of the sort here. Jesus Christ never owned, bought, or sold slaves. Nor did He or His disciples ever speak one word in advocacy of slavery. St. Paul did enjoin upon those who were " under the yoke " to "count their masters worthy of all honor," etc.; not, indeed, as justifying slavery, but as inculcating the necessity on their part for submission to God's providential orderings, and the performance of Christian duty even under adverse circumstances. But Jesus Christ *did drink wine*, according to His own statement. John "came neither eating bread nor drinking wine." He, however, in marked contrast, came " both eating and drinking." If words mean anything, it was in consequence of the *reality* of the fact as thus stated, that a class of men existing in every age, and never more than at the present time, charged Him with being a " wine-bibber." The modern exegesis which destroys this contrast, and empties His words of all sense and application, is too pitiable for any serious notice.

The writer of letter No. 20 states that the Synoptists refer to γέννημα τῆς ἀμπέλου, *i. e.*, "the fruit of the vine," and maintains that by using *must* he is obeying the command of Christ, for he is using "the fruit of the vine." It is remarkable how a fallacy, once fastened in the popular mind, will retain its hold, especially if adopted in support of some favorite theory. The argument has long been used by the advocates of the generic theory. In the " Temperance Bible Commentary," p. 285, Dr. Lees states: " Unfermented wine is, in literal truth and beyond all question,

the only 'fruit of the vine.' That designation it may challenge,
without fear of contradiction." By the same logic we may claim
that unfermented cider is, "in literal truth and beyond all question," the only fruit of the apple-tree. Literally, the only fruit
of the vine is the grape itself, of which wine is a product. Men
do not drink grapes, any more than they drink apples. The fruit
and its product, wine, are not identical. Besides the expressed
juice, there are the stones, skin, and other refuse matter, which
have an equal right to be called "the fruit of the vine." But
these are small things—too small to be noticed by men absorbed
in their fancies.

All scholarly and reliable commentators have regarded the expression γέννημα τῆς ἀμπέλου as a periphrasis for οἶνος, or wine.
Why our Lord used it as He did, we have abundantly shown.
(App. B, p. 163.) That it is a mere inference, as this writer
maintains, that the wine was fermented, IS NOT TRUE. It is as
positive a fact as that the bread was unleavened, or any other
provable fact in the economy of Jewish social and religious life.
(App. B, pp. 157–163.)

Another writer, while admitting that the wine used at the
institution of the Eucharist by Christ was fermented, is unable to
see why it must be used now, any more than unleavened bread,
or, received reclining at the table. This reasoning, we would
say, makes no distinction between accidentals and essentials. In
baptism, water, the natural element of bodily cleansing, and the
emblem of spiritual purification, is essential to the validity of the
sacrament. Whether the water be warm or cold, salt or fresh, is
a matter of indifference. In like manner, bread, the generally
recognized "staff of life," and the emblem of spiritual sustenance,
is an essential. Whether it be leavened or unleavened, made
from wheat or barley, is also a matter of indifference. As in
baptism, moreover, no other element, such as milk, oil, wine, can
be used; so in the Eucharist, neither cheese, meat, nor any other
element, may be substituted for the bread. The same holds true
with regard to the wine. It is essential that it be *wine, i. e.,* the
fermented juice of the grape. That it should be red or white,
sweet or tart, strong or weak, is likewise a matter of indifference.
In saying this, we have, of course, no idea that Divine grace and

blessing are confined to sacramental ordinances, or that the humble, loving, trusting soul will ever famish through defect in sacramental elements. God's power, mercy, and grace infinitely transcend all covenant provisions and privileges, no matter how important and full with blessing they may be to the faithful and obedient. Our contention is with that Manichean spirit, which *locates evil in matter itself*, rather than in the abuse of it—which regards wine that is brought by God, as the psalmist says, out of the earth, to make "glad the heart of man," as "a devil's drink."

The same writer charges upon "the sticklers for fermented wine," that they have some taste or desire to gratify. This is a discourteous fling, unworthy of a Christian gentleman, which we will not designate as it deserves. We recommend, instead, for him "to read, mark, learn, and inwardly digest" St. Matt. vii. 1. This correspondence abundantly shows that some of the most strenuous "sticklers" are total abstainers; but as honest, scholarly men, having the courage of their convictions, they are not afraid to speak the truth, even though it be to their own hinderance.

The writer of letter No. 9 accuses the undersigned of "twisting definitions to his advantage," and states, by way of illustration, "In his definition of Tirosh, he quotes Gesenius as far as will favor his view. He neglects to quote the same author on page 428, Lexicon, where Tirosh is translated *must, new wine*." As we had nothing to gain or lose by making the quotation, having given the final, and manifestly the deliberately-formed opinion of Gesenius, from page 1129 of his Lexicon, we regarded that as sufficient. But, if it will be any satisfaction, we will give it now, and see what will be made of it. Under the root word, ירש, Gesenius gives as the primary definition, "*To take, to seize, to take possession of*," etc. He then states, in opposition to Fürst, on whose authority the two-wine advocates mainly rely, "That this, and not 'to inherit,' is the primary signification is apparent from the derivatives רֶשֶׁת, *net*, and תִּירוֹשׁ, *must, new wine;* as also from the syllable רֵשׁ, which, like רַם, רַץ, has the force of *taking, seizing*."

The writer of No. 9 would have been wiser if he had let this reference alone, as it helps to strengthen the definition as given in the pamphlet. Gesenius has in no way contradicted himself, nor have we misrepresented him in the least. Can *must*, freshly pressed, in any way seize, or get possession of, in the sense intended? With Gesenius, as is evident from the above definition and statement, Tirosh as *must*, or *new wine*, was not the freshly-pressed juice preserved in that condition. In a loose sense it might perhaps be so used; but accurately, in his idea, it had already progressed so far in the process of fermentation as, in accordance with the root definition given on page 428, "to seize," "get possession of," to justify his statement as quoted in the pamphlet (App. B, pp. 120, 127), "Tirosh, so called, because it gets possession of the brain, and inebriates." That *mustum*, like *gleukos*, had this meaning in ecclesiastical usage, we have abundantly shown. (App. B, p. 171.)

In letter No. 10, the writer, after mentioning that one of his elders told him, " I spent the whole communion hour praying for J—— B—— that he might not fall through the wine," he gives expression to the shocking language already referred to, " At last, simply that the Lord's Table might not prove a trap of the devil, we have voted for unfermented wine." Did the writer of this reflect who instituted the Lord's Table and prescribed the materials to be used? Is he aware that the nature of those materials is as certain as any fact narrated in the domestic or public life of our Lord? The proof is too clear and abundant ever to be overthrown, that the wine used at the Passover solemnity was the fermented juice of the grape. And what are his thoughts of Christ? Whose Son is He? To a believer in Christ's divinity, such language verges very closely on blasphemy. Could He whose eye ranges through eternity—He who is not subject to the limitations of time, foreseeing every possible contingency until the last chapter of human history is closed, and whose heart is love —have made such a mistake as to "set a trap of the devil" in the instituting of that solemn feast designed for His own perpetual memorial, and the spiritual upbuilding of His followers? To what greater lengths fanaticism may go, it will be hard to realize.

The writers of letters 11 and 12, as friends of Dr. Samson, see only through his glasses. The former says, "I have read his book, and entirely agree with him, Dr. Jewett to the contrary notwithstanding." To both these writers, in justification of all that we have said about his book, we propose for their candid consideration the following question: Why was Dr. Samson so grievously smitten in the house of his friends? His book was published and extensively circulated by the National Temperance Society, and was highly lauded as a "new and thoroughly scholarly book," etc. (See App. B, p. 117.) Now, however, it cannot be bought over their counters. Why is this? Because the managers of that society have been made sensible—and mainly by those who sympathize with and aid in their work—how utterly untruthful, unreliable, and contemptible it is. It has been *thrown out* from their list of publications! We commend also the following for their consideration. Dr. Lees, an acknowledged leader in the two-wine delusion, wrote some time ago in the Canadian *Critic*, with regard to Dr. Samson's book: "On the appearance of this work, some years ago, I warned the Temperance Society against circulating it, and told the Secretary very plainly that it was a wild and unreliable book." This is decidedly refreshing! We are amusingly reminded of the traditional compliment which the pot paid the tea-kettle. For, certainly, the T. B. C., although more systematic in its arrangement, is no less a "wild and unreliable book." In many instances it is equally "wild" in its exegesis, and no less dishonest in dealing with authorities. In fact, because of its greater show of learning, and plausibility in argument, it is far the more dangerous book of the two.

The writer of letter No. 21 has evidently been handling tools to which he is not accustomed. Of four Greek words used, one is misspelled and all are without their proper accent marks. In a Hebrew sentence of two words, one is incorrect; and in a Syriac sentence of two words, both are incorrect.* Taking this in connection with his ungentlemanly personality, we will say, in his own words, "Comment is unnecessary!"

In letter No. 22, the writer states that he has not received or read the pamphlet, but is "inclined to think Dr. Jewett mistaken." This will do! It is a fitting close to such a weighty body of adverse criticism. We are quite satisfied with the whole, and trust its friends will be.

EDW. H. JEWETT.

---

* Unfortunately, Syriac type could not be obtained.

CORRESPONDENCE.

PAGE.

DR. CROSBY'S LETTER TO DR. JEWETT, ... 18

TWO HUNDRED AND SIXTY-SIX LETTERS AGAINST TWO-WINE
    THEORY, ... 19 to 99

TWENTY-TWO LETTERS IN FAVOR OF TWO-WINE THEORY, . 100 to 108

NOTE ON LETTER NO. 4, FIRST SERIES, ... 109

New York, August 9, 1888.

My Dear Dr. Jewett:—

I have had correspondence with ministers of all denominations in the State of New York and elsewhere, asking their opinion of your pamphlet on the subject of "unfermented wine." The result of that correspondence I herewith transmit to you, and beg you to prepare it for publication.

Your essay is a most convincing argument against this strange and utterly unfounded theory of two wines (one fermented and the other unfermented), and the correspondence shows that the great majority of Christian ministers repudiate the theory.

The publication of the correspondence with your pamphlet will be a good work for truth, and against the perverseness and effrontery of fanaticism.

I need not say that I sent the pamphlet indiscriminately to all the ministers whose names I could find, so that the result fairly shows the proportions of clerical opinion among us.

Yours very truly,

HOWARD CROSBY.

CORRESPONDENCE.

[1]

Diocesan House, 29 Lafayette Place, New York, June 6, 1888.

MY DEAR DOCTOR CROSBY :—Pardon my delay in replying to your inquiry of May 15th. Of late I have been much driven.

Dr. Jewett's pamphlet seems to me entirely conclusive now, as it did when I first read it, some time ago. One of the older authorities on the other side was my grandfather, Dr. Nott, but I was long ago constrained to confess that, in this matter, his scholarship was more ingenious than accurate.

There is a very simple remedy for the difficulty of our radical friends, viz., to follow the very ancient custom of mixing water with the wine. But this new "denial of the Cup to the laity," and also to the clergy, is an impressive illustration of the way in which extremes meet. In Dr. Barton's church in Boston, they place the bread and wine on a table, and, I have been told content themselves with looking at them. Are we coming to this?

I am, dear Dr. Crosby, with affectionate respect, faithfully yours,

H. C. POTTER.

[2]

Cardinal's Residence, 408 N. Charles St., Baltimore, July 5, 1888.

To REV. HOWARD CROSBY, D.D.

MY DEAR SIR :—You desire to elicit from me an expression of my opinion on the merits of the pamphlet on Communion Wine, by Rev. Edward H. Jewett, S.T.D.

I take pleasure in stating that, in my judgment, it is good and sound, fortified in its positions by the Old and New Testament texts, which texts are interpreted according to well-established canons of hermeneutics.

The general tone of the learned writer's disquisition is all that can be desired in treating such a subject. I beg to remain, my dear sir, with much respect,

Faithfully, yours in Christ,   J., CARDINAL GIBBONS.

[3]

Congregational Parsonage, Groton, N. Y., May 22, 1888.

MY DEAR SIR :—I have read Dr. Jewett's pamphlet on "Communion Wine" with intense pleasure.

I did not need to be convinced of the fallacy of the unfermented-wine theory : Dr. F. R. Lees, in a course of lectures given in England some twenty years ago, when he tried by numerous *suppressiones veri et suggestiones falsi* to prove that the wine used by the Corinthian Church was unintoxicating, converted me to the view of the question held by Dr. Jewett.

It is high time that all this jugglery and insane mangling of God's Word, as practiced by unscrupulous and fiery fanatics, should receive a check (for sometimes, on the part of scholars, patience ceases to be a virtue), and this check has been given by Dr. Jewett in a masterly fashion.

The cause of temperance does not need to be bolstered up with falsehoods. Dr. Jewett has made the entire Christian Church his debtor because of his marvelously able and etymological treatment of this important subject.

I remain, with respect and thanks, yours sincerely,

WILLIAM A. SMITH, Congregational Minister, Groton, N. Y.

[4]

115 E. Seventy-first St., New York, May 22, 1888.

HONORED SIR :—I am in possession of your circular letter, as well as of Dr. Jewett's pamphlet on Communion Wine, and beg to state that I read the two articles in question with a good deal of interest, and fully indorse his views and statements regarding the "TWO-WINES" theory, which no Hebrew scholar familiar with Semitic, and particularly Rabbinical lore, can look upon except with an ironical smile. It is so utterly absurd that only men who lack all historical conception of things of the past can earnestly hold the idea that wine (οἶνος, יַיִן), a product, the very (Semitic) name of which indicates its character, "fermentation," should have been unfermented, that is, no wine. I wonder whether any of the Scripture distorters read the story of Noah, or of Lot and Nabal, or the Book of Esther, not to mention the fact, scarcely known to them, that the very intoxicating character lent the wine in the eyes of the primitive Semitic tribes, as it did the Soma or Mead in the eyes of the Aryans, its sacred or DIVINE character.

The lamentable fact is that most of our theologians, particularly in America, are extremely poor linguists, and far less historians and archæologists, or else they would not commit so many blunders. They see the entire past through their grandmothers' spectacles. Dr. Jewett is an honorable exception. His arguments are telling, not merely by the power of their logic, but also by scholarly accuracy and by historical perspective. In making a few comments on some remarks, it is more for the sake of corroborating than correcting his statements.

So p. 6. While יַיִן wine (from which the Greek or Latin οἶνος or *vinum* is derived) means FERMENTATION, and likewise the Syro-Arabic חֲמַר, the word תִּירוֹשׁ used only in POETICAL language for wine, is most probably MUST, or new wine still in the press, the root of the same being (not as Jewett, according to Gesenius, thinks, יָרַשׁ, "taking possession of the brains," but) תָּרַשׁ, of Arabic and Syrian = ταράσσω = excite, agitate, the agitating, foaming, FERVESCENT drink. In this respect, Thayer and Samson are right against Jewett, p. 9.* Nor is the word שְׁמָרִים, p. 7, always used in the plural, anything but the lees, and characteristically used by the prophet (Is. xxv. 6) for the wine.

Now, as to the main question : Is intoxicating or fermented wine displeasing to Jehovah? Why, the very same יַיִן, wine which is used as libation at every sacrifice, is (Lev. x. 9) forbidden to the priests previous to their service, in order that they may be able "to distinguish between what is holy and profane." Consequently, intoxicating wine was in legitimate use on all ordinary occasions.

In regard to the wine used on Passover eve, I wish to add to the almost exhaustive remarks made by Dr. Jewett with reference to Lightfoot, p. 43, that the Talmud Pesachim, p. 108, quotes the traditional law from TOSIFTHA that " no less than four cups of wine should be given to every Israelite that night to drink, no matter whether the wine is OLD or NEW, mixed with WATER, or PURE." Now, is this rule in any way applicable to unfermented wine?

The climax of absurdity, however, is reached by Dr. Lees's statement, that FERMENTED GRAPE-JUICE was included in the interdict of שְׂאֹר and חָמֵץ, "yeast" and "leavened bread" on PASSOVER.

But whether the Temperance literature will, notwithstanding the masterly refutation by Dr. Jewett, to which I know not what to add, still quote Lees as an authority, I know not. Certainly, those who "love the Truth more than they love Plato" will, in the future, resort to better arguments than those drawn from Scripture.   With sincere regards,   Yours,   D. K. KOHLER.

P. S.—It is interesting to compare ch. xiii. 6, of the teaching of the Twelve Apostles : "Likewise, when thou openest a jar of wine or of oil, take the firstling and give it to the prophets." This shows that the wine, laid up in jars, as we to-day would in barrels, was *given to the Apostles or Prophets* to drink at the table, the first outpouring being considered too holy for common use. Now, is it likely that UNFERMENTED WINE was laid up in jars?

* See note at end of correspondence.

. [5]
North Malcolm St. Methodist Episcopal Church, Sing Sing, N. Y.
DOCTOR HOWARD CROSBY.

DEAR BROTHER :—I do not accept the two-wine theory. But would say, in addition, that I believe this question of the use of fermented wine at Communion is deeper than Greek and Hebrew exegesis. It is one of Christian ethics. "IF EATING MEAT CAUSE MY BROTHER TO OFFEND," etc.

With sincere regard, GEO. II. SMITH.

[6]

DEAR BROTHER :—I received your note and Dr. Jewett's pamphlet, and have reviewed it with some care. Its exhaustive research into all known sources of information is highly commendable, and should receive the thanks and endorsement of all ministers of every name. I have long looked for some really reliable treatise on the subject of "The Two Wines"—a theory that in the face of Bible truth is to me most flimsy, and even wicked.

Dr. Jewett has gotten hold of the root of the matter, and I only wish his pamphlet could be placed in the hands, not only of the clergy, but of all intelligent church members, many of whom are being led away from fundamental principles of truth to simply superficial views of *the social, religious, political and domestic* questions of the day.

If there ever was an "epoch of exegesis," I hope Dr. Jewett's pamphlet will prove to be one on the subject treated. Yours fraternally,

L. W. BEATTIE, Pastor Presbyterian Church, Cambridge, N. Y.

[7]
Fort Wayne, Ind., May 22, 1888.
DR. HOWARD CROSBY.

DEAR SIR :—Your kind letter and pamphlet of Mr. Jewett received. You are well aware the Catholic Church has always understood the scriptural term " Wine " as advocated in the pamphlet mentioned.

Yours, most respectfully, JOSEPH DWENGER,
Bishop Fort Wayne.

[8]
No. 405 W. 20th Street, May 28.

REVEREND AND DEAR SIR :—I have carefully read the argument of Dr. Jewett, and it seems to me to be conclusive in every particular. He has exhausted the learning on the subject, and made the very best use of his materials. The important word in the discussion is *Tirosh*, and the view of Gesenius, which Dr. Jewett adopts, is the view of the older lexicographers, Buxtorf and Simon. Buxtorf says, *"Tirosh—mustum, sed dictum quod potum hominem facillime possideat et occupet mentemque o recta sua sede expellat;"* and much to the same purpose Simon, *"Sic dictum quod ce possessorem hominis faciat ejus cerebrum occupando ut ille non amplius sui compos sit."*

I am inclined to think that the wish of Drs. Samson and Thayer is the father to their exegesis.

I am, reverend and dear sir, very respectfully yours,
ANDREW OLIVER.
Rev. HOWARD CROSBY, D.D.

[9]
Rochester, May 24, 1888.

MY DEAR DR. CROSBY :—I have looked with some care over a considerable portion of Mr. Jewett's article, and cannot but regard it as unquestionably sound in its general positions. It seems to me that every renewed examination only makes additionally clear the fact that seems to lie on the face of the

New Testament, that the wine of Scripture is that fermented fruit of the grape which the words *oinos* and wine ordinarily express.

I have never doubted that the wine which our Lord made at Cana was wine of the very best quality.

Very truly yours,   A. C. KENDRICK.

[10]

Yonkers, N. Y., May 28, 1888.

DEAR SIR:—In answer to your circular of May 15th a. c., allow me to state that I read Dr. Jewett's arguments when they first appeared in the *Church Review.* They very strikingly and clearly set forth my own sentiments in the matter, but they bring far more learning and acumen to bear upon the subject than is at my command; therefore I admire Dr. Jewett's effort very much, and gladly subscribe to everything he puts forth. However, in a matter like this I am less influenced by intricate and ponderous arguments, than by some principles of common sense. Few men are more deeply impressed by the crying evil of intemperance and the shocking ravages of "King Alcohol" than I am, but I also know that these conditions have prevailed, more or less destructively, through all ages.

The Apostles, the Fathers and Christian Reformers have all denounced them and worked against them. Intemperance was with all of them as burning a question as it is with us. How is it possible, then, that the Holy Ghost could have failed to reveal this important fact of two wines to the apostles, and have allowed the Corinthians to get drunk at their "Sacred Feast"? How is it possible that this vital fact escaped the knowledge of all the General Councils and such holy and learned men as St. Chrysostom and St. Augustine? Such a thing is unreasonable. If there is any chance of erring, I rather err with the Apostles, Fathers, Saints, and, in fact, with all united Christendom, than with a parcel of men whom we know to be very small in learning and true spirituality, but very large in self-conceit, vivid imagination and fanaticism, and withal unscrupulous in the use of their means to reach a certain, frequently selfish, end.

Respectfully yours,   AUG. ULMANN, Rector Christ Church.

[11]

I have read Dr. Jewett's pamphlet, and must say that, historically, philologically and logically, as well as in its spirit of candor, it fully satisfies me. Long since, when reading upon the subject, out of mere curiosity and without any desire in any way to build up a theory, I was impressed with the idea which Dr. Jewett places beyond question.

Very truly yours, for the Truth,

J. W. MALCOLM, Pastor Park Cong. Church, Brooklyn, N. Y.

[12]

Piermont, Rockland Co., N. Y., May 23, 1888.

ELDER HOWARD CROSBY.

DEAR SIR:—Yours addressed to me in Brooklyn reached me here 21st inst., without Mr. Jewett's pamphlet.

I regard the two-wine theory as without the support of the Holy Scriptures, and as an effort of extremists, who retard truth when they would advance its claims.

Yours, with respect,   J. B. TAYLOR.

[13]

Faith Presbyterian Church, New York, May 24, 1888.

DEAR DR. CROSBY:—I desire to thank you for the valuable pamphlet of Dr. Jewett's on the Wine Question, which you were kind enough to send me.

I have read it with great interest, and am more strongly confirmed in the opinion that he is right in all his conclusions, viz., that the wine of the Bible, both in the Old and in the New Testaments, was fermented, and hence intoxicating.

I wish the pamphlet could have a wide circulation.

Very sincerely yours,   JAMES H. HOADLEY.

[14]

31 Linden St., Rochester, N. Y., May 22, 1888.

REVEREND AND DEAR SIR:—Please accept my thanks for Dr. Jewett's pamphlet which you have sent me. I have read it with lively interest, and deem it a thoroughly fair and satisfactory answer to the advocates of the two-wine theory. I never believed in that theory, not being able to find any evidence for it in the Bible. And it is a great satisfaction to have the true and common-sense view so strongly supported and enforced as it is in these able articles.

Dr. Jewett has shown himself quite competent to discuss this question, and has employed his scholarship to good purpose.

Yours very truly,   ALBERT WOOD.

[15]

The Rectory, Church of the Holy Communion, No. 47 W. 20th St.,
New York, May 26, 1888.

DEAR DR. CROSBY.—I have read very carefully the two papers on Communion Wine, by the Rev. Dr. Edward H. Jewett.

If I had ever entertained a doubt concerning the use of fermented wine in the Communion, I am sure his presentation of facts, based upon the most erudite learning, would have convinced me of the correctness of his position.

Permit me to thank you very sincerely for the service you have rendered in the issue of those articles in pamphlet form.

Faithfully yours,   HENRY MOTTET.

[16]

Fonda, N. Y., May 22, 1888.

DR. HOWARD CROSBY.

DEAR SIR:—Accept my thanks for Dr. Jewett's pamphlet. The argument seems to be unanswerable, and the circulation of such a work appears to be timely.

I have always entertained the views expressed in this work, and in my ministerial experience have known a mild form of persecution, because I have uniformly refused to sign the temperance pledge, and to urge any upon others, except the divine one to lead a "sober, righteous, and godly life."

Yours,   J. C. BOYD.

[17]

Geneva, N. Y., May 21, 1888.

MY DEAR SIR:—I am in receipt of Dr. Jewett's pamphlet kindly forwarded by you. I do not consider myself competent to express any criticism upon it. I may venture, however, to make two observations. 1. That it is too scholarly for those to whom it is addressed. 2. That in my humble judgment—and on the principle of Cicero, that the first duty of an advocate is to conciliate his audience—certain passages in regard to opponents (though I have reason to believe them just and true) are calculated to deepen the prejudice and animosity which have grown around this question.

As to the rest, if any scholarly man, whose instincts and judgment are not blinded by preconceptions, needs to be convinced, this pamphlet seems to me excellently adapted to accomplish that desirable end.

If you desire my opinion on the merits of the question it discusses, I can only say, that, in my judgment, the two-wine theory is only one of many fatal examples of the evil influence of that biblical exegesis which lays the Scripture on the Procrustean bed of prejudice or dogma in the attempt, not to find out what it really does teach, but to make it teach what it ought.

Any careful reader of the Bible, with the literary sense well developed, ought to detect the falsity of this theory with the help of Young's Concordance, and it gives me a sensation of sadness that a man like Dr. Jewett should be compelled to waste so much valuable labor in combating a theory whose inconsistency ought to be apparent to all.

I am, my dear sir, yours truly,   PAUL VAN DYKE.

[18]

Elmira, N. Y., May 20, 1888.

MY DEAR DOCTOR :—Jewett's paper on Wine affects me as my brother Edward's on Baptism did. I marvel at the learning and industry squandered on a subject that for me can have but one side, and that, moreover, of no importance or interest.

Of course (*meo judice*) immersion was apostolic baptism, and wine was wine. But at what time the sacrament of baptism is desecrated by a jangle of tongues as to how to apply water, or the communion of the Lord's body and blood sets participants on smelling for alcohol—that moment the sacraments are gone more fatally than any blunder could accomplish.

I WON'T dote on words, nor preach for doctrine any truth that stands or falls by help of grammars and lexicons.

Therefore I do nothing on either side of the controversy. Clearly persuaded in my own mind, I easily allow all others to be clearly persuaded.

If they get to remission of sins by a plunge, and to the body of Christ by raisin water, I am glad of it.

Doubting that this reply to a printed circular will ever reach your eye or get beyond your tabulating clerk, I none the less add the expression of my heartiest fellowship with you in your conclusions and courageous testimonies at sundry times and on divers questions—heartier than you can have known or had reason to suspect.   I am, dear doctor, repectfully yours,

THOS. K. BEECHER

[19]

St. Mary's Retreat, Dunkirk, N. Y., May 21, 1888.

DEAR SIR:—In my opinion, Dr. Jewett has the right view on wine. He is lucid in his explanations of Scripture.

Yours respectfully,   STEPHEN KEALY.

[20]

Johnstown, N. Y., May 26, 1888.

REVEREND AND DEAR SIR:—Dr. Jewett's pamphlet is unanswerable, and would utterly demolish the two-wine theory were that theory amenable to argument. I only regret to see so much learning and research wasted on a theory that never had any standing among competent men. It was born, not of exegesis, but the exigencies of a fallacious position. It was a foregone conclusion before the first pseudo-scholar patched up an argument in its favor. It will survive all scholarly missiles, I fear.

Here is the real argument behind the two-wine theory :—

1st. It is a sin to drink any alcoholic beverage (save as a medicine, some would add).

2d. Christ made wine of water at Cana; he was also in the habit of drinking wine as a beverage. He came eating and DRINKING.

3d. As Christ was free from sin, he could not have made or drank an alcoholic beverage. What he made and drank must have been a different wine than that which biteth as a serpent.

Now, the first proposition is, with many, an axiom and not open to argument. Inexorable logic forces such to the two-wine theory, and I have little hope from Jewett's argument, which has been filed in my library since its publication originally.

D. McLANE REVES, Pastor Presbyterian Church.

[21]

208 Eagle St., Buffalo, May 23, 1888.

DEAR SIR:—In compliance with your request, let me say that Dr. Jewett, in his pamphlet on "Communion Wine," seems to have entered into his subject very carefully, and the results which he reaches appear to be wholly conclusive. I can not see how any unprejudiced person can differ with him, or how any prejudiced person, who is willing to be ruled by reason, can cling to his prejudice any longer after reading this work.

I thank you for sending me the work.

I am, yours very truly,   CHAS. H. SMITH.

[22]

Waterloo, N. Y., May 21, 1888.

DEAR SIR :—I have read Dr. Jewett's pamphlet, and consider it a learned and masterly argument against the Prohibition fanatics.

Yours,   L. A. LAMBERT.

[23]

Flushing, L. I., N. Y., May 25, 1888.

RESPECTED SIR :—The unsettled "question," so well and truly argued by Dr. Jewett, is not at all unsettled for Catholics, as the Doctor very well shows.

If ever there were a "question" about it in the Catholic Church, it was, as far as I know, but a CURIOUS question.

If there be such a thing as unfermented wine, we do not know it at all for church purposes.

Thankfully yours,   J. M. MacKENNA.

[24]

Church of the Redeemer, 117 E. 82d St., New York, May 24, 1888.

REVEREND AND DEAR SIR :—The pamphlet of Dr. Jewett on "Communion Wine" seems to me entirely conclusive, and, in my judgment, should settle this much-discussed question for all unprejudiced persons.

Sincerely yours,   J. W. SHACKELFORD.

[25]

First Presbyterian Church, 120 First St., Troy, N.Y., May 21, 1888.

DEAR BROTHER :—I have read Dr. Jewett's pamphlet, and express my hearty concurrence with its conclusions. I have never been able to understand the exegesis that brought out the "two-wine" theory; but if there is any value in it, why may it not be used to discover "Price's" or "Royal" baking powder? If this could only be done, what a help it would be in the interpretation of the parable of the woman and the leaven !

Our Lord certainly MUST have used some kind of baking powder—for he NEVER COULD have countenanced the eating of FERMENTED bread. Or shall we say that he was a total abstainer from fermented bread one day in the year, but that all the rest of the year he took his bread and wine in a wholesome condition ?

Isn't it worth while, in order to redeem our Lord's character from any possible suspicion, to set some of those wonderful exegetes—like Dr. Samson and the editor of the *Voice*—to work and see if they can't find a "two-leaven" theory?

Fraternally and respectfully yours,   T. P. SAVIN.

[26]

Dunkirk, N. Y., May 22, 1888.

DEAR SIR :—I have read carefully Dr. Jewett's Pamphlet on Communion Wine.

It is certainly very able, and, I think, exhaustive and conclusive. He well maintains the view which I have held for almost fifty years, that the wine commended in Holy Scripture was undoubtedly fermented wine, and, if taken in excess, intoxicating.

Yours sincerely,   PASCAL P. KIDDER.

[27]

Rochester, N. Y., May 25, 1888.

DEAR SIR :—Accept my thanks for the pamphlet of Dr. Jewett on Communion Wine. Inasmuch as it accords with views I have held and expressed for a number of years, it could not fail to meet my hearty approval. I am glad the work has been done so thoroughly. Whether the same thing will have to be done over and over again, before the two-wine theory people are ready to adopt reasonable and scriptural methods of temperance work, is the melancholy question I am forced to ask.

Very respectfully yours,   MYRON ADAMS.

[28]

56 Quincy Street, Brooklyn, May 21, 1888.

MY DEAR DR. CROSBY :—Thanks for the very able and scholarly article of the Rev. Mr. Jewett. I received it this morning, and have just finished reading it, and I imagine it will make the temperance cranks in Reade Street squirm.

It is the best and most exhaustive treatment of the wine question I have seen, and I have seen several on the other side, but none that have convinced me that our Lord proved himself a trickster at the marriage in Cana, or that such noble and devoted men as Drs. Van Dyke, Smith, Thompson, Calhoun, Jessup, etc., were men addicted to making statements they knew to be false. The common-sense view set forth by Mr. Jewett, that grape juice, to be wine, must be fermented, is a view of the subject that leaves the defenders of fresh grape juice with a stock in trade that they had better hasten to christen, unless they desire it to be placed in the category with Barnum's What Is It ?

I think Dr. Cuyler might study the pamphlet with profit ; and many others, who have been giving their OPINIONS as LAW to the CHURCH and the WORLD, might find it very helpful in aiding them to find the rock-bed of truth, which will prove a far better foundation than the sand on which they are now building, and which Mr. Jewett (as a first-class tempest) has so thoroughly removed.

Again I thank you for the pamphlet. Yours for the truth,

SAM'L P. HALSEY.

[29]

Newburg, N. Y., May 21, 1888.

DEAR SIR :—I have read Dr. Jewett's Essay on Communion Wine, containing a critical examination of the Scripture words on the subject, together with historic testimony ; and it seems to me so ably to defend my own life-long views, based on reading the entire Scriptures in their original languages, that nothing more need be said to forever put to rest the opposite theory.

Yours respectfully,   S. H. JAGGER.

[30]
St. Luke's Church, Catskill, N. Y., May 28, 1888.
DEAR SIR:—I have carefully examined Dr. Jewett's pamphlet, reprinted from the *Church Review.* With very inferior scholarship, I had some years ago arrived at the same conclusions.
Dr. Jewett's very able examination of the question confirms me in the opinion I had formed.
Very respectfully, W. H. HARRISON.

[31]
Fayetteville, N. Y., May 10, 1888.
REV. DR. CROSBY.
DEAR SIR:—I have carefully read the admirable essays of the Rev. Dr. Jewett, on "Communion Wine," in the pamphlet you kindly sent me.
I regard his arguments as exceedingly able, and, indeed, conclusive on this subject. They serve only to confirm the opinions I have long held, and are strongly corroborated by those honored Syrian missionaries whose witness he quotes (page 28). Further controversy on this subject by extremists is to be deprecated.
Most respectfully and truly yours, I. K. BROWNSON.

[32]
Mechanicville, N. Y., May 24, 1888.
REVEREND AND DEAR SIR:—Your circular note reached me here (directed to Malone, N. Y.). I may say in reply that I read the articles referred to in the *Church Quarterly,* when published, and that I have held the same general opinion for the last forty years in regard to the subject as expressed by the learned writer. All my life an advocate and practicer of total abstinence, I can only wonder at the lengths of obstinacy and intolerance and (perhaps not willful) misrepresentation men will reach while riding a hobby. The whole subject is to me a test, not merely of scholarship, but of charity and common sense. I regard the position of the advocates of unfermented wine as utterly untenable. Yours respectfully,
WM. G. N. LEWIS, Rector St. Luke's Church.

[33]
New York, May 22, 1888.
REVEREND AND DEAR SIR:—You ask my opinion of the merits of Dr. Jewett's pamphlet on the question of two wines; that is, as I understand the matter, whether the Jews and the early Christians used the juice of the grape in two conditions, the one fermented and the other unfermented.
I think the pamphlet is of the highest merit, not only as showing conclusively that only the fermented juice of the grape was regarded and used as WINE, but as showing, also, a most commendable spirit of fairness and courtesy towards those whose arguments are controverted.
Respectfully, D. M. FACKLER, 137 West 63d Street.

[34]
Grace Church Rectory, Lockport, N. Y., May 22, 1888.
MY DEAR DR. CROSBY:—In reply to your circular letter dated May 15, anent the pamphlet by Dr. Jewett, I must answer that I am not accustomed to printing my opinion upon subjects of current interest in the local press, and it would seem uncalled for, perhaps, to many people should I change my habit in a single respect. I willingly write to you, however, to say that I think Dr. Jewett is unanswerable. His learning is not second-hand, his style is clear, and his arguments are convincing. Still, I am aware that I have not come to the reading of his essay without prejudice. Some ten or twelve years ago, I

carefully went over the whole of the Holy Bible to form my own opinion on the two-wine theory. I still have the lists of the texts in both Hebrew and Greek which refer to wine, but the result of my inquiry, which I cast in the shape of an essay, I have mislaid or loaned. I read it before the Ministerial Association of the City of Kingston, N. Y., where I resided at the time, and, as I remember, it was well received. Still, the advocates of the two-wine theory were not convinced in their hearts, I fear, doubtless owing to my unskillfulness in argumentation. Since that time I have not hesitated to deny the two-wine theory on all occasions.

I would like to have Dr. Funk read the pamphlet, and review it in the *Voice.* Sometimes I think he is inclined to be quite fair, and again, on the contrary, quite the reverse.

Wishing you every success in your undertaking, I am your brother in Christ,

C. W. CAMP, Rector Grace Church.

[35]

House of the Paulist Fathers, 415 W. 59th St., New York, May 21, 1888.
REV. DR. CROSBY.

DEAR SIR :—I acknowledge the receipt of your circular letter, with Dr. Jewett's pamphlet. In reply to your request that I should give you my opinion as to the merits on the question of two wines, I have the honor of saying, after having read it, that I regard it as able and conclusive.

Yours respectfully,   A. F. HEWITT.

[36]

144 E. 65th St., New York, May 23, 1888.

REVEREND AND DEAR SIR :—Both your circular letter and Dr. Jewett's pamphlet were received at the close of last week ; but owing to a pressure of duties, I have not, till to-day, found opportunity to reply to your interrogatory.

Dr. Jewett's opinion as to the meaning of יין used in the Sacred Scriptures, as describing the fermented and intoxicating juice of the grape, is perfectly correct and impregnably true. Any attempt, by uncritical assumptions, to give the word a contrary meaning is absurd, and is the product of a jugglery which would play havoc with the authority of God's Word, if carried out in other cases to the same end—of making the Bible prove what we want to have proven. Such logic (?) would be ruinous and destructive, and would strike a cruel blow at the sanctity and reliability of that which is promised "to stand forever."

That יין means "wine," in our accepted sense, cannot be denied by any sane man possessed of the slightest knowledge of Hebrew. Its intoxicating qualities are shown (Gen. ix. 21), "And he drank from היין and got drunk." The priest is forbidden (Lev. x. 9) to drink יין and strong drink when he goeth to the tabernacle, etc. The Nazarite is commanded to separate himself from "יין and strong drink." But I shall not weary you with further quotations, which are available to you. Could 1 Sam. i. 14 have been overlooked? Is this not also direct and palpable proof?

In the usages of the Hebrew ritual, יין, "wine," in the popular and reserved sense, has a definite meaning as such, both historically and traditionally. It is simply absurd to give it any other than that of being the fermented product of the grape, or to ascribe to it two definitions. As well might it be said that מים means "water" in one passage and "milk" in another. The temperance people injure a good cause by seeking to prove too much. All rational men must take the Scriptural view, that it is in the abuse and not the use of God's gifts that the danger and sin lie.

In conclusion, then, let me say that I fully and unqualifiedly support the statement of Dr Jewett (page 7), that "it is evident that the word WINE, as usually understood by the Jews, referred primarily and etymologically to a fermented liquor."   Yours respectfully,   HENRY S. JACOBS,
Minister of the Madison Ave. Synagogue.

[37]

256 Clinton Ave., Brooklyn, May 25, 1888.

MY DEAR DR. CROSBY:—Thanks for the copy of Dr. Jewett's pamphlet on the Wine Question. I am grateful, as every man who loves truth more than hobby must be, to the author. His exegesis is both scholarly and candid—his logic irresistible. I cannot see how any unprejudiced mind can follow him and remain unconvinced. It is refreshing to examine so honest a bit of work. As it proceeds, one is struck with the contrast between the method of explaining, and that of explaining away, the truth.

I regard Dr. Jewett's paper a most valuable contribution to the cause of truth and temperance.

Yours sincerely, THOS. B. McLEOD.

[38]

1389 Washington Ave., N. Y., May 21, 1888.

MY DEAR DR. CROSBY:—Yours of the 15th inst. came with Dr. Jewett's pamphlet on "Communion Wine," an unanswerable refutation of that theory, which some temperance people hold, that the wine of the Bible was of two kinds—fermented and unfermented; the former an evil, the latter only a good. And I cannot see how any sane man can come to other conclusions than Dr. Jewett's own, after reading his argument.

I have always regarded the theory which Dr. Jewett so ably *refutes* as an unwarrantable assumption on the part of those who maintain it ; worse than this, a "handling of the Word of God deceitfully"—a perversion of the truth.

Some of the good temperance people are honestly ignorant of what the Scriptures teach, and may be excused for their fanaticism on the temperance question. But those who pretend to be TEACHERS of God's Word are not to be excused for such perversion of Holy Writ to maintain a cause, however good and dear to them ; and they must be indeed blind not to see that such a course is to defeat the very end for which they strive. I have no patience with those who suppose they can advance truth through deception or trickery.

We are but of one mind in my own congregation. We have those in the congregation who never taste wine except at the Communion table, but I do not know of a single individual among them who abstains from wine, EVEN AS A BEVERAGE, on the ground of its use being anti-scriptural. The subject has been thoroughly discussed from my pulpit, both from a moral and scriptural view; and we are all convinced that the wine of the Scriptures means WINE; that the Lord Jesus made it and drank it ; and that we cannot improve upon his preaching or his practice. Thanking you for the pamphlet,

I am, fraternally yours, L. P. CUMMINGS.

[39]

Lockport, N. Y., May 22, 1888.

DEAR BROTHER:—Thanks for Mr. Jewett's treatise on Communion Wine. It is exhaustive and unanswerable.

I am sorry that good people should try to serve a good cause by bad arguments. Such results must always be evil.

I have letters from four distinguished Jewish rabbies in accord with Mr. Jewett's account of Passover Wine.

E. P. MARVIN.

[40]

Vernon, N. Y., May 22, 1888.

DEAR SIR :—I thank you heartily for the pleasure and privilege I have had in reading Dr. Jewett's pamphlet on "Communion Wine." His argument is the most thorough and convincing proof that I have seen against the theory of two wines. He leaves no room to doubt. I shall henceforth have a surer ground for a dislike of "unfermented wine," regarding it in the same light as "dry water" and "unelectric lightning."

Gratefully yours, E. C. LAWRENCE.

[41]

West Sand Lake, N. Y., May 23, 1888.

HOWARD CROSBY, D.D., New York City.

DEAR SIR AND BROTHER:—Your letter of the 15th inst., and Dr. Jewett's pamphlet on "Communion Wine," have both been received.

I wish to say that I have read Jewett's articles, and regard them as masterly and unanswerable on the subject of which they treat. Undoubtedly the Scriptures speak of but one kind of wine, in the proper sense of that word—fermented, intoxicating wine. I pity those who, in the Lord's Supper, must resort to RAISIN JUICE, MUST, and even WATER; they are benighted, and I question their guiltlessness just a little.

I am a temperance man through and through, but I am not a fanatic. I have no sympathy with the raisin-juice idea in the Communion, even though some weak Lutherans sometimes use such juice on sacramental occasions. I fear, and I say it in all charity, in such cases faith is often as weak as the juice. WINE ought to be used, not slop!

I thank you very much for the pamphlet of Dr. J.

Very truly and sincerely yours,   F. T. HOOVER.

[42]

180 West End Ave., May 21, 1888.

MY DEAR BROTHER:—I have read very carefully Dr. Jewett's pamphlet on COMMUNION WINE, and I have been both interested and instructed by it. I thank you for sending me a copy.

It is one of the most severe, searching and scathing criticisms I have ever read; at the same time it is just, candid and discriminating.

I most heartily concur in the conclusions of the writer, which are well sustained by varied, cumulative, conclusive, and irrefragable testimony. It is a most valuable contribution to the recent vexed controversy on the question.

Yours faithfully,   W. ORMISTON.

[43]

94 Charlotte Street, Utica, May 25, 1888.

DEAR SIR:—I have carefully read Dr. Jewett's pamphlet on the Wine Question with much satisfaction. While I had not critically examined the points he discusses, his conclusions but confirm my own long-established opinions with reference to the subject. In the mind of the common reader of the Bible, I do not think a doubt is raised as to the use of fermented wine, where its use is spoken of. The teachings seem explicit. The use is sanctioned—the abuse is condemned. That the evil from the abuse will ever be overcome, may be, when human nature undergoes as thorough a regeneration as a well-meaning but somewhat zealous Methodist preacher once told his audience they must be the subjects of, in order to enter heaven: "You must be PHYSICALLY, CHEMICALLY and SPIRITUALLY regenerated."

For example's sake, abstinence from intoxicants as a common beverage is a safe concession to the Temperance Reform.

Fraternally yours,   ELIAS CHILD, Pres. Clergyman.

[44]

Brooklyn, N. Y., May 26, 1888.

DEAR SIR:—I thank you for favor of 15th inst., and also for pamphlet. I have merely had time to run over the arguments in a general way. Dr. Jewett's position is the only correct one upon the question of the two wines. I fully agree with him: all the more as it has been my conviction all along, though of course not so clearly defined as this incomparable treatise on the subject puts it. The whole truth, or no cause! The holy cause of temperance must never be degraded to sanctify unsound means for its worthy end. It is not necessary nor wise. Yours truly,   J. C. GRIMMELL,

General Secretary General Missionary Society of German Baptist Churches.

[45]

Cazenovia, N. Y., May 26, 1888.

REVEREND AND DEAR SIR:—Rev. E. II. Jewett, in the treatise before me, gives an exhaustive and learned discussion on the subject of the wines of the Bible. His command of the languages is quite extensive and reminds me of the great Catholic theologians, such as Saints Augustine, Thomas of Aquinas, with Suarez Bellarmino De Liguori, &c., &c., when treating of Church subjects. Like them, he leaves nothing more to be said, as far as he goes.

It is much to be regretted that all Protestant writers do not go as exhaustively into biblical subjects, and give also, like him, the historical and traditional, as well as the Judaical testimonies of religious subjects. This is the way with the Catholic writers, from whom Roman Catholic clergymen draw their information. They simply give the biblical, traditional and historical testimonies of dogmas.

I would beg to suggest that the traditions of the Catholic Church be searched, in order to strengthen the proofs already given by him in this pamphlet. In that case it would be found that there is and always has been but ONE kind of wine, and that is the fermented juice of the grape. Before fermentation it was never considered as wine, and would NOT be considered as the right material for Mass. This the whole voice of the traditions of the Church proclaims.

In the early ages the Church easily solved this difficulty by denying the chalice to the laity, as they began to abuse it. So that the discussions relating to FERMENTED or UNFERMENTED wine never disturbs us, but is entirely confined to Protestant Churches.

A long and interesting article could be written on the practices, customs and traditions of the Catholic Church on this subject, and would be a valuable addition to the learned work before me.

Please excuse this hurried note, just penned while people are waiting for me to attend them at church services.

Sincerely yours, JAS. L. MEAGHER, Pastor St. James.

P. S.—Coming from the church, it strikes me that an investigation of the Catholic, Greek, Coptic, Nestorian, Syrian, Maronite, etc., Churches, with the study of the early Christian Fathers, the Councils, Synods of the East and of the West, the customs of the first Christians as found in histories of the different nations, soon after Christ, would throw great light on this subject. It is all nonsense to think that Christ and the Apostles used any but FERMENTED WINE.

Nor can any one say that they fostered drunkenness. The reason that all Catholics, EXCEPT THE DYING, are allowed to receive Communion when fasting, is because they used in apostolic times to come to receive the Sacrament when drunk with wine, and the wine used at Mass increased that drunkenness. Therefore two regulations were made: first, that all must be fasting from midnight; second, that no one but the clergyman celebrating could partake of the chalice. This is our discipline at the present day, and has been for centuries.

All these and numerous other customs show that only FERMENTED wine was used in the Catholic Church since the apostolic times.

Alas for the weakness of poor human nature! Men exaggerate and ride hobbies, and one of these is the use of unfermented wine in church services.

Sincerely yours, JAS. L. MEAGHER.

[46]

Troy, N. Y., May 21, 1888.

DEAR DR. CROSBY:—It would be quite unpardonable did I not recognize your kindness in sending the article on Communion Wine. Thank you for calling my attention to it.

I have read it with much pleasure, and find that it expresses precisely my own views on the two-wine question.

Yours truly; GEORGE FAIRLEE.

[47]

Hamilton Theological Seminary, Hamilton, N. Y., May 19, 1888.

MY DEAR SIR :—I desire to express to you my thanks for a copy of Dr. Jewett's pamphlet, received yesterday. I think it is an able and satisfactory discussion of the subject treated. This view is the one to which my own studies have forced me—that there is not, in the Old Testament, the slightest evidence in favor of the two-wine theory. I speak only of the Old Testament, because that is now my special study. I am sure, however, that the same can be truly said of the New Testament. I am myself a life-long advocate and practicer of total abstinence, an uncompromising foe to the liquor business in all its forms, and believe the saloon to be the deadliest foe to American civilization. But I do not believe in lying to make a good cause succeed.

Very truly yours,   S. BURNHAM,
Prof. of Hebrew and Old Testament Exegesis.

[48]

HOWARD CROSBY, D. D.   Lima, N. Y., May 21, 1888.

DEAR BROTHER :—I most heartily agree with the conclusions of Dr. Jewett in his article, "Communion Wine," a copy of which your kindness has placed in my hands. Only fanatical blindness can assert a two-wine theory, in the face of such research as has been given by the scholarship of a Jewett and a Hovey. YOU ARE IN THE RIGHT, and may God bless you in your work of accomplishing *something of material and practical benefit* in the cause of Gospel Temperance.

Yours fraternally,   EDWIN F. HARD, Pastor Baptist Church.

[49]

American Baptist Home Mission Society,
Temple Court, Beekman St., New York, May 23, 1888.

DEAR SIR AND BROTHER :—Yours, with the pamphlet of Dr. Jewett, to hand. I am decidedly a Prohibitionist and a third-party man, willing to see intoxicating liquors banished from the land, and yet I am frank to say that I have not seen anything on the "two-wine theory" to convince me that the wine so often spoken of in the Bible wa_ *not* intoxicating if taken in sufficient quantities. Dr. Jewett has the better of the argument. I do not think anything is gained for temperance or total abstinence by strained constructions of plain language.

Respectfully,   O. C. POPE.

[50]

Cape Vincent, N. Y., May 23, 1888.

DEAR BROTHER:—I received and have read the pamphlet by Dr. Jewett.

I have believed for a long time that the two-wine theory could only be maintained by torturing the Scriptures from their true meaning.

I agree fully with Dr. Jewett, and think he has made an unanswerable argument against this misleading theory.

Yours sincerely,   JAMES W. HILLMAN.

[51]

Rouse's Point, N. Y., May 24, 1888.

DEAR SIR :—I have read the pamphlet of Rev. Mr. Jewett, and I think it both timely and conclusive.

For Catholics this question has never been of any moment, as our church practice never thought of any other wine than the fermented.

But I am glad to see the truth so well vindicated against the dangerously foolish assumptions of scriptural prohibitionists.

Sincerely yours,   J. T. SMITH, Pastor St. Patrick's.

[52]

Gloversville, N. Y., May 29, 1888.

Reverend and Dear Sir :—I beg you to accept my sincere thanks for the copy of Dr. Jewett's Review article on the subject of Communion Wine, which you kindly sent me.

I have hardly time to write a formal OPINION, and therefore briefly declare to you my full and hearty agreement with the conclusions of Dr. Jewett.

That the Church has always used wine (i. e., the fermented juice of the grape) as an essential element in the Holy Communion, is to me an all-sufficient reason against substituting anything else. I have not the slightest doubt but that Our Blessed Lord used in the Institution a strong fermented juice of the grape, which (after Jewish custom) he slightly diluted with water.

His use of wine for the Holy Communion was like his bidding to use water in Baptism.

Baptism is not valid in any element other than water; so, also, the Holy Communion is not consecrated without WINE. Very truly yours,

C. P. A. BURNETT, Rector of Christ Church.

[53]

911 President Street, Brooklyn, May 22, 1888.

Dear Sir :—Your book of "Communion Wine" I received a few days ago. Please accept my thanks. I thoroughly agree with the Rev. E. H. Jewett.

Yours truly, HERMANN RAEGENER (P. Emeritus).

[54]

Clinton Grammar School, Clinton, Oneida Co., N. Y., May 23, 1888.

My Dear Sir:—I have read Dr. Jewett's pamphlet, and am convinced —against my wishes—that he has the truth on his side as to the two-wine question.

The Christian Charity argument is the strong argument for abstinence, and also for unfermented wine at Communion.

Respectfully yours, ISAAC O. BEST.

[55]

256 Second Street, New York, May 23, 1888.

Reverend and Dear Sir:—Your favor of 19th inst. received. Have had no time to closely examine Dr. Jewett's pamphlet; besides, my scholarship does not entitle me to an opinion when doctors disagree. Still, I am free to say that, having read a good deal on the subject of the two-wines theory, *pro* and *con*, I can not accept it, though I would gladly do so, being a teetotaler.

Will you permit me to ask a question? My church—German Methodist Episcopal—is on Second Street, about 125 feet from corner of Avenue C. On the corner is a saloon, where not only men but also women congregate and leave at all hours of the night. The side-door is not fifty feet from the church, and not more than fifteen from the door to my own residence. Now, I have lodged complaints with the police Captain of the precinct and with the Excise Commissioners, but to no purpose. What can I do? The place is a bad one, but, of course, I have no legal proof of its character.

Permit me to assure you of my high esteem.

Yours very truly, PAUL QUATTLANDER,
Pastor German M. E. Church.

[56]

The Second Memorial Presbyterian Church, Scranton, Pa., May 22, 1888.

DEAR DR. CROSBY:—The Jewett pamphlet has come, and I have read it with care. It is scholarly and exhaustive in the treatment of the subject, but it only confirms my former opinion. I went over the whole argument, years ago, in a private correspondence with an old friend, and was more thoroughly convinced than before that there was nothing in it. And last year, in Egypt and Palestine, getting all the light I could from the missionaries, I was still more confirmed in my belief, if that were possible.

Very cordially yours, CHARLES E. ROBINSON.

[57]

The Presbyterian Church, Goshen, N. Y., May 29, 1888.

MY DEAR SIR AND BROTHER :—I have never believed in the theory of "two wines," and Dr. Jewett's argument only renders my previous conviction deeper and more intelligent. Yours cordially ROB'T B. CLARK.

[58]

Portland, May 25, 1888.

DEAR SIR :—The pamphlet on Communion Wine is the result of much research, but I consider it as labor thrown away. For those who believe in the continued existence of the Church as founded by a divine Lord, the tradition- ary custom as regards the sacramental wine is entirely sufficient. For those people of one idea, who feel bound to correct the Lord himself, no evidence, no argument, is of any use. For those who think that the Church and Christian religion were buried for centuries and reformed or refounded by men, neither this pamphlet nor any amount of historical evidence can be a defense, for the living witness is wanting. Yours truly,

JAMES AUG. HEALY, Bishop of Portland.

[59]

Sauquoit, N. Y., May 19, 1888.

DEAR SIR :—Dr. Jewett's pamphlet received. Thanks. Have read with interest and care. Am fully prepared to accept his position. Was so before seeing his pamphlet.

Some years ago I read Dr. Sampson's book, and at first thought there might be something in his theory. But I soon found that the all but unanimous ver- dict of scholarship was against it. I am one of the many who have to be scholars at second hand, not having means or ability for original investigation. But I flatter myself that I am able to recognize the evidence of scholarship in others. And I cannot see how Dr. Jewett's argument can be answered, or his position be invalidated. I have for years had no doubt that the wine spoken of in Scripture, made at Cana, used habitually by Christ, and contained in "The Cup" at the Eucharist, was fermented and intoxicating. Nor can I see any- thing wrong, *per se*, in using this wine at Communion. Yet, I don't see any necessity for it. I have no cosmopolitan or millenial experience, yet I have never seen UNLEAVENED BREAD on the Communion table. If not wrong to change the character of the bread, why should it be to change the character of the fruit of the vine? And if using fermented wine causes my weak brothers to stumble (as it may, and, I presume, has done), it seems more charitable to substitute the unfermented juice of the grape. To use the first in such a case seems to me to be one of those things that are lawful, but not expedient.

I am a total abstainer from wine as well as all other intoxicants; not so much from apprehended evil consequences to myself from drinking, as for sake of influencing others who need to abstain for their own good. I don't sit in judgment on your conscience, but mine doesn't allow me to drink wine as yours does you. Hence I can't see any necessity for fermented wine as Communion wine. I am well content to let it alone.

GEORGE HARDY, Pastor Pres. Church.

[60]

St. Stephen's College, Annandale, N. Y., May 29, 1888.

DEAR DR. CROSBY:—I have read Dr. Jewett's pamphlet on "Communion Wine." I entirely agree with it. I have long entertained the same views, and was about to make a more thorough investigation of the question for my own satisfaction. What investigation of the Bible I have made has led me to the same conclusion as that of Dr. Jewett. I have no doubt from my reading of the Bible that there is only one kind of wine there referred to.

Very truly yours, R. B. FAIRBAIRN.

[61]

St. Meinrad's Abbey, St. Meinrad, Spencer Co., Indiana, May 21, 1888.

DEAR SIR:—I am very thankful to you for having sent me Dr. Jewett's pamphlet, the perusal of which has given me much pleasure. It is a most excellent and solid refutation of the queer and dishonest arguments of the Prohibitionists, who dare to blame the Creator of the noble wine, and blasphemously contradict our Blessed Redeemer in trying to correct his divine institution. Yours respectfully,

FINTAN MUNDWILER, Abbot.

[62]

St. John's Rectory, Rochester, N. Y., May 22, 1888.

DEAR SIR:—I received your note and the "pamphlet" last week, and in accordance with your expressed wish, forward to you my opinion

Personally, I have no doubts about fermented wine; if I had, Dr. Jewett's essay would settle the question. I do not see what can be added to the opinions of Bishops Williams, Seymour, Paddock, and Dr. Beardsley.

The opinions of the Jewish rabbies are simply overwhelming as to what was used in the time of Christ, and must first be overthrown before any other arguments can be heard. The pamphlet is most valuable and timely, and I trust it will be universally read. Such, dear sir, is my humble opinion, if it be of any value to you. Thanking you, I remain sincerely yours,

ARTHUR SLOAN, Rector.

[63]

64 Pitt Street, New York, May 22, 1888.

REVEREND AND DEAR SIR:—I have read the pamphlet from Dr. Jewett carefully, and it is an excellent document. For my part, I do not believe in unfermented wine. Yours truly,

CONRAD D'OENCH.

[64]

American Baptist Home Mission Society, Troy, May 23, 1888.

DEAR DOCTOR:—I have examined the pamphlet of Dr. Jewett on the subject of "Communion Wine." I think his discussion of the question is thorough, candid and exhaustive. He shows conclusively that the theory of "two wines" has no foundation in the Bible, and is exegetically and historically untrue. His conclusions are substantially the same as those of Rev. Alvah Hovey, D.D., of Newton Theological Seminary, as given in the able article published by him recently in the *Baptist Quarterly*. The true course of Temperance needs no evasions or perversions of scriptural or historic truth for its support. All attempts to thus aid it are pernicious and dangerous. Truth alone will ultimately stand and prevail.

Yours truly, C. P. SHELDON.

[65]

St. Matthew's Church, East Syracuse, N. Y., May 21, 1888.

DEAR DR. CROSBY:—Dr. Jewett seems to have the bulk of tradition and public opinion upon his side. Yet, neither that nor his pamphlet seems to me conclusive. The consensus of mankind was absolute for the literal days in Genesis, for the Ptolemaic Astronomy, for the Julian Calendar, etc., etc., etc.

I am by no means decided by the enthusiastic assertions of the theorists for *Must.* But may not time reveal further data? The biblical literature gives us no idea why the Gospels were written in Greek. We say that the Greek thought and language had permeated Judea, but we say it without the formal approval of the text.

So Greek social customs may have permeated Judea, and among them the use of *Must.* I think we should hold to the fermented wine until grave reasons induce the change. The Catholic Church, whose humble servant I am, showed her radical willingness to adapt herself to the needs of her children by abolishing the cup in the Communion of the laity. Pius IX gave permission to Polish missionaries to say Mass with the juice of raisins.

Sincerely yours,   MICHAEL CLUNE.

[66]

Glens Falls, N. Y., May 28, 1888.

DEAR BROTHER:—Whatever special pleaders may say, the opinion of genuine scholars undoubtedly is that *yayin* is *oinos*, and *oinos* is wine, and wine is a fermented liquor.

Dr. Jewett's articles are able, but not more so than those on the same subject by President Alvah Hovey, D.D., of Newton Theological Seminary.

Yours truly, '   G. B. GOW.

[67]

Fredonia, N. Y., May 24, 1888.

MY DEAR SIR:—Dr. Jewett's pamphlet on Communion Wine finally came to hand, and as you wished, I have read it with care, and am satisfied that the author has settled the matter so completely that there is no chance for further discussion. As I am absent from home, and can not consult my Bible, I wish the author had made the distinction between wine and STRONG DRINK, on page 10. Still, the opponent can get no aid by the omission.

Yours truly,   N. W. BENEDICT.

[68]

Germantown, N. Y., May 25, 1888.

DEAR BROTHER:—I have read the pamphlet on Communion Wine which you were pleased to send to my address.

I heartily agree with Dr. Jewett in his views on this important matter; they are very logically, and, therefore, to all reasonable minds, convincingly expressed. In my judgment, it is violating the integrity of the holy sacrament of the Lord's Supper to use, on the occasion of its celebration, any other liquid element than the kind of wine that the dear Lord himself sanctified for the purpose it contemplates.

I thank you for your kindness in mailing to me a copy of the ablest and most satisfactory discussion of the perplexing subject of "Communion Wine" that I have ever read.

Yours fraternally,   W. H. LUCKENBACH,
President of the N. Y. and N. J. Synod of the Evangelical Lutheran Church.

[69]

RESPECTED SIR :—Since you may not receive many letters from Catholic clergymen with regard to the pamphlet about the Communion Wine, for the simple reason that with Catholic theologians no other practice from the beginning did obtain and no other will obtain, than to use for altar purposes only fermented wine, I, though not pretending to be a spokesman, can assure you that that pamphlet will be found by them in its results a fully satisfying one. The author of that pamphlet deserves the full acknowledgment for his great toil in examining so many and even so various books, and I especially feel bound to him, as I some time ago (having been favored by Dr. John Ellis with his new book, "New Christianity") was induced to try the "unfermented wine," which I found to be a pure grape juice, a liquid to which I would always instinctively deny the name of "wine." Whilst the pamphlet states that the Copts in Egypt used fermented wine for church purposes, Dr. Ellis says on the reverse (pages 218 and 248) that they use only the juice of soaked raisins. Your maxim, that all things created by God are good in themselves (wherefore God hates none of them), and that therefore only the bad use of them is detestable and so sinful, is a thoroughly scriptural, consequently a fully Christian, one. The intention of Dr. Ellis to contribute towards the checking of alcoholic substances for drinking purposes is a very good one too; but to denounce absolutely, as he does, the taking of fermented wine, is surely an outdoing.

In case you would make any public use of this, my statement, please to put only the initials of my name (and perhaps place also).

Respectfully,   P. F. K.

[70]

Gustavus Adolphus Sw. Luth. Church, New York, May 25, 1888.

DEAR BROTHER :—I have read with attention and pleasure Dr. Jewett's pamphlet which you kindly sent me. The arguments are convincing, and prove that the "unfermented-wine" theorists have a poor doctrinal structure on a sandy foundation. Yours truly, CONRAD EMIL LINDBERG, Pastor.

[71]

St. Stephen's Rectory, 43 West 47th St., New York, May 24, 1888.

DEAR DR. CROSBY :—You have done me a favor by inducing me to read again the articles on Communion Wine which I had examined in the *Church Review* three years ago.

It appears to me that the ability and learning of Dr. Jewett have left the sophistry of his opponents not a foot of fact to stand on. That the wine at the Last Supper was fermented wine is shown by the immemorial usage of the Church.

The words for wine in the Old and New Testaments, fairly understood; the language of the Talmudists, of contemporary rabbins, of the early Christian theologians, and of the writers of classical antiquity, all prove the declaration of the learned Jewish Seminarians of Breslau to be true, that " *Ungegohrener Wein wird nicht als Wein betrachtet.*"

You are doubtless aware that our House of Bishops have spoken—not in commendation—of "the unfermented juice of the grape" for sacramental use.

Yours very truly,   A. B. HART.

[72]

Syracuse, May 25, 1888.

DEAR SIR :—Your favor of the 15th ult. reached me in due course of time, with Dr. Jewett's pamphlet.

I saw Dr. Jewett's papers when they first appeared, and without intending to commit myself in detail, I have no hesitation in accepting his general conclusions with regard to the character of the wine used and to be used in administering the Holy Communion.

Very truly yours,   W. D. WILSON, P. Emeritus.

[73]

Pastor West Side Pres. Church, Buffalo, N. Y., May 29, 1888.

DEAR SIR:—As far as I am fitted to judge, Dr. Jewett's position on the question of the two wines seems to me the only tenable one, and he seems to me to have presented the matter in a most able way. On that basis our Session changed some eight or nine years ago from the so-called unfermented wine in use when I became pastor to the wine only properly so called, *i. e.,* fermented. Either it is that or it is water. By all means, no lie at the table of the Lord of all truth and righteousness.

Yours most truly,   HERBERT G. LORD.

[74]

May 23, 1888.

REVEREND AND DEAR SIR:—Yours of the 15th inst., as also Dr. Jewett's monograph on "Communion Wine," came duly to hand. Please accept my sincere thanks for the favor.

As to my opinion of the merits of the discussion, I can only say that it seems to be both fair and conclusive. When some time ago I began studying the question of two Bible Wines, I had hoped that the advocates of the double theory would at least prove the possibility of their being right, but I fail to see that they have done so.

Their strange assumptions and *non sequiturs* led me to question, if not their logical powers, at least their conceptions of those of their readers, while their use of Scripture evidence prompts the query whether they have to good effect studied 2 Cor. iv. 2.

I would most gladly see the powerful force of Scripture truth brought to bear against intemperance, but I would not wish, with a prophet's good intentions, to have the crushing verdict of 1 Kings xiii.18 pronounced against my method.

In all charity, I must say that I think that our Nazarite, while he may have kept his vow, has already lost his eyes, and that the "Wines on the Lees" is exceedingly well refined.

Yours in the cause of righteousness, temperance and judgment to come,

L. J. D., Pastor of First Baptist Church.

P. S.—Please do not publish this over my signature.   L. J. D.

[75]

HOWARD CROSBY, D.D.   Forest Port, N. Y., May 24, 1888.

REVEREND AND DEAR SIR:—I have read with great satisfaction the articles of Prof. Jewett in review of the new "two-wine" theory.

I have never thought it worth while to read the class of works in question, but have taken for granted that innovations so contrary to the traditional common sense of the world were fit only to irritate a candid scholar.

No doubt, however, there is a degree of skill and plausibility in these books which is making them dangerously influential, and we owe thanks for such perfectly finished and adequate defenders of the truth as Dr. Jewett.

Very truly yours,   WM. N. CLEVELAND.

[76]

Binghampton, N. Y., May 26, 1888.

MY DEAR BROTHER:—I have read with much interest Dr. Jewett's pamphlet, "Communion Wine."

His examination of Scripture terms and historic testimony seems to me to be both critical and conclusive; the more so, perhaps, because it reaches results which so perfectly accord with my own convictions touching the question of "two wines."

I find myself coming more and more under the power of this threefold belief—that the Scripture terms for wine always signify the fermented juice of the grape, though recognizing different degrees or stages of fermentation ; that the Passover wine used by Christ in the institution of the Lord's Supper was the fermented juice of the grape mixed with water, just such as the Jews have always used in their sacred feasts ; and that the substitution of any other " cup " in the observance of the Lord's Supper is an unwarrantable inter-meddling with a divine and most holy appointment, which the will of man has no right to change.   Yours fraternally,   HERMAN C. RIGGS.

[77]

Newburg, N. Y., May 26, 1888.

REVEREND AND DEAR SIR:—I received your note and Dr. Jewett's pamphlet, and it gives me pleasure to say that the pamphlet seems to me ab-solutely conclusive, if argument were, indeed, necessary. Any one who pro-pounds a theory so strange and new as that of two wines, is bound to prove his point. 1 have never seen anything approaching this, and all attempts be-gin by begging the question.

All individuals that I have heard advocate the theory, based their argu-ment on the fact that "scholars" said so. Dr. Jewett has shown how little claim they have to scholarship.

I am yours faithfully,   GEORGE W. LAY.

[78]

St. John's Rectory, Medina, N. Y., May 19, 1888.

DEAR SIR:—I have read Dr. Jewett's pamphlet, and regard it as present-ing the argument against the fanatics on this question of unfermented wine in a most satisfactory manner. An unbiased reader can not fail to be convinced by it. Perhaps I am biased, for to me the thought of a DOCTORED article for the Holy Communion is most revolting. The pure blood of the grape can be had to-day, and if God wills it to ferment, I don't believe any artificial means should be used to prevent it. In our blessed Lord's institution of the Sacra-ment I find no order to use unfermented wine, and the Church has no right to go beyond it. I wish the Jewett pamphlet success.

Very truly yours,   WARREN W. WALSH.

[79]

Rising Sun, Indiana, May 23, 1888.

REVEREND AND DEAR SIR:—Your note of the 15th inst. received this P. M., with accompanying pamphlet of Dr. Jewett. Agreeably to your re-quest, I have examined the document, and my opinion of it may be briefly stated in the following notes, to wit :—

1. So far as Dr. Jewett's pamphlet argues, by inference or otherwise, a justification of the practice of moderate drinking, I deny the validity of his conclusions and consider the inference irrelevant to the main question and pernicious. The main question I understand to be whether the Scripture precepts touching the use of wine are based on the assumed fact of there being or having been two wines.

2. So far as Dr. Jewett's pamphlet confines the discussion strictly to the refutation of the theory of two wines, I think it is strong and valuable, though not the strongest possible

3. My observations in the East led me to note particularly what appears to be the weakness of *partial* statement of facts on page 26. He says: 'In short, the juice of the grape, kept permanently unfermented, was, in so far as anything can be shown to the contrary, as unknown *anciently* in Bible lands as in the Bible record itself." To prove this statement he cites the testimony of missionaries in modern times, Van Dyke, *et al.* But Van Dyke is not writing of all uses of the "juice of the grape," but of wine strictly so-called. All juice of the grape is not necessarily wine, or necessarily fermented.

There is a juice of the grape kept unfermented in Eastern lands, which will not intoxicate, but no one would class it with wine, nor under the terms used in the Bible for wine. Dr. Jewett corrects *in part* the sweeping statement above quoted, on page 27.

I have not time now to write further on the subject, except to say that there seems to be great igorance on the subject among the people of our country churches. I find the specious and fallacious arguments of the publications of the two-wine, or double-barrel, men have been widely accepted by pastors and people, and in this and another church I have been treated as ignorant of the latest interpretations because I have denied the correctness of the two-wine theory.   Yours respectfully,

JAMES BASSETT.

[80]

37 East 39th St., City, May 21, 1888.

DEAR DR. CROSBY :—I have read Rev. Jewett's pamphlet on the wine of Scripture you were so good as to send me, with a request that I would send you my opinion of it. I began to skim its pages, and ended by reading every word.

I think it is an admirable treatise on the subject, learned, rational, philosophical and devout. I know of nothing so thorough and good on the subject. It is written with a trenchant pen, wielded by a keen intelligence and a kind heart. It is of real service both to temperance and the Scriptures, and its exposure of unfair and prejudiced tricking of philological and historical facts is most valuable.

I can sympathize with those who honestly hold erroneous views, but I have no sympathy with that fanatical *a priori* logic which assumes that certain things must be true because we wish them to be true and because we hold they ought to be true. The world, as Dr. Bacon used to say, was not created on Mohammedan principles, but on Christian principles, which demand virtue in face of temptation, not in the absence of it, and which refuse to deny the use of what may be abused.

Yours sincerely,   C. C. TIFFANY.

[81]

Syracuse, N. Y., May 21, 1888.

DEAR DR. CROSBY :—I have read with renewed interest the very able and exhaustive discussion of the wine question, which you were so good in sending to me. I read it at the time of its first appearance, and was amply convinced of its sound scholarship and candid spirit. I am a thorough-going temperance man, and feel very sure that no real temperance work is to be advanced by wresting Scripture and the lexicon and common sense, as is being done by too many men at the present day.

Somehow, the Bible stands, notwithstanding the foolishness and fanaticism of its friends.

With sentiments of profound esteem, I am yours,

GEO. B. SPALDING.

[82]

St. Mary's Rectory, Albany, N. Y., May 25, 1888.

DEAR SIR:—I have received your letter of the 15th inst., and also the copy of Dr. Jewett's admirable pamphlet. In answer to your inquiry, let me say, that I agree perfectly with that learned gentleman, who leaves little to be said on the question. The idea of two wines in the Scripture language—the one fermented and intoxicating, the other unfermented grape juice, and only the latter praised as good, or even tolerated—I hold to be pure nonsense. It is a ground unworthy of any true scholar, injurious to the divine record, and calculated to lead rapidly to moral and religious mischief. It is, to use the words of a poet,—

> " Much wrestling with the Holy Word,
> To make it yield the sense of the Lord."

A special evil is, that by this course one only plays into the hands of interested and disorderly dealers, who have, to sustain their trade in its present state, no arguments so telling as those derived from the fanaticism of heedless and hot-headed temperance advocates. It also plays into the hands of political demagogues, and especially those possessed of official power. It helps these latter to evade their duties to the country. It furnishes them with plausible excuses for opposing all laws really and efficiently restrictive, such as could change this trade from a disorderly aggregation of drinking resorts to a legitimate merchandise.

In fine, the distinction must always be maintained between temperance and total abstinence. The former is a necessary virtue. The latter is simply a prudent expedient, not only useful, but sometimes made actually necessary by circumstances, to save men from closely pressing occasions of sin.

There is no need for me to enlarge any more upon the questions you have proposed. Dr. Jewett has treated the subject learnedly, thoroughly and in a masterly manner. I trust his pamphlet will be widely read.

Very truly yours,　　C. A. WALWORTH.

[83]

Hoosick Falls, N. Y., May 29, 1888.

REV. DR. HOWARD CROSBY.

DEAR SIR :—Your name, well-known and honored, affixed to the circular concerning "Two Wines," induces me to comply with its courteous request. Having no desire for ANY publicity, I address this note to you privately.

I read with great satisfaction the articles of Rev. Dr. Jewett when they first appeared in the *Church Review*. I have now examined them again with increased approval for their sound learning, manifest truth and soberness. The use of unfermented grape juice in the Holy Sacrament of the Lord's Supper was repugnant to the mind of the Church for eighteen hundred years. In this historical fact lies the truth of the resolution passed by the House of Bishops on the fourteenth day of the session of the General Convention of the Protestant Episcopal Church, 1887, viz., "The use of the unfermented juice of the grape as the lawful and proper wine of the Holy Eucharist is unwarranted by the example of our Lord, and an unauthorized departure from the custom of the Catholic Church." The anti-wine theory (unfermented grape-juice is not wine) seems—being wise above measure—to be pursuing that Jesuitical maxim of doing evil that good may come. So did Eve. When attempting to be more wise, more good—wise above God and his ordinance,—she ruined a world. If the "cup" which the Son of God used in instituting the Holy Sacrament of the Lord's Supper did not contain wine (fermented grape juice), the Church, which is his body, through her whole existence, although illumined by the Holy Ghost, has been deceived !

The mere thought seems almost blasphemous.

With great respect, I am, dear sir, very truly yours,

[84]

Albany, N. Y., May 23, 1888.

MY DEAR SIR :—I have received your circular-letter and Dr. Jewett's pamphlet on "Communion Wine."

I have read the pamphlet, and it seems to me he has left the advocates of the two-wines interpretation no ground to stand upon.

F. M. GRAY, Canon in All Saints' Cathedral.

[85]

Cazenovia, N. Y., May 24, 1888.

DEAR DR. CROSBY:—I thank you for sending me Dr. Jewett's pamphlet on Bible Wine.

I did not need it to convince me of the truth of his view of the question, but it confirms my convictions and increases the degree of my enlightenment.

I have long been persuaded that the wine of both the Old and New Testaments became wine by alcoholic fermentation, and that no liquid otherwise was ever properly called wine.

I wrote years ago to a physician at Vineland, who was widely advertising "Communion Wine, unfermented and unintoxicating," and asked him if he regarded the article as properly "wine" at all, and he frankly said No; that he used the word because it was customary, and he presumed that it would be understood as used in a loose sense for convenience. But he had no thought that there was ever any wine that was not fermented and alcoholic.

My impression is that Dr. Herrick Johnson became convinced of this view of the case either in connection with or soon after his discussion with Dr. Atwater, a dozen years ago.

Prof. Beecher has knowledge, specific and abundant, about the untruthfulness of many of the publications of the National Temperance Society, IN THE LINE OF STATISTICS.

Prof. Moses Stuart was understood by his friends, I believe, to be too largely characterized by the *ingenium fervidum* to be the safest of exegetists.

     Cordially yours,   D. TORREY.

[86]

Chapel of the Comforter, New York, May 24, 1888.

REVEREND AND DEAR BROTHER:—Permit me to thank you for having sent me Dr. Jewett's pamphlet. I have read it with great interest, and regard the arguments as unanswerable. It ought to convince any man who is not invincibly ignorant.

Though I have never had any doubt in regard to the unlawfulness of the use of the UNFERMENTED product of the grape (you can not call it wine) in the Sacrament of the Lord's Supper, yet I am very glad to have my views supported by such able and scholarly arguments as Dr. Jewett's pamphlet contains.

     I am, very truly yours,   C. H. VAN WINKLE.

[87]

535 Quincy Street, Brooklyn, N. Y., May 28, 1888.

THE REV. DR. H. CROSBY:—Your note of the 15th inst. was followed on the 25th by Dr. Jewett's pamphlet.

I have read it somewhat carefully. The facts derived from Jewish authority and custom with respect to the use of wine at the Passover, &c., are IN PART new to me.

I regard Dr. Jewett's conclusion, critically, historically and inferentially, in opposition to the so-called "two kinds" of wine, as sound and scriptural. In fact, it is unanswerable.

As the pastor of a mission chapel, I have had some "tribulation" from enthusiasts in the matter of "Communion Wine," because I would not change the scriptural doctrine and use of wine at the Lord's Supper.

I have always noticed that those who were loudest in their denunciations of the scriptural idea were the least liable to be tempted by fermented liquors at any time and under any circumstances. I am, with highest assurance of respect, truly yours,   CHAS. WOOD.

[88]
83 14th Street, Buffalo, N. Y., May 21, 1888.

My Dear Sir:—I thank you very sincerely for the valuable and exhaustive article of Dr. Jewett on Communion Wine. It settles the dishonest temperance argument as effectively as Bishop Lightfoot, in his edition of St. Ignatius, does the Presbyterian claims as to two orders of the ministry. I fear, however, there are some who will be convinced by neither. Again assuring you of my thanks for your courtesy, I am, yours very sincerely, WALTER NORTH.

[89]
Passaic, N. J., May 25, 1888.

Dear Doctor :—I read Dr. Jewett's tractate on the wine used in the Holy Communion at the time of its first appearance, and was satisfied that he had well established the point he had set out to prove. On a second reading (at your request), I see no cause to change the judgment originally formed.

For myself alone (without intending to interfere with the liberty of others), I have for a dozen years or more rejected alcoholic drinks of every kind; but I never dared to think of such a thing as doing otherwise with the Lord's Supper than as the Lord himself commanded.

Just now I am visiting some grandchildren in Passaic, or I should have answered your letter more promptly. With cordial greetings, as of old,
Very faithfully yours, J. A. SPENCER.

[90]
256 West 54th St., New York, May 21, 1888.

Dear Doctor :—I have read with interest and care Dr. Jewett's pamphlet, which you were so good as to send me.

I have had occasion to give this subject a very thorough examination some years ago, and a re-examination only serves to confirm and strengthen the convictions then formed.

I most heartily concur both in the argument and conclusions reached by the writer, that we have absolutely no warrant, either scriptural or historical, for the assumption that unfermented wine was used on the occasion of the Holy Supper, or that it was in common use among the Jews at that time. On the other hand, I think the New Testament clearly teaches by necessary inference that the kind of wine used on that and all other occasions would intoxicate if abused and used in excess.

I think the effort so persistently made to commit Christian people to this new dogma is both unwise in its teachings and hurtful in its tendency, the main reason urged for it in practice being that a great danger may be removed out of the way of those who may have acquired an appetite for strong drink.

I do not know how it may strike others, but to me it seems a monstrous idea that a man who might have such an appetite would be endangered; if, with that feeling of dependence upon God, and holy reverence for the ordinance he had instituted, he came in the way he had appointed, he should suffer harm.

It seems to me a poor, low, mean conception of the character of God to suppose he would allow a child to stumble in the use of a means of grace which he himself has appointed.

I regard this question of unfermented wine, and many others like it with which our times are afflicted, as an effort to be wise above what is written.
Faithfully your servant, SPENCER L. HILLIER.

[91]
Rome, N. Y., May 21, 1888.

Dear Sir and Brother :—In your favor of May 15th, you ask a question about a double kind of wine in the Bible. I did not receive your pamphlet referred to, but will give my opinion nevertheless, if so accepted.

Wine—vine—vineyard—the most noble product of *terra firma nostra*—is described in the Bible as one of those precious gifts the Lord God bestowed on the chosen land, and therefore so many likenesses and parables are derived from it—as in Ps. lxxx. 9-16; Hosea x. 1. The land itself is called a vineyard, Jer. xii. 10.

According to its excellent climate, Canaan was especially fitted for the vine; that it grew even to an enormous size, as we read in Num. xiii. 24.

There were two kinds of grapes, one, a very noble kind, with small, sweet, white berries, called Sorek, קֵרֹשׂ-בֶּן, in Gen. xlix. 11; Is. v. 2 (choicest vine); Jer. ii. 21 (a noble vine). In Acts ii. 13 and 15, μεμεστωμίνοι and μεθύουσι, μεθύ is sweet, and rather a strong wine, or people could not get drunk on it.

The vineyards of Engeddi, Hebron, and the Lebanon were of special quality, surrounded by walls or fences and protected against wild animals (Sol. Songs ii. 15)—take us the foxes, those little foxes, that spoil the vines.

In Is. lxiii. 1-3, reference is made as in other places (Gen. xlix. 11), "He washed his garments in wine, and his clothes in the blood of grapes;" to the juice of the red grape, "Their blood shall be sprinkled upon my garments;" etc., etc.

This vine-tree, with its precious fruit and balmy flowers, and its thick foliage spreading far around it, is—like the olive and fig-tree—an emblem of earthly blessing (1 Reg. iv. 25), where it says that "Juda and Israel dwelt safely, every man under his vine and under his fig-tree—from Dan even to Beersheba, all the days of Solomon." So also Mic. iv. 4, "They shall sit every man under his vine and under his fig-tree, and none shall make them afraid." Zech. iii. 10, "In that day shall ye call every man his neighbor under the vine and under the fig-tree."

Even the housewife (Ps. cxxviii. 3) "shall be as a fruitful vine by the sides of thine house."

The kingdom of Heaven is made similar to a vineyard in Old and New Testament. Song of Sol. vi. 8; Is. v.; Matt. xx. 1; xxi. 33; and in John xv. the Lord calls God a husbandman, γεωργός, and himself a vine-tree, ἄμπελος; his disciples the branches thereof (κλήματα).

That strengthening and heart-quickening beverage derived from said plant —the wine—*oinos*—*vinum*—*wein*—יַיִן—is mentioned very often on account of its salubrious and health-giving qualities (Ps. iv. 7): "Thou hast put gladness in my heart, more than in the time that their corn and their wine increased." Ps. civ. 15, "And wine that maketh glad the heart of man." Eccles. ix. 7, "Eat thy bread with joy, and drink thy wine with a merry heart." 1 Tim. v. 23, Paul even advises—as our best medical authorities do in our time —again to take wine as a cordial for stomach disease. Is. lv. 1, "Buy wine and milk (a kind of milk punch) without money and without price"—or any other high license, either!

Our Lord Himself changed water into the best kind of wine (John ii.), and as Melchizedek of old (Gen. xiv.) offered bread and wine to Abraham, he made and used these elements of daily nutrition as mediums of his own Mystic Communion and Union.

From these and other "*locis probandis*" we truly find that there are different kinds of wine mentioned, but both kinds were, if used immoderately, intoxicating, and the prophets of old were just as strict and loyal towards any and every abuse of the fruit of the vine (Hab. ii. 15), "woe unto him that giveth his neighbor drink, that puttest thy bottle to him, and makest him drunken also, that thou mayest look on their nakedness." (See also Is. xxviii. 1-7) as our Lord Christ rebukes the unfaithful servant (Matt. xxiv.) who eats and drinks with the drunken, and Matt. xi. 19, he himself speaks of his own eating and drinking, although they called him a man gluttonous and a wine-bibber. (There ought to be also, according to some modern hair-splitters, a distinction made between one kind of meals of plain, innocent character, and another meal that is surfeiting?)

The same Apostle Paul who advised Timothy to take some wine for a cure, earnestly rebukes his Ephesian friends (v. 18) not to be drunk with wine, wherein is excess, but to be filled with the Spirit.

The Scripture does not exhibit any token or sign of a double kind of wine in this regard, as to its use ; it allows the use of strong drink with that only restriction not to abuse it. All things are yours, but you belong unto Christ, and Christ to God.

There is nothing unclean by itself, says the Apostle (Rom. xiv. 14); and it is good neither to eat flesh nor to drink wine, nor anything whereby thy brother stumbleth.

Let everybody be fully persuaded in his own mind, etc.

Yours respectfully,   O. F. EBERT.

[92]

Syracuse, N. Y., May 23, 1888.

REVEREND AND DEAR SIR:—I have read Dr. Jewett's pamphlet with some care, although I have never had any difficulty in regard to the question which he discusses. It seems to me that with any fair-minded man his argument must be an end of controversy.   Very truly yours,

H. R. LOCKWOOD, Rector of St. Paul's Church.

[93]

Clinton St., cor. Third Place, Brooklyn, N. Y.

MY DEAR DR. CROSBY :—Dr. Jewett's paper on "Communion Wine " is an exhaustive discussion of a subject upon which good and learned men differ. The argument, drawn from a critical analysis of the root-meanings of Bible words, is very convincing. I think he brings from this source abundant proof to establish the "fermented-wine" theory. The historical grounds of his theory are carefully explored, and the evidence adduced therefrom goes to buttress the etymological argument. It is also made clear that the best scholarship of the past and present is pledged to the views so ably advocated by Dr. Jewett.   Truly yours,

FRANK ROGERS MORSE.

[94]

Albany, N. Y., May 19, 1888.

MY DEAR DR. CROSBY :—You asked my opinion of Dr. Jewett's pamphlet, on the question of the proper wine for use in the Holy Communion. I am most free to say that I think it deals with a question of the gravest importance in a most thoughtful and thorough way. Its arguments seem to me respectful and exhaustive, and I hope the friends of true temperance will some day come to learn that its best interests can not be promoted by the fanaticism which denies the wisdom of God the Father in creation, and of God the Son in the system that his love chose to redeem mankind.

Very truly yours,   W. C. DOANE, Bishop of Albany.

[95]

Rochester, N. Y., May 21, 1888.

REVEREND AND DEAR SIR :—Certainly no unpredjudiced person would, from the statements of Scripture, reach any different conclusion about the kind of wine our Lord used, than that of Dr. Jewett.

If the disclosure should be made to us through natural law, that there was danger for us in using fermented wine, i should think we ought to respect the fact as a divine revelation; but this is another matter, concerning which my opinion was not asked. Thanks for the pamphlet.

Very truly yours,   AMOS SKEELE.

[96]

11 and 13 Waverley Place, New York, May 19, 1888.

REVEREND AND DEAR SIR :—Your favor of the 15th inst. reached me on the 17th. I thank you for sending me the pamphlet of the Rev. Dr. Jewett, whom

I remember very well as a theological student more than thirty-five years ago. I have read what he has written carefully and with much interest, and I feel sure that his position is impregnable. I am heart and soul in sympathy with the movement for the suppression and prevention of intemperance, and I would, if I had the power, close every saloon in this great city. At the same time, I am fully assured in my own mind that the great evil of excess in the use of strong drink cannot be done away by the intemperate methods of some of the so-called temperance advocates, or by the sacrifice of any portion of revealed truth. With much respect, I am, faithfully yours, E. M. PECKE.

[97]

133 East 35th Street, New York City, May 19, 1888.

My Dear Dr. Crosby :—You must excuse me if I do not read the pamphlet you have been so kind as to send me. I never had any doubt but that wine in the N. T. means wine, and not raw grape juice. It is scarcely possible that anybody could have ever taken any other ground except for some ulterior purpose, and in the interest of some anti-wine theory that is strong enough to twist exegesis and warp the Word of God.

Yours very cordially, C. H. PARKHURST.

[98]

May 19, 1888.

My Dear Dr. Crosby :—I have read the pamphlet of Dr. Jewett on the wine question. It seems to me a scholarly, fair and unanswerable argument against the "unfermented-wine" nonsense. Very truly yours,

(*Signature illegible.*)

[99]

St. Joseph's Church, Amsterdam, N. Y., May 19, 1888.

Dr. Howard Crosby, New York City.

Dear Sir :—I beg leave to thank you for your kindness in presenting me with Dr. Jewett's pamphlet.

Dr. Jewett, as is evident from his very scholarly essay, is a highly respectable scholar, and fully competent to treat the subject. All I regret about him is that I see him arrayed against such shallow praters and comical exegetes as Thayer and Samson.

I should like to see him battle against more redoubtable adversaries. But this is no fault of *his*.

I shall assign to the pamphlet a permanent place in my library. It is one of the most solid and clearly written treatises I have seen for many a day, and fully settles the question from the standpoint taken.

Yours very respectfully, DR. EDWARD HIPELIUS.

Pastor St. Joseph's, formerly Professor of Hebrew.

[100]

St. Ann's on the Heights, Brooklyn, N. Y., May 18, 1888.

Reverend and Dear Sir:—I have already read Dr. Jewett's article on the "two wines," and from that reading, as from some other careful study of the subject, have long been of the opinion that the theory that two wines are spoken of in Scripture, one intoxicating and the other not, is utterly untenable. To thus force Scripture words and texts in defense of temperance is to carry the Ark of the Lord into battle with the Philistines. It is the surest way to lose the battle. Respectfully,

REESE F. ALSOP, Rector of St Ann's Church, Brooklyn.

[101]

1 East 9th Street, New York, May 18, 1888.

Reverend and Dear Sir:—In acknowledging your note and the pamphlet containing Dr. Jewett's articles, I beg leave to say that I read them with great interest at the time they appeared in the *Church Review,* and they impressed me as being very thorough and convincing.

I hope to read them again, and if my opinion should be in anywise different I will let you know.

But I give you now from recollection the strong impression which was made upon me when I read them. With highest respect, yours very truly,

CLARENCE BUEL.

[102]

130 W. 13th Street, New York, May 19, 1888.

REVEREND AND DEAR SIR:—I have your note, politely asking my opinion as to the merits of the Rev. Dr. Jewett's pamphlet on "Communion Wine," also the copy of said pamphlet so kindly sent by you.

By the courtesy of the learned author, I had the pleasure of reading his treatise on its first publication.

It seemed to me then exhaustive of the subject.

The argument to prove that the wine used at the Passover Supper was and must have been ordinary fermented wine, is, in my humble judgment, unanswerable and perfectly conclusive.

With great respect, I am, yours truly, THEO. A. EATON.

[103]

Grace House, 802 Broadway, New York, May 18, 1888.

REVEREND AND DEAR SIR:—I have read the pamphlet which you have kindly sent me, and, as you ask my opinion, I beg to say that Dr. Jewett's argument seems to me clear and conclusive.

Very respectfully yours, GEO. F. NELSON.

[104]

117 West 87th St., New York, May 18, 1888.

MY DEAR DR. CROSBY:—Yours of May 15th was duly received, followed in the next mail by the pamphlet to which you referred.

I have hastily glanced over the articles in question. So far as a superficial look at the reasoning can go, the argument seems conclusive. I do not care to go into a more close examination of the question, as for a long time it has seemed to me strained and foolish to attempt a distinction between the two kinds of wine in biblical usage. Also there are other reasons which make me think that the sacramental wine should be fermented wine.

I am glad, however, to have on hand and for reference an exhaustive statement of the arguments on this point, and thank you for sending me the pamphlet. Yours very truly, ANSON P. ATTERBURY.

[105]

Deansville, May 18, 1888.

REV. HOWARD CROSBY, D.D.

DEAR SIR:—I have never been able to find any hint of the "two-wine" theory in the Bible.

Yours, etc., SAMUEL MILLER.

P. S.—I claim to be as good a temperance man as there is.

[106]

27 Kingsborough St., Gloversville, N. Y., May 19, 1888.

THE REV. HOWARD CROSBY, D.D.

DEAR SIR:—Accept my sincere thanks for the monograph on Communion Wine, which I have just read. I think it unanswerable. I was in need of just such a collation of the facts, and shall put it to immediate use. This question must be settled, but "we can do nothing against the truth."

Very sincerely yours, ISAAC O. RANKIN.

[107]

161 Butler St., Buffalo, N. Y., May 18, 1888.

MY DEAR DR. CROSBY :—Dr. Jewett's pamphlet—for which I am greatly indebted to you—settles for me, as a historical fact, what, indeed, I have never doubted, that the wine of the Scriptures was fermented.

It is like God to give good things to man. It is like man to abuse them.

Yours sincerely, ANSON G. CHESTER.

[108]

The Utica "Lutheran," Utica, N. Y., May 19, 1888.

DR. HOWARD CROSBY.

REVEREND AND DEAR SIR:—For Dr. Jewett's pamphlet on "Communion Wine," recently received, I desire herewith to express my hearty thanks. I have read it with deep interest. Its presentation against any two-wine theory in Holy Scriptures is, in my judgment, complete—the truth, the whole truth, and nothing but the truth. It bears testimony to the position held and maintained almost unanimously by the great Evangelical Communion of which I have the honor to be a member. Wishing you God speed in your crusade against fanaticism, I am, very cordially yours, THEO. B. ROTH.

[109]

St. John's Rectory, Canandaigua, N. Y., May 19, 1888.

REVEREND AND DEAR SIR :—I thank you for Dr. Jewett's pamphlet on "COMMUNION WINE." The question of "two wines" is to me the same as the question of two hands. As to the merits of the article, it is, in my judgment, correct in its examinations and conclusions.

I have had occasion to traverse the same ground as Dr. Jewett, but not as thoroughly—wanting his erudition. I have in a public discourse impaled the so-called CHRISTIAN GOSPEL Temperance Reformers on these four points, looking at the QUESTION as a Christian man :—

1. Making a nullity of temperance as a virtue.
2. Misinterpretation of Scripture words.
3. Discredit of a miracle.
4. Invalidation of a sacrament.

Are you not of the opinion that Dr. Jewett proves all these? At least, are they not logical deductions from the Scripture in the light of his article?

I trust you will be of service in dispelling this heresy which is vexing the souls of Christians. Yours sincerely, E. J. BABCOCK.

[110]

Diocese of Central New York,
Bishop's Residence, Walnut Place, Syracuse, May 19, 1888.

DEAR BROTHER :—Dr. Jewett's article or pamphlet expresses, for the most part, my view of the subject, and, as I suppose, those of our clergy generally.

Yours sincerely, F. D. HUNTINGTON.

[111]

MY DEAR DOCTOR CROSBY :—I have read the paper of the Rev. Dr. Jewett which you were kind enough to send me.

It is able, scholarly, candid and conclusive, exposing the utter futility of the two-wine theory. Years ago I studied the Scripture carefully on the matter, and arrived at the same conclusion. And I was confirmed in my opinion by all that I saw and heard when traveling in Palestine in 1874. There is but one wine mentioned in the Bible, and that is always a product of fermentation.

It is very hard to see how any competent and fair-minded scholar can think otherwise. Yours faithfully,

TALBOT W. CHAMBERS.

New York, May 19, 1888.

[112]

Parsonage, Nanuet, May 19, 1888.

REVEREND AND DEAR BROTHER:—Your kind letter of the 15th of this month, as also Dr. Jewett's pamphlet, came to hand, and I read it with great, very great, interest. It would and must do incalculable good if it would be read by all ministers of the Gospel. I am ever so thankful that you sent it to me, and would beg of you, if possible, to send it to all the members of Hudson Presbytery. It is needed there, I am very sorry to say. In our spring meeting in 1887, a brother Elder, tinker by trade, got up and made the proposition that this Presbytery shall use unfermented wine for sacramental purposes. The Presbytery voted FOUR in the majority for the proposition. We have a number of able and highly educated ministers, but sadly misguided and very short-sighted on this question. Please send each of our ministers Jewett's pamphlet, and I know their manly spirit and Christian judgment will direct them to correct their error. With thankfulness, I remain, yours truly,

ADOLPH SCHABEHORN.

[113]

Brooklyn, N. Y., May 19, 1888.

REVEREND AND DEAR SIR:—In answer to your circular of the 15th inst., I beg to say that my convictions that there is only one kind of WINE, strictly speaking, which is referred to in Holy Scripture, have only been strengthened by a careful reading of the Rev. Dr. Jewett's articles upon the subject. It seems to me that the result of his research is such as to leave no ground for his opponents to stand upon. The etymology of the original words of Scripture and the facts of history, all appear to be on the side of his argument. Apart from the question of the SOCIAL usages of the Jews, the one so important to the Christian Church, "what is meant by the fruit of the vine, in connection with the Holy Communion," ought to be considered as definitely settled by the results of his research. He has adduced most important and disinterested Hebrew testimony to the effect that since its introduction into the Paschal Feast (so far as information can be gained) WINE has been exclusively the fermented article; he has strengthened the position by showing that it was ordered to be mixed with water, in order to lessen its strength. It is not disputed that the wine of the Passover was that which was used by our Lord in the institution of the Holy Communion. The inference would seem obvious, that the introduction of unfermented grape juice, or any other article, which would appear to criticise our Lord's act, will be both impertinent and irreverent.

Very truly yours, HENRY B. CORNWELL,

Rector of the Church of the Good Shepherd, Brooklyn, N. Y.

[114]

Buffalo, N. Y., May 18, 1888.

MY DEAR DR. CROSBY:—I admire Dr. Jewett's patience of research and agree with his conclusions.

It seems strange to me that such labor was necessary in such a cause. That WINE is the NAME for FERMENTED grape juice, that the juice of the grape became wine only by fermentation, is something which a very ordinary scholarship ought to know, and a very ordinary HONESTY ought to admit.

Yours truly, L. S. MITCHELL.

[115]

Presbyterian Parsonage, Centre Moriches, L. I., May 19, 1888.

MY DEAR DOCTOR:—I have just read Dr. Jewett's "Communion Wine," and with much satisfaction. I have long felt convinced that the two-wine theory had LITTLE to commend it, but now I know it has absolutely NOTHING. The simple fact that some people used to drink grape juice was just enough of a straw for intemperate temperance men to catch at. If our Lord had not made that wedding gift of "GOOD WINE" they would have let even that straw go by.

Query: Why make three barrels of unfermented juice, which must have *fermented* long before it could possibly have been used down to the lees?

Why can't they let the whole question rest where the Scriptures put it?

Hollow straw doesn't compare with solid ground!

I could only wish that some of our hot-headed, third-party, temperance-or-nothing friends would carefully read Dr. Jewett's calm reasoning.

Sincerely yours, HAMILTON B. HOLMES.

I want to add one line of thanks for the pamphlet. I hope you sent it into the General Assembly.

[116]

St. Nicholas Place, 151st St., New York, May 20, 1888.

REVEREND AND DEAR SIR:—I read Dr. Jewett's articles at the time of their publication, and have seen no answer to them. In my judgment, the argument in them is conclusive.

Very respectfully yours, M. VAN RENSSELAER.

[117]

New Rochelle, N. Y., May 19, 1888.

MY DEAR DR. CROSBY:—I have received the pamphlet on the scriptural wine question, and beg leave to reply to your inquiry briefly. The result of a very careful examination of the matter twenty years ago was the conviction that the arguments in favor of two kinds of wine (as presented by the advocates of a change in the Communion Wine) WERE NOT SOUND—in short, that the attempt at proof was a complete failure. I have not changed my views since, although I have read what I could find on the subject. I never would allow the change to be made from WINE to any of the strange concoctions now in use, in any church of which I was the pastor.

When I was at Lane Seminary, for two years under Dr. Lyman Beecher, a venerable gentleman of my acquaintance (this was in 1844–'45) returned to his home (where I was on a visit) from the Communion in the Second Presbyterian Church, of which Dr. Hays is now pastor, at Cincinnati, with a very dejected countenance. I asked him what was the matter. He said in substance that "he had been nearly poisoned that morning at the table of his Lord. He went there in good faith, hoping to find a blessing. Instead of the blood of the Lord, however, or anything to represent it, they had fed him on the POISON OF DRAGONS!" It turned out that, in trying to brew some new article as a substitute, a mistake had been made, and a fearful decoction produced, which tasted worse than the worst wine ever manufactured in a New York or Cincinnati gin-mill.

Poor old Mr. Tichenor (Newark family) was deeply grieved and offended, and I, for one, could not blame him. Dr. Beecher was not then pastor, but I think Dr. Cleveland was. I have watched the operation of the new principle in our churches for more than thirty years. I have been in the ministry over forty years. I have never known a SINGLE INSTANCE of its being a benefit to any one.

This is the best examination of the question, and the most thorough, I should think, which the controversy has produced so far. The argument meets my views PRECISELY, and I hope it will be given a very wide circulation.

Yours most sincerely, CHARLES E. LINDSLEY.

[118]

7 East 31st Street, New York, May 17, 1888.

DEAR DR. CROSBY:—I have read very carefully Dr. Jewett's pamphlet. My own views have always been such as Dr. Jewett most lucidly sets forth, and his pamphlet must carry conviction wherever and whenever read. It settles the question beyond the shadow of a doubt—in my humble opinion.

Very truly yours, REUBEN W. HOWES, JR.

[119]

314 Second Avenue, New York, May 18, 1888.

MY DEAR DR. CROSBY :—I read Dr. Jewett's pamphlet on "Communion Wine" when it appeared in 1886, and deem it one of the most admirable treatises on the subject. Its position, that the Hebrew *Yayin* and Greek *Oinos* of Scripture signify common or fermented wine, and that no rational or honest exegesis can force upon these terms, whenever one chooses to wish it, the meaning of another and unfermented wine, is unassailable.

Dr. Jewett's pamphlet is moderate in temper, scholarly in citation, and in argument absolutely conclusive. It is quite time that the unanimous verdict of European and American scholars, should dispel this illusion of the "two-wine theory," and with it the untenable exegetical methods of its advocates, which, if applied to other words and doctrines of Scripture, would invalidate them all, no matter how precisely and definitely stated.

Faithfully yours,　　　J. B. REIMENSNYDER.

[120]

Wassaic, N. Y., May 18, 1888.

DR. HOWARD CROSBY :—Many thanks for Dr. Jewett's pamphlet. I have read it with interest. It is clear and convincing, and should be scattered and read everywhere.　　　Yours truly,

WILLIAM J. McCORD.

[121]

245 West 48th Street, New York, May 17, 1888.

DEAR DR. CROSBY :—Let me thank you for the pamphlet on "Communion Wine," by the Rev. Dr. Jewett. I read the article shortly after it was published, and regard it as an unanswerable argument, exposing the absurdity of the "unfermented-wine" theory.　　　Very truly yours,

RANDELL C. HALL.

[122]

Protestant Episcopal Seamen's Society, 7 Coenties Slip,
New York, May 18, 1888.

DEAR SIR :—I thank you for the pamphlet which you have sent me and which I have received this morning. I read Dr. Jewett's articles at the time that they were published in the *Church Review*, and the opinion which I formed then has not changed since. I believe his argument for the use of fermented wine in the Holy Communion is scriptural, reasonable, and convincing to any person not influenced by prejudice or preconceived opinions. I think, sir, that the weight of learning, scholarship and history is all on the side of the question which Dr. Jewett advocates.

Yours respectfully,　　　ISAAC MAGUIRE.

[123]

Church of the Heavenly Rest, 551 Fifth Avenue, New York, May 17, 1888.

REVEREND AND DEAR SIR :—I read Dr. Jewett's articles very carefully at the time they were published, as they touched a question of most serious import. I can only say in this brief note, that, according to my light and conscience, the position taken by Dr. Jewett is most certainly in accordance with the mind of God, and, I think, as revealed in the Old and New Testaments.

I am, dear sir, yours very truly,　　　D. PARKER MORGAN.

[124]

The Lexington Avenue Baptist Church, Corner of 111th Street,
New York, May 18, 1888.

MY DEAR BROTHER :—I thank you for Dr. Jewett's pamphlet. Having had occasion, as chairman of a committee appointed by the "National Tem-

perance Society," to examine Dr. Samson's book. " The Divine Law as to Wines,"
I found it impossible to come to any other conclusion than that arrived at by
Dr. Jewett. His pamphlet is, in my opinion, unanswerable. I am also convinced that the efforts of good men to help a good cause, by advocating the
false theory of two wines, are worse than fruitless. Though belonging to the
company of total abstainers, and believing in the doctrine of Prohibition, I
have long ago abandoned the teaching of Dr. Samson's mischievous school.

Permit me to call your attention to two facts which (if you do not know
them) will be of interest to you. First, Dr. Samson's book, after a careful and
painstaking examination by competent scholars, was condemned as worse than
useless, and stricken from the list of the " National Temperance Society's "
publications. President Alvah Hovey, D.D., LL.D., of Newton, wrote the
criticism. This paper is in the possession of the Society. Second, Dr. Hovey
has contributed two very valuable articles on the general subject of the two
wines, which you may find—one in the *Baptist Quarterly Review* for July, 1887,
the other in the same publication for January, 1888.

With kindest regards, yours fraternally,   HALSEY MOORE, D.D.

[125]

37 West 125th St., New York, May 18, 1888.

REVEREND AND DEAR SIR:—I agree entirely with Dr. Jewett's pamphlet, as
the Church has done through all countries and as the Evangelical Lutheran
Church (of which I am a pastor in the " General Council ") has always done as
a whole body.   Most respectfully,   JULIUS EHRHART.

[126]

St. Paul's Church, Trinity Parish, New York, May 18, 1888.

REVEREND AND DEAR SIR:—It gives me pleasure to say, in reply to your
note with Dr. Jewett's pamphlet, that I had read his articles on their appearance
in the *Church Review*, and considered them then, as I do now, thoroughly
learned and almost exhaustive on the scriptural Wine Question.

I do not believe that unfermented wine ever had any existence except in
the muddled brain of " temperance " fanatics. At the same time it has always
seemed to me to be a noteworthy fact in this matter, that the art of distillation
was utterly unknown in our Lord's day and for about a thousand years thereafter.
Consequently, the wine used by him at the Paschal feast and the marriage in
Cana could have been only the pure juice of the grape fermented, not fortified
—as most of our imported wines now are—with brandy or any other preparation of distilled alcohol.

Travelers tell me that Eastern wines are even now, for the most part,
similarly light and pure, and that they can not ordinarily be kept more than two
or three years without becoming vinegar.

Excuse this long note, and believe me very truly and respectfully yours,
JAMES MULCHAHEY.

[127]

New York, May 17, 1888.

DEAR SIR:—I heartily endorse the book above mentioned. Its conclusions
are in full accord with my early education, ministerial training and individual
study, observation and experience for the past twenty years.

Yours sincerely,   E. H. CLEVELAND.

[128]

Seneca Falls, N. Y., May 18, 1888.

DR. HOWARD CROSBY.

DEAR SIR:—Yours received, and pamphlet carefully and profitably read.

It corroborates my opinion formed long ago on the basis of common sense,
rather than of personal study or of linguistic knowledge.

I have no doubt that our Lord used and made fermented wine.

I have no doubt that "the fruit of the vine" Christ used was fermented. There was no such popular occasion then, as now, for the use of any other kind of drink to represent his shed blood.

I believe scriptural temperance to be in accordance with the literal meaning of the word, and not in accordance with the modern and popular use of the word.

Nevertheless, I teach and practice total abstinence. At our communion we use prepared juice of the grape—unfermented. Habits and facilities have changed in respect to intoxication since Christ's days. In his day there was no discussion (reported to us) about one or more kind of wine. The discussion in our day proves the existence of a MODERN occasion.

The occasion seems to me real, but the discussion which has grown out of it, with a view to exonerate our Lord and the Bible, seems to me useless.

The frank acknowledgment of the scriptural view, with a Christian application of it to the exigencies of the times, seems to me all that is necessary.

At least, beyond that course I do not venture to go.

Respectfully and fraternally yours,   LEWIS H. MOREY.

[129]

Office of St. Paul the Apostle, 59th Street and 9th Avenue,
New York, May 21, 1888.

REVEREND AND DEAR SIR:—I am in complete accord with Dr. Jewett in the matter discussed in his pamphlet. The arguments of his opponent I consider forced, far-fetched and little short of ridiculous.

Very truly yours,   EDWARD B. BRADY.

[130]

New York, May 20, 1888.

MY DEAR DR. CROSBY:—I thank you for Dr. Jewett's pamphlet on "Communion Wine."

My own independent study years ago led me to the same conclusions, but I have derived great satisfaction from the erudite and finished demonstration of the futility of notions which seem to be pernicious alike to national morality and to religious faith.

Yours truly,   JAMES M. WHATON.

[131]

Saratoga Springs, N. Y., May 18, 1888.

DEAR SIR:—I have given my attention to Dr. Jewett's pamphlet.

It is, perhaps, the most exhaustive and vigorous treatment of the question of two wines that has come to my notice. It has come to be a conviction with me that it is not exegesis, but eisegesis, that places the Bible under contribution to the craze for unfermented wine. The wine which our Lord made at Cana, and which he used at the Supper, was fermented wine, if great scholarship is worth anything in the study of this question.

The theory of unfermented wine is a bad argument injuring a good cause, as bad arguments have a habit of doing.

Yours, etc.,   G. B. FOSTER, Pastor First Baptist Church.

[132]

Garfield, N. Y., May 19, 1888.

REVEREND AND DEAR SIR:—The pamphlet and your letter have been received and contents noted. I cannot say that the pamphlet has converted me, as I did not need conversion on that subject.

I will not be surprised if the next life and death struggle in which the country engages, and in which it will be carried to a successful issue by good men and pure, of all parties, will be for prohibition or total abstinence, as the last one was for slavery or freedom. But the coming conflict must be carried on along other lines than the "sin-*per-se*" or the "two-wine" theory, as the last one was for other reasons than the "sin *per se*" of human slavery. If it is attempted on the "sin-*per-se*" theory, it will deservedly come to nothing.

I perceive no reason whatever for holding on to the authority of the Bible, or from any other trustworthy source, to the "two-wine" theory. If there was non-intoxicating wine it certainly was not used either at the Passover, the marriage in Cana of Galilee, or at the institution of the Lord's Supper.

I would that all men were even as I myself am on this whole subject, *i. e.*, unable even to tolerate the attempt to prove the two-wine theory from the Bible; but convinced from personal experience, reading, observation and otherwise, that alcohol adds nothing to the strength and continued healthy working of either mind or body (even if it does add, the addition is, as Prof. Loomis used to say about the heat of the morning rays, so small as to be inappreciable), and that it is the prolific parent of poverty, sin, sickness and sorrow to manifold myriads of my fellow-men, and I abstain from it altogether for such reasons. Conscience, I say; pleasure, profit, gratification, liberty, I say.

With very pleasant and appreciative recollections of your influence in the class-room, prayer-meetings and chapel, I am, affectionately,

Your old pupil,   SAMUEL DODD.

[133]

Lancaster, N. Y., May .8, 1888.

DEAR DOCTOR CROSBY :—I thank you with all my heart for the copy of Dr. Jewett's admirable articles on "Communion Wine." I have just read them carefully through with great interest.

With large learning, accurate quotation of the original tongues, conspicuous fairness and candor, temperate language, Christian dignity, and utterly overwhelming argument, he so thoroughly demolishes the "two-wine" theory, and so plainly exposes the tricky quibbling advocacy of Dr. Lees and Dr. Samson, together with their utterly false assertions, that it is difficult to understand how any honest man, who has read Dr. Jewett's pamphlet, can ever again allow himself to give countenance to this pious fraud of the "two wines." I am rejoiced that the two articles are given to the public in pamphlet form. They ought to put to shame those pragmatical and dangerous people who would be wiser and more righteous than Christ himself, and who think they can promote good morals by lying for God. With many thanks,

I am, fraternally yours,   WILLIAM WAITH,
Pastor of the Presbyterian Church.

[134]

General Theological Seminary, 401 West 20th St.,
New York, May 17, 1888.

REVEREND AND DEAR SIR:—I was so well acquainted with Dr. Jewett's pamphlet on the use and allowableness of wine for sacred purposes, and on the qualities of the wine so used, that I might have saved you the trouble of sending me a copy, for which, nevertheless, I certainly thank you. In answer to your inquiry, I would simply say that I agree with Dr. Jewett in every view that he takes of the matter. And I think, moreover, that the last two sentences of Dr. Jewett's pamphlet give a most salutary warning to all Christian men who adopt or advocate the views which Dr. J. both opposes and exposes.

I am, dear sir, very respectfully yours,   SAM'L BUEL.

[135]

St. Luke's Rectory, Troy, N. Y., May 18, 1888.

DEAR SIR:—Many thanks for your copy of Dr. Jewett's pamphlet on "Communion Wine."

I have read it carefully, and suppose it to be abundantly sufficient to prove his case.

Whoever thinks that "wine" has two meanings should be convinced of his error by reading this pamphlet. At least, he must be convinced that the proof of "unfermented wine" is very uncertain, and needs stronger evidence and more of it.

The treatment accorded to our Blessed Lord is dreadful, in the case of all those who decide confidently just what he could do and what he could not do.

Certainly, the central service of his holy Church compels great caution and reverence in those who desire to "do in remembrance" of him the very thing he wishes to be done. And such caution and reverence seem to me to be lacking when men of abundant opportunity to learn the truth corrupt the ancient customs on such feeble pleadings as I have been able to find.

I retain the pamphlet for further use, unless you desire its return.

Hoping you may increase more and more in the good work of sound teaching, and be satisfied with the result of this circular letter,

I remain sincerely yours, JAMES OTIS LINCOLN.

[136]

St. Andrew's Church, Rector's Office, 108 East 128th St.,
New York, May 18, 1888.

MY DEAR DR. CROSBY :—I have already read Dr. Jewett's pamphlet, and am strengthened in my conviction, that, unless one has a theory to support, he never would find " two wines " in Holy Scripture.

It is nothing less than sinful to insert a meaning into God's Word in order to advance a moral cause ; and this, I fear, our fanatical friends of temperance reform have done in their teaching the "two wines" of Scripture.

Faithfully, GEO. R. VANDEWATER.

[137]

28 West 15th St., New York City, May 17, 1888.

REVEREND AND DEAR SIR :—I have your favor of the 15th inst., and, although the pamphlet has not yet reached me, I hasten to reply.

I had the pleasure of reading Dr. Jewett's monograph very carefully when it first made its appearance, and the facts and arguments which he brings forward are perfectly conclusive.

Having been for the last thirty years a diligent student of Hebrew and Greek, and at one time a professor of these languages in the Seabury Divinity School, I trust that I am not utterly incompetent to form some judgment on the merits of the question. The simple fact is, that the "two-wine" theory is a "FAD" to bolster up an extreme view and give it plausibility in the eyes of the unlearned. Dr. Jewett bursts this soap-bubble very neatly, and deserves great credit for the skill and courtesy with which he performs the useful labor of an iconoclast.

I am, respectfully yours, JOHN ANKETELL, A. M.

[138]

Cooperstown, N. Y., May 18, 1888.

DEAR SIR :—Accept my thanks for Dr. Jewett's pamphlet on the "two wines," or rather his very convincing demonstration that there is but *one wine ;* generically speaking, of course, and not considering the unfermented juice of the grape to be wine at all. The maxim, *in vino veritas,* is doubtful ; but it might seem that the conclusion, *de vino veritas,* ought to be easily reached, as in fact it would be, but for the "lying spirit," the very spirit of pious frauds in every age, who, in the person of more than one eminent prophet of the Temperance Reform, has offered himself to the Lord, to "lie for the truth." Respectfully yours,

W. W. LORD.

[139]

St. Stephen's Rectory, Olean, May 21, 1888.

REVEREND AND DEAR SIR :—In commenting briefly upon the pamphlet which you kindly sent me (Dr. Jewett on Communion Wine), and in answer to your communication of the 15th inst., I beg to call your attention to a paper which you may have already seen, by Prof. Atwater, in the April number of the *Century Magazine*, in which the writer makes the following pertinent observations : "I have been unable to find evidence that the composition of the juice of the grape, the laws of fermentation, or the practice in the making and using of wine were different in that country (Palestine), at that time, from those in other countries ; and I believe it safe to say, that the theory that Bible wine was different from other wine, and that it had not the alcohol which other wines contain, is without any basis to support it, in the opinion of the student of science." (*Food and Beverages*, pp. 139 and 140.)

Not long ago an article appeared in one of our local papers containing a severe criticism from a member of the W. C. T. U. of those Christian people who use wine (*i. e.*, fermented juice of the grape) in the Holy Communion, to which a layman of my congregation made reply, as follows : "I notice in your Saturday evening's issue that the Women's Christian Temperance Union objects to the use of fermented wine at the Lord's table. I cannot regard this otherwise than meddling with a subject entirely beyond the scope of their prerogative. The House of Bishops of the Protestant Episcopal Church, at the general convention of 1886, in reference to this question, adopted the following resolution, viz.: 'That in the judgment of the House of Bishops the use of the unfermented juice of the grape, as the lawful and proper wine of the Holy Eucharist, is unwarranted by the example of our Lord, and an unauthorized departure from the custom of the Catholic Church. Bread and wine are, by our Lord commanded, the material elements to be used, and any minister who would substitute others for these would be committing nothing less than sacrilege.' The above resolution was introduced by Bishop Littlejohn."

I would likewise call your attention to the exegetical fact, that the wine of the Holy Communion in the Corinthian Church, when St. Paul wrote his first Epistles to that congregation, must have been intoxicating. We read in chapter xi., verse 21, the following language : "For in eating, every one taketh before his own supper, and one is hungry, and another is drunken." This is given as an explanation of the Apostle's condemnation of the sacrilegious act of an unworthy partaking of the Lord's Supper.

Can anything be done to put a stop to the insane ravings of fanatical defenders of the temperance cause ? There is still ringing in my ears the profane utterance of an excited platform orator of the extreme wing, whom I heard say, among other wild speeches of like character, that the chief cause of intemperance in this country was the constant use, by certain churches, of fermented wine (?) at the Lord's Supper. He tried to argue (?) that, until that practice was broken up, there could be but little hope of the success of the temperance (?) work.

I have very little hope of the success of the temperance work so long as it counts among its so-called promoters men and women who favor the substitution of raisin water for grape juice, and vinegar for wine, in the Blessed Sacrament. But then, remember, that it is not the Sacrament to many of them.

I should like to resume this correspondence at some future time. I had the honor of being associated with Mr. Robert Graham, of the Church Temperance Society, of which he is the able secretary, when he introduced the glorious work of that society in the City of Philadelphia.

I should like to speak of the merits of Dr. Jewett's pamphlet, with the substance of which, as articles in the *Church Review*, I had some previous acquaintance. I hold an opinion very favorable to its scholarship and the soundness of its conclusions upon the Two-Wine theory.

I am, very truly yours,   JAMES W. ASHTON.

[140]
Poughkeepsie, N. Y., May 21, 1888.

My Dear Dr. Crosby:—For awhile, in my earlier ministry, I adopted, in a hesitating and tentative way, the two-wine theory, but I long since abandoned it as wholly untenable. Dr. Jewett's pamphlet on the subject seems to me quite conclusive.

Very sincerely yours,   J. R. KENDRICK.

[141]
Riverdale, New York City, May 22, 1888.

REVEREND HOWARD CROSBY, D.D.

Dear Brother:—Dr. Jewett's pamphlet, which you sent me, seems to me an exhaustive and conclusive argument on the two-wine theory. I think Dr. Jewett is right, without question.

But is not such a discussion a little like threshing of old straw? Those to whom such a scholarly argument as this appeals, are, I should think, all convinced already, and are all on our side—the same side with this pamphlet.

Very sincerely yours,   IRA S. DODD.

[142]
Nyack-on-Hudson, N. Y., May 23, 1888.

My Dear Brother:—In reply to your note of the 15th inst., and relative to Dr. Jewett's pamphlet on "Communion Wine," I would state that his examination of the subject seems to be exhaustive, and is satisfactory.

I regard it as a matter for deep regret that the words of Holy Scripture, and the testimony of the Church from the beginning, have been called in question, and thus occasion given for doubting our Lord's wisdom in the use of wine as a part of the Holy Communion institution.

Skeptics are always delighted to see Christians in controversy among themselves. I have long thought that the most plausible objections against Christianity are those its alleged advocates supply.

The unhappy divisions among those who name themselves after the name of the Lord and Saviour, make a sort of hot-bed for the growth of all sorts of strange doctrines and practices.

The testimony of a united Christendom, at least of so much of it as hold to "the faith once for all delivered to the saints," would dispel many vagaries; and it is just such sort of testimony all long and pray for who believe that in religious as well as in other matters, not merely union, but unity, is strength.

Very sincerely yours, in Christ,   CHARLES SEYMOUR.

[143]
Flatbush, N. Y., May 25, 1888.

Dear Sir:—I have carefully read the Rev. Dr. Jewett's articles on "Communion Wine," which you have been so kind as to send me, and regard his exegesis of scriptural words and phrases bearing on the subject as entirely correct, as well as exhaustive and incontrovertible.

I am, yours very truly,   T. S. DROWNE.

[144]
Syracuse, N. Y., May 20, 1888.

Reverend and Dear Sir :—Dr. Jewett's pamphlet is a very scholarly and able production. Until μεθύω can be proved to signify TO BE GORGED, as well as TO BE DRUNKEN, 1 Cor. xi. must be regarded, I think, as positive proof that WINE and not MUST was used at the Lord's Supper.

Yours respectfully,   J. E. JOHNSON.

[145]

333 Clinton Street, Brooklyn, May 19, 1888.

DEAR SIR :—I have read Dr. Jewett's admirable pamphlet on "Communion Wine."

It is inconceivable how any SCHOLAR, unless his mind were turned to a hobby, or rendered incompetent by fanatical prejudice, could reach any other conclusion than that which Dr. Jewett so unanswerably demonstrates. The Doctor has left nothing more to be said.

Respectfully,   WM. ALLEN FISK.

[146]

Durham, N. Y., May 23, 1888.

DEAR SIR :—I thank you sincerely for putting into my hands the most excellent article of Dr. Jewett's.

It is the most scholarly, candid and honest treatment of the two-wine THEORY that I have seen.

I maintain Prohibition principles for the sake of the weaker brother and his family's welfare. I believe most heartily in "high license" and "local option" as a means of curtailing the evils of intoxicating liquors, and perhaps controlling some of the evils connected with the saloons. Personally, I have no objections to allowing my congregation to decide whether they want "grape juice" or "fermented wine" for sacramental purposes, although I believe that Jesus used fermented wine at the Last Supper.

When a set of men tell me that the Bible teaches two kinds of wine, and that Jesus would not or did not tempt men to drink intoxicating wine, I must beg to infer that their scholarship is at fault or that their zeal in the TOTAL ABSTINENCE cause savors of a fanatic or jesuitical spirit. And I have no doubt if we should ask these wiseacres if the Bible was the only infallible rule of belief and practice, they would reply "yes." And hence they seek to make it agree with their individual conscience and the right of their personal interpretation upon the liquor question.

Sometimes, in discussing the temperance question, I have asked a zealous total abstinence man if he had ever preached a sermon from the text as found in the Book of Proverbs xxxi. 6, 7.

Hoping that the above will give you my idea of the two-wine THEORY in answer to your printed request, and thanking you again for the valuable pamphlet, I am, sincerely and fraternally yours,

FRED. J. POHL, First Presbyterian Church.

[147]

433 Fifth Avenue, New York, May 26, 1888.

MY DEAR DR. CROSBY:—I have read Dr. Jewett's articles on "Communion Wine" as carefully and with as much patience as I could command in the discussion of a doctrine so absurd and untenable as that of the "Two-Wine" theory.

After Dr. Hovey's articles, recently published in the *Baptist Quarterly*, I felt that that theory was no longer an open question, and had been laughed out of court. Dr. Jewett, with even greater skill and learning, has, forever, I think, settled the matter to all candid and unprejudiced minds, who have not a preconceived theory of temperance to uphold and who believe in making such a theory a Procrustean bed, for which even the Word of God is to be mutilated in order that it may agree therewith.

I thank you for giving me such "ammunition" in permanent form.

I am, cordially yours,   HENRY M. SANDERS.

[148]

Hygienic Institute, Geneva, N. Y., May 24, 1888.

REVEREND AND DEAR SIR:—I have carefully read Dr. Jewett's pamphle and am convinced that his arguments are unanswerable. I would add tha have a tolerable knowledge of the Hebrew and other Semitic languages, and am not unacquainted with Rabbinical literature. I venture to assert that the two-wines theory is baseless; that wine in Hebrew and other Semitic languages means and can only mean fermented wine, and to assert the contrary is betraying either a lack of knowledge or a willful perversion of facts.

Yours respectfully,

S. J. J. SCHERESCHEWSKY, formerly Bishop of China.

[149]

DEAR SIR:—The arguments on the Two-Wine Question were familiar to me. I have no doubt of the substantial correctness of Dr. Jewett's views as given three years ago.

My reasons, however, for total abstinence, Prohibition, exclusion of fermented wine from the Communion Table, rest on foundations in no way affected by the Two-Wine argument. Truly yours,

WAYLAND SPAULDING, Pastor Cong. Church, Poughkeepsie, N. Y.

[150]

Rochester, N. Y., May 24, 1888.

REVEREND AND DEAR SIR:—When Dr. Jewett's article was published in the *Church Review* I read it with peculiar interest.

His argument is clear, convincing and overwhelming; and its basis is, without a doubt, Scriptural Truth.

With respect, I am most sincerely yours,   WM. D'ORVILLE DOTY.

[151]

170 Spring Street, New York, May 29, 1888.

DEAR SIR:—Your note, with the pamphlet, was duly received. I have read it over carefully and consider it a very able and scholarly document. It is, to my mind, as complete a demonstration on the fermented wine being the proper wine to use in Communion as any problem in Euclid. And, if it were in my power, I would place it in the archives of the Church, to be referred to as a chief authority to settle the question in all time to come.

I had already seen some articles on this discussion in the *Church Magazine*, but still I thank you very much for the copy you sent me, and also your note calling my attention to the question, as I had not before given it sufficient attention to express any opinion on the subject.

I remain, yours truly,   W. STIRLING.

[152]

321 Seventh Street, Brooklyn, N. Y.

REVEREND AND DEAR SIR:—With great satisfaction I have read Dr. Jewett's pamphlet on "Communion Wine," which was sent so kindly to me.

In our Fatherland, where the vine is growing more than a thousand years, we never heard of "two classes of wines," so-called "fermented and unfermented." The classification is only in regard to quality.

We know by experience that the juice (must) of the grapes in a shorter time than three days will ferment, which fermentation will last from three to six weeks continually in the spring-time of two or three successive years. Without special preparation (chemical), you can never keep an unfermented juice.

We never can nor will believe that the Jewish Nation, with their laws of purification, have used the unfermented juice (must) of the grapes, which latter were, as is customary in the Orient, pressed with the feet.

The purification of the unfermented juice is effected by fermentation.

Above all, we stand as strong against the "Trinkteufel" as our greatest predecessor, Dr. M. Luther, but we are also against those who irreverently juggle with the words and deeds of our Lord Jesus Christ.

It is a wrong, not only against the Holy Scripture, but also against all personal freedom (mentioned by St. Paul, Rom. xiv.), which I believe is and should be the foundation of every Christian life in a free Christian country like ours. " It is defective logic which would show that because excess in any matter is denounced, all use whatever is forbidden."

My hearty thanks for your kindness. I am, yours truly,

C. LEB. WISSWAESSER, Ger. Evan. Luther. Pastor.

[153]

Plattsburgh, N. Y., May 28, 1888.

REV. DR. HOWARD CROSBY.

DEAR SIR :—I have read the pamphlet of the Rev. Dr. Jewett sent me by you, and at your request herewith write my opinions upon the subject matter.

In the first place, the pamphlet strikes me as an elaborate and exhaustive piece of exegesis on the Wine Question, but a useless logomachy about words which engender strife. It does not appear necessary to a mind whose judgment is not warped by prejudice to debate the question that WINE means WINE, whether it be derived from "Yayin," "Thavin," or "Tirosh," or any other foreign term.

In the second place, as to the proper documental element, I am disposed to hold that the unfermented juice of the grape, and for that matter wine much mingled with water, is more proper than any other substance, for the following reasons :—

1. Communion WINE is a misnomer. That word WINE, to the best of my ability to find, is not used in any of the statements "received of the Lord" concerning the institution of the Sacrament.

"*This Cup* ($\tau o \tilde{v} \tau o \ \tau \grave{o} \ \pi o \tau \acute{\eta} \rho \iota o \nu$)," not this Wine ($o \tilde{\iota} \nu o \varsigma$), "is the N. T. in my blood." "I will not henceforth drink of the FRUIT OF THE VINE ($\gamma \iota \nu \nu \acute{\eta} \mu a \tau o \varsigma \ \tau \tilde{\eta} \varsigma \ \dot{a} \mu \pi \acute{\epsilon} \lambda o \nu$) until I drink it new with you in my Father's kingdom." I should like, when you have leisure, to have you give me an exegesis of the last part of the promise as to the "new wine in the Father's kingdom."

"This cup is the N. T. in my blood," *i. e.*, the emblem of the promise and potency of his sacrificial death; but from the Saviour's side water *and* blood flowed. Why may not one or the commingling of both be as typical of his sacrifice as the other, since the washing of regeneration is typified by "pure water" as well as by the "blood of the Lamb." I am not a Greek-Churchman, but an old-fashioned Presbyterian, after the straitest sect.

2. The force of EXPEDIENCY for unfermented fruit of the vine has been often, more forcibly than I can put it, elaborated; for "conscience' sake," and to prevent temptation to tingling palates, I have latterly been constrained to use the "new fruit of vine in this dispensation of the Father's kingdom."

Very respectfully and admiringly yours,   JOSEPH GAMBLE.

[154]

158 South Fifth Street, Brooklyn, May 23, 1888.

DEAR SIR:—Your circular note of the 15th inst. and pamphlet on Communion Wine came duly to hand.

The pamphlet is a masterpiece of learning and research.

I will take some time to study it, and probably "favor" you with my opinion on the subject.

Yours respectfully,   W. J. MacDOWELL.

[155]

Annandale, N. Y., May 22, 1888.

DEAR SIR:—I received a few days since the pamphlet of Dr. Jewett, which you were kind enough to send me, and have read it with much interest. It is a scholarly production, and seems to me conclusive with regard to the question at issue. There is no doubt in my mind that our Lord used fermented wine when he instituted the Sacrament of the Holy Eucharist, and that we may with propriety follow his example when we celebrate the Lord's Supper. I quite agree with you also in many other phases of the temperance question.

Very truly yours,   GEO. B. HOPSON.

[156]

48 Eighth Avenue, Brooklyn, June 28, 1888.

DEAR SIR :—I am indebted to you for Dr. Jewett's pamphlet on the wine controversy. It is a comprehensive and a masterly treatment of the whole subject, and only confirms me in the opinion I have always held, that the theorists who condemn the use of fermented wine for sacramental use as unscriptural have not a leg to stand on. On grounds of expediency only, my church uses a non-intoxicating wine, which, having undergone a sort of artificial fermentation, has sufficient of the wine flavor to be agreeable to the taste, and yet not be a source of temptation to any who are weak through former indulgence of the appetite. This wine is procured from Mr. A. W. Pearson, of Vineland, N. J. I am free to say that the "stuff" used for sacramental purposes in some of our Brooklyn churches is simply nauseating, and has a tendency to divert one's attention from the spiritual it should represent to the stomach which it has roused into rebellion.   Very sincerely yours,

T. A. NELSON, Mmeorial Presbyterian Church.

[157]

New York, June 28, 1888.

DEAR BROTHER :—A month ago, perhaps, I received a pamphlet on Communion Wines, etc., by Dr. E. H. Jewett, with request to report my view of the same, after careful reading, to you.

I have only to say that I have carefully and with great pleasure read the same, and that it only in clearer and larger way CONFIRMS the view I have always held of that subject.

In the clear and simple terms of the Scripture, and the historical evidence, it is a masterly statement, which it seems to me no impartial mind can refuse.

With many thanks for the favor, I am, truly yours,   F. S. BRADNER.

[158]

Newburg, N. Y., June 20, 1888.

MY DEAR DR. CROSBY :—Dr. Jewett's pamphlet, which you so kindly sent, was mislaid, and not forwarded for some time, which must be my excuse for so long delaying to answer your inquiry.

Such data as I myself possessed had made me come very decidedly to the same conclusion as Dr. Jewett, and I was glad to be fortified in my belief by so able and convincing a treatment of the subject.

A statement, made to me by a very intelligent lady in France, made me wonder as to how soon the intoxicating property might be developed even in *Must*. When a young girl, she told me, she went to visit a vintage in her own country, and was given to drink of the freshly pressed liquor taken from the vat, and became "thoroughly drunk" (" bien ivre ") in consequence.

While holding the view before mentioned, I would state that I am almost a total abstainer from all alcoholic beverages.

I am, very sincerely, your friend and brother,   SAM'L M. AKERLY.

[159]

Tarrytown, N. Y., June 26, 1888.

Your circular and pamphlet, kindly sent me some time since, have been received. The subject of which the essay treats is most interesting and important; the able author has handled the matter with convincing skill. I believe his conclusions correct; they tally with all my previous study and reading on the question; I think the two-wine theory is untenable.

As to the practical application of such a conclusion, it may easily be unwisely and unfairly made; every truth is influenced by every other truth; only in such light is it truth; a fact of experience is of as much importance as a fact of Scripture. Sin perverts what righteousness can enjoy. God made everything good—the wheat, the grapes, the wine; but not until the spirit of goodness reign everywhere can man be kept from debasing and destroying himself; hence safeguards are necessary. High license? Yes. Better yet—menaced by the fact of universal weakness,—Prohibition

Respectfully and fraternally, BENJ. L. HERR, Pastor Baptist Church.

[160]

First Presbyterian Manse, Dryden, N. Y., June 26, 1888.

REVEREND AND DEAR SIR:—Permit me herewith to acknowledge, with thanks, the receipt of Dr. Jewett's pamphlet on the wine question.

He discusses it in a most scholarly and somewhat elaborate manner, presenting, it seems to me, from the scriptural point of view, an irrefutable argument and as positive a conclusion as it is undeniable.

Very truly yours   G. V. REICHEL.

[161]

346 West 28th Street, New York, June 4, 1888.

DEAR DR. CROSBY:—Dr. Edward H. Jewett has done an excellent service. His exegesis of the Scriptures on the "Wine Question" is so scholarly, candid and conclusive as to carry conviction to the unprejudiced mind. The question of two wines from one juice of the grape is neither scriptural nor scientific. The juice of the apple from the press to vinegar we call cider, and nobody mistakes our meaning. We speak of its properties as sweet, sour, etc., etc., but never as two liquors. So the Scripture speaks of the juice of the grape. Unmixed with any other ingredients, and not spoken of symbolically, it is only and always wine. There may be two or twenty mixtures, but they are not what the Bible specifically calls wine. Its commendation as a blessing, and condemnation as a curse, relate strictly to its use. The wedding wine at Cana was exceptional—miraculously made to certify the divinity and illustrate the power of him who came to seek and save the lost.

Faithfully yours,   J. SPAULDING.

[162]

119 Avenue B, New York City, June 4, 1888.

DEAR REVEREND DOCTOR:—In accordance with your desire, I have looked through the pamphlet of Dr. Jewett, in which he holds that it is right to use fermented wine for the Holy Sacrament of the Eucharist, and supports his opinion with numerous texts and testimonies.

In common with all Catholics, I agree with the reverend gentleman in this matter. We never use, or did use, as far as I know, any but fermented wine, although unfermented juice of the grape is regarded as valid matter, but to be used only in case of necessity.

As, no doubt you know, we hold the doctrine of the Real Presence, and hence attach immense importance to the use of valid matter.

The species of wine is still used by the priest in the Mass, but it is no longer used in communicating the laity, this right having been abolished by the Supreme authority of the Church on account of the abuses which are likely to follow, one of which is the difficulty of giving Communion to such multitudes without irreverence. The species of bread alone (unleavened) is now used for giving Holy Communion in the Western or Latin branch of the Catholic Church, but the United Greeks and other rites, which are still in

Communion with the Roman Pontiff, continue to give Communion under both the species of bread and wine.

I am surprised that anybody should maintain that by wine in the Script ures unfermented grape juice was meant, and was amused at the innocence of some Total Abstinence ladies who sent me an exhortation to cease using the fermented kind in the Mass. Of course, such matters are with us regulated by the highest authority only.

Moreover, it looks as if the good Total Abstinence people ought to have enough to do with the drunkards without paying so much attention to the moderate drinkers. They seem somehow to have less toleration for the latter than for the former, and are so bitter and *intemperate* sometimes that one is tempted to follow the example of St. Paul to Timothy and counsel them "to take a little wine for the stomach's sake." They appear to need some such tonic to enable them to live in a brotherly way with their fellow-men. If Prohibition were to make us all like them in disposition, I fear we would have to get up anti-total-abstinence societies.

Your High-License Bill was in the right direction, and I regret its failure.

Yours truly, P. F. McSWEENY.

[163]

Poughkeepsie, June 2, 1888.

REVEREND AND DEAR SIR:—Your letter of May 15th was forwarded to me while in Philadelphia, but not having the pamphlet to which you refer in your letter, I was compelled to defer my reply to the present time. The ground covered by Dr. Jewett's pamphlet has been for years quite familiar to me. The attempt of Edward C. Delevan, of the Town of Ballston, Saratoga County, to induce the church of which he was a member, and neighboring churches, to cease the use of wine in the Sacrament of the Lord's Supper aroused the attention of many fifty years ago. As he was living near, and as he was well known to me and my father's family, you will not be surprised that his views and efforts made a deep impression upon my mind. About this time he persuaded Dr. Eliphalet Nott, President of Union College, to write and publish his lectures on the wine question.

About this time appeared certain papers written and published by several clergymen of the City of Albany combating the views of Mr. Delevan and Dr. Nott.

Those papers gave no uncertain sound, and did much to shake my confidence in the views and doctrines of Mr. Delevan and Rev. Dr. Nott. I soon after entered college, and in my classical reading I never lost sight of this subject, and afterwards, in my training during several years in the Trenton Theological Seminary under Dr. Archibald Alexander and Dr. Charles Hodge, and other illustrious men, I was fully convinced that there was no true basis for the belief in " unfermented wine." It seems to me a *misnomer.*

I fully believe that *oinos* always means intoxicating wine ; such wine I believe the Saviour made at the marriage in Cana in Galilee, and such wine we are advised to use for "our stomach's sake."

The highest scholarship of the age, I believe, knows nothing of this modern exegesis. I fully approve of the sentiments and exegesis of the pamphlet you sent me. I believe it will do much good if sent widely among the clergy of our land.

Furthermore, I will say that a residence of several years in India, and mingling at times with people from various parts of Asia, have confirmed me in my belief in the words set forth in the pamphlet of Dr. Jewett.

I have been a steady and hard worker in the great temperance movement of the day, and not without a good degree of success in that field. I have never signed a temperance pledge, but fully co-operated with those temperance workers who believed in it. While there were some sentences in your widely known Boston lecture that I regretted to see, I had no sympathy with or approval of the outcry that it called forth.

With high respect for your courage and scholarship and truly Christian spirit, as manifested in our Assembly at Philadelphia, I remain,

Yours most truly,   A. H. SEELEY.

[164[

"The Church Eclectic," Utica, N. Y., June 2, 1888.

DEAR DR. CROSBY—I desire to thank you for sending me Dr. Jewett's pamphlet. He has been a contributor to my magazine, but not on that subject. Some time before he wrote I reprinted the substance of an article from the *Church Quarterly Review* on the Scripture view, and also a tract on "Wine in the Holy Eucharist," by Messrs. Dowling & Martin, both of which I send you herewith. I think they fairly represent the philological and scientific aspects of the question.

Is there not too much of the old Manichean dualism in our popular religion, which places the seat of evil in THINGS rather than in the evil heart of man, which makes evil use of them? Saint Paul had to release his Gentile converts from their heathen bondage, who consecrated even all food and drink to idols to spite the Christians, and told them to ask no questions for conscience' sake. The most fearful feature in this matter is the disposition to call in question our blessed Lord's own conduct as the Pharisees did in contrasting it with the asceticism of John the Baptist, under Nazarite vows. He "kept the best TILL last," directly against the rule that was intended to secure against excess. It is a sublime thought that his teaching builds no external fences against temptation, but endows us with the spiritual power to overcome it, and to keep our bodies in "temperance, soberness and charity." Force and compulsion never produced a VIRTUE of any kind—are incompatible with the very quality of a grace or virtue. All our history protests against compulsory outward conformity. The Seventh Commandment takes in all sins of the flesh, but we see the strange phenomenon in these days of men, and women too, running to and fro in crowds, to all manner of meetings, professedly for moral purposes, but INCIDENTALLY to enjoy themselves, have a good time, with the special objective point of plenty of good eating and drinking. In most cases the money so spent is MORE than that directly raised for the object. I can't help seeing a sort of GROSSNESS and worship of the body in many of our modern reforming bodies. The moral sense is becoming unbalanced, if not ATROPHIED.

I have reclaimed a number of drunkards in my time, but ONLY under God, by their CONVERSION to a Christian life. It is only Divine Grace that can make a man conqueror of this vice, as well as some of the powerful LUSTS of the body, which are still more terrible, and more pampered by the fashions and habits of society, until faces that are perfectly natural and unconscious are seldom to be met.

Of course, I favor legislation. I believe the High License to be a great step up, and perhaps sufficient to allow full play to a moral crusade. My son lost his election because he would not pledge himself against it, and FOR the repeal of the Sunday Laws. We have arrived at a point at which public opinion will sustain both, and ought to become our settled policy. But those who denounce the use of wine or its manufacture as A SIN, even in the Sacrament, fly in the face of Scripture, of history, and of common sense, and are trying themselves to manufacture an artificial conscience. There are sins enough already without making new ones, or making sad whom the Lord hath not made sad. The worst of it is, such extremes are ALWAYS followed by great reactions, as in Chas. Second's time, equally overwhelming to sober truth.

Yours very faithfully,   W. T. GIBSON.

[165]

Rochester, N. Y., June 2, 1888.

MY DEAR DR. CROSBY :—I am once more obliged to you, as I have been so frequently before. This time it is for sending me and calling my attention to Dr. Jewett's pamphlet on the question of Two Wines.

It expresses my long-cherished convictions and the conclusions in which I rest, except that as a matter of EXPEDIENCY, regardless of what is lawful, or of early ecclesiastical precedent, or of the sort of wine used by our Lord at the Last Supper, I favor the use, at our Communion Table, of a liquid not intoxicating. I am indifferent to its character so long as it is not unwholesome nor intoxicating. I am, with great respect and affection, yours,

HENRY H. STEBBINS.

[166]

Astoria, L. I., June 1, 1888.

REVEREND AND DEAR SIR :—I have read Dr. Jewett's pamphlet, which you kindly sent me, on the subject of Communion Wine, and do not hesitate to pronounce his argument, in my opinion, completely unanswerable. In order to support the novel theory of "the two wines," one must go, as he shows quite conclusively, I think, very far out of the way, and tamper with language and history in a manner utterly unworthy of a Christian, and fatal to any unprejudiced pursuit of Truth.

Yours truly, CHARLES M. BELDEN.

[167]

Elmira, N. Y., June 2, 1888.

DEAR SIR :—By your request I have read Dr. Jewett's pamphlet on the wine question,

To me his argument is satisfactory and unanswerable, and to my mind, in regard to this and all other things which are not sinful *per se*, the apostle's rule is the infallible guide, viz., that we are to use the things of this world, and not abuse them. Yours truly,

GEO. H. McKNIGHT, Rector of Trinity Church.

[168]

DEAR BROTHER :—Your letter of May 15th came to me, forwarded from Rushville, N. Y., my former residence. Jewett's argument on Wine came also. I have read it, and regard it as conclusive. Two years ago I went over the question of two wines in the Bible pretty thoroughly, and settled the question that the whole theory is a myth, never thought of by men before the present century, and is the result of the present temperance agitation. Every reformation is liable to such extremes. The same was true of the anti-slavery agitation. These attempts to force the Bible into service in its letter rather than in its spirit are a weakness which will die out in due time.

Thanks for the pamphlet. It is a good strong argument.

Yours fraternally, H. B. FRY.

[169]

342 East 42d St., New York City, May 31, 1888.

DEAR SIR:—Having carefully examined the pamphlet you had the kindness to send me, I feel no hesitancy in giving my opinion, both historically and linguistically. Dr. Jewett is perfectly right. There is certainly a difference between *Yayin* and *Tirosh*, the former denoting old wine, the latter the fruit of a recent vintage. But that the "old" was considered the "best," is evident from the fact that *Yayin*, and not *Tirosh*, was prescribed for sacrificial purposes. The natural meaning of Hosea iv. 11 is decisive against *Fürst*. Evidences are yet wanting that it was must, and not real wine, fermented grape juice, Christ drank at the Passover.

As regards leaven, Dr. Jewett might have mentioned that modern science discountenances the notion that fermentation, such as is caused by leaven, is the natural action of the body fermenting, resulting from its tendency to decay. Its cause is, as botanists have shown, the introduction of a new life-force, a plant technically called TORULA, but more commonly known as yeast. Leaven is, therefore, a symbol, not of corruption, but of something good or bad, that grows by organizing surrounding elements. This is the reason why both the Kingdom of Heaven and the doctrine of the Pharisees can be compared to leaven.

The question, of vastly more importance, what should be one's attitude to the liquor power, must be determined upon other grounds.

Respectfully yours, in Christ,

NATHANIEL SCHMIDT, Pastor of First Swedish Baptist Church.

[170]

Hoosick Falls, N. Y., June 6th, 1888.

DR. HOWARD CROSBY.

REVEREND AND DEAR SIR:—I have always regarded the "two-wine" theory as without support in Scripture. While, therefore, I cannot say that Dr. Jewett's argument convinced me of the correctness of the opposite view, it did convince me of its own entire soundness, and greatly enlightened and strengthened my convictions on this subject. I have read the pamphlet twice with care and all possible candor, and I do not see how any unprejudiced mind, or, indeed, any prejudiced mind, can resist its conclusions.

Recently the W. C. T. U. here petitioned my Session to discontinue the use of wine at the Communion. The Session replied that they had no scruples against this use of wine, but that they would make the change desired as an open and avowed concession to the opinions and wishes of the women if they could be assured that the request was supported by the general body of the Church. The petition was at once withdrawn, and we have heard no more of it.

Respectfully and truly yours,   JOHN TATLOCK, Pastor Pres. Church.

[171]

1640 Ave. B, June 1, 1888.

DEAR SIR:—I thank you for directing my attention to Dr. Jewett's pamphlet on "Communion Wine." It did not require all this erudition and acuteness to convince me that the author's view of the question is the true one. But the labor is well bestowed, and I trust it will make peace in the Churches and wisdom among temperance workers.

Yours very truly,   E. J. MORRIS.

[172]

Presbyterian Church, Waterville, N. Y., May 30, 1888.

DEAR BROTHER:—Heartily approve of Dr. Jewett's views, and believe, with Father Gavazzi, that the expression "unfermented wine" imparts downright nonsense. Have resided in Palestine many months.

T. R. G. PECK, Pastor.

[173]

Auburn Theological Seminary, June 4, 1888.

REVEREND AND DEAR SIR:—At your request, I have read Dr. Jewett's pamphlet, which you kindly sent me with your favor of the 15th ult. Without criticising particular points, the argument, or rather "the critical examination," etc., is conclusive, unanswerable. That it was intoxicating wine which our Saviour habitually drank, must be so, or his words—Matt. xi. 18, 19; Luke vii. 33, 34—would have no meaning.

I often dwell upon one particular, with regard to the use of *Tirosh* and *Yayin*, which, with me, had great weight. It is that, as a rule, to which there are very few, if any, exceptions. *Tirosh* is used in connection with the fruits of the earth NOT YET GATHERED, or, if gathered, NOT YET PREPARED FOR FOOD OR OTHER USE; e. g., Gen. xxvii. 28, 37, "corn and wine" (*Tirosh*); whereas *Yayin* is used with PREPARED ARTICLES, or at least partially prepared; e. g., with BEATEN or THRESHED wheat and barley, with flour, bread, oil, etc., Gen. xiv. 15, 27, 25, etc, etc.

With me, "Do thyself no harm," and "It is good neither to eat flesh, nor to drink wine, nor to do anything whereby thy brother stumbleth, or is offended, or is made weak"—these are sufficient reasons for total abstinence.

Fraternally yours,   E. A. HUNTINGTON.

[174]

First Presbyterian Church, Fowlerville, N. Y., June 5, 1888.

MY DEAR SIR AND BROTHER:—I have just read with great interest, ardor and profit Dr. Jewett's pamphlet on Communion Wine, which you have so kindly sent me.

Trained in the conservative school of Princeton theology, and imbibing as a part of my very life the principles of God's Word as I believe they are there most accurately interpreted in harmony with our principles and polity, and having been nurtured in these views by a father and grandfather who were Presbyterian clergymen, I do most heartily indorse every word and every syllable of Dr. Jewett's monograph.

Although it contained nothing new to me, and although I have carefully reached his conclusions from the same and other premises, I regard his position as impregnable and unanswerable. I hope that every minister of our denomination may receive a copy of the same, and every student in our theological seminaries.

I utterly repudiate the gospel of Francis Milliard, *et id omne genus,* who would supplant the Gospel of Jesus Christ, and dictate to Embassadors of Christ what we shall use in the holy of holies of the Communion, to exhibit the dying love of our Saviour. As for me, I would not KNOWINGLY administer anything else but real and true wine at the Lord's Supper, in imitation of MY MASTER. I cordially reiterate the words of my late Professor, Dr. A. A. Hodge:—

"Whosoever puts away true and real wine, or fermented grape juice, on moral grounds, from the Lord's Supper, sets himself up as more moral than the Son of God who reigns over his conscience and than the Saviour of Souls who redeemed him." On the grounds of expediency, as well tell me that ladies must not wear jewelry to the Lord's Table for fear that some Christian brother (?) will be tempted to steal their diamonds; as well tell me that beauty must not adorn the Lord's Table for fear that some Christian (?) will be tempted to lust by its presence. That man or woman who cannot come to the Lord's Table and eat the bread and drink the cup without falling, if there is such a weakling on earth, has no business at the Lord's Table, and I would warn such a one to remain away.

The very idea and claim of zealots on this point is as great a libel on Christ and his Word as any device of Satan conceived in modern times. It is blasphemy.

I desire to give you an instance which has come within my knowledge recently, of unimpeachable authority, which discloses the unquestioned absurdity of using the so-called "unfermented" wine. In a church (Methodist) here in Western New York, they use the so-called unfermented wine. A man who had formerly been an inebriate professed conversion and joined that church, but would never commune, on the ground that he was afraid he would go back to drinking if he did. Remember, this was the so-called "unfermented wine!" He was finally urged to go to Communion, consented, and on the following day engaged in the most brutal debauch he had engaged in for years! So much for the moral benefit of this "bastard wine," which 19th-century fanaticism has invented for the saving of souls! So much for expediency, as superior to the example and teachings of Christ, and the concensus of every scholar, missionary and he Church Catholic! God bless you in your efforts to stem the tide of fanaticism. I am for temperance and godliness (1 Cor. x. 31), but the age demands men who are loyal to Truth and the old path.

Very cordially yours,   B. D. SINCLAIR.

[175]

First Congregational Church, Ithaca, N. Y., June 5, 1888.

DEAR DR. CROSBY:—The pamphlet of Dr. Jewett is decisive as to the nature of ancient and modern wine of the Orient, in my judgment. Since Governor Andrew's discussion with Dr. Minor, I have had no doubt that the Lord and his apostles used fermented wine—indeed, had no doubt before I read that debate.

The only reason for yielding, as we have done here, to the brethren who desire some substitute for wine in the form of a decoction of grape syrup—for Communion use—is that "the strong must yield to the weak," and that perhaps the Master himself, were he here, would say, "Better have no Communion whatever in outward form if you are to fall into contention." But the large majority feel that they are the victims of an ill-timed scrupulosity.

With great regard and esteem, yours,   CHARLES M. TYLER.

[176]

Broadalbin, N. Y., June 7, 1888.

DEAR SIR :—Dr. Jewett's argument on the subject of Communion Wine seems to me sound, so far as I am able to judge. I never took much stock in the so-called two-wine theory at any rate; but not being in a position to make my influence felt, I have not said much on the subject. Perhaps at some time I may have more to say.   Truly yours,   J. H. TRUSSELL.

[177]

Clinton, N. Y., June 5, 1888.

DEAR DR. CROSBY :—I have read with care, for the second time, the articles written by Rev. Dr. Edward H. Jewett, and reprinted from the *Church Review* of April and July, 1885, and published by the Church Review Association of New York, in 1886, under the title of " A Critical Examination of Scriptural Words and Historical Testimony."

It seems to me to be thoroughly scholarly, and particularly in maintaining that there was BUT ONE KIND OF WINE ever spoken of in the Old Testament, or in the New, and that this was FERMENTED in its nature, and probably intoxicating in its effects.

The testimony which he superadds from American and English missionaries abundantly, of large scholarship and acquaintance with Oriental life and manners, is of the most satisfactory kind, in opposition to the contrary ideas and opinions of Drs. Lees, Samson and Prof. Stewart.

I think with Bishop Seymour, of Springfield, Ill., that Dr. Jewett's argument on " Communion Wine " is both CONVINCING and CRUSHING, and that the whole round of false ideas, often called biblical, which Dr. Jewett effectually attacks and demolishes, is full of unsound assumptions and deductions.

I am, dear sir, always yours,   BENJ. W. DWIGHT.

[178]

First Baptist Church, Greenport, L. I., June 5, 1888.

DEAR SIR :—The pamphlet sent came duly to hand. Thank you for it. I was long ago convinced that all sound argument was *against* the "two-wine" theory, and have not hesitated to say so both in public and in private.
Dr. Jewett only strengthens that conviction. Sincerely,

C. E. HISCOX.

[179]

Evangelisch-Lutherisches Ministerium vom Staate New York
und Angrenzenden Staaten und Laendern,
Rochester, N. Y., June 4, 1888.

REVEREND AND DEAR DOCTOR :—I have taken great pleasure in examining the treatise on " Communion Wine," by the Rev. Dr. E. H. Jewett, pursuant to your request. I reviewed the same in one of our Lutheran church papers several years ago, when the "two-wine" theory was advocated in some of our church periodicals. I took occasion to examine into the meaning of the several Hebrew words translated "wine," and their use in connection with the services in the temple and the eating of the Passover, and found that the claims advanced by the friends of the "two-wine" theory were not supported by facts. The paper of Dr. Jewett is most thorough and scholarly.

Thanking you for the copy sent to me, I am, with sentiments of the highest esteem, Very truly yours, J. NICUM, President Conf. 4th District.

[180]

MY DEAR SIR :—Thanks for the pamphlet on "Communion Wine" by Rev. Edward H. Jewett, S.T.D. I have read it with great care and interest. His argument is sound and incontrovertible. It is refreshing to follow so careful a student, and feel when his work is done that his position is impregnable.

This paper ought to end the discussion on the "two kinds of wine," if language and history are of any worth.

Nevertheless, I think it well, FOR THE SAKE OF WEAK BRETHREN AND YOUNG PEOPLE IN OUR CHURCHES, TO USE THE MILDEST KIND OF WINE in celebrating the Lord's Supper, and even prefer the preparation which is CALLED "unfermented wine" for that purpose.

No, I do not understand that that militates against the position of the essayist ; it does not claim scriptural example or deny that Christ used wine in its proper sense.

Cordially yours, SAMUEL H. VIRGIN, Pilgrim Church, Madison Ave., cor. 121st St.

[181]
New York, June 5, 1888.

REVEREND AND DEAR SIR :—Absence from home and attendance at Synod must be my excuse for not giving an earlier reply to your favor of the 15th ult.

I thank you for Dr. Jewett's pamphlet, which I have read with the greatest satisfaction. I heartily agree with the highly commendatory notices printed on the cover of the pamphlet, and especially with the language of Bishop Seymour, when he says that Dr. Jewett's article on "Communion Wine" is "CONVINCING AND CRUSHING." The last paragraph, on page 60, is a well-deserved rebuke to all intemperate advocates of temperance who want to be wise above what is written, and holier than the Lord who did his first miracle in Cana.

Yours truly, G. F. KROTEL.

[182]
New Brighton, N. Y.

DEAR SIR :—The pamphlet expresses my convictions entirely, as, of course, I could not express them myself. Since in the ministry, I have given such study to the subject as every minister ought to give, and while the pamphlet of Dr. Jewett has not formed my opinions, it has confirmed them.

Its arguments are certainly unanswerable.

The time has come for every educated man to KNOW the right or the wrong of the subject discussed. Ever sincerely,

T. A. LEGGETT, Pastor Presbyterian Church.

[183]
Rome, N. Y., June 4, 1888.

REVEREND DOCTOR :—There is not the slightest foundation for the superinduced distinction of modern zealots between a wine unfermented and fermented, and that the former was in use at the time of our Lord or before the

Christian era among the Jews, or at their feasts of a religious character. For two thousand years no such an issue has ever been raised, and hence it would be a fruitless task to search for proofs to prop up a modern theory of rather sentimental fancy. The dissertation of Dr. Jewett on the subject is fully borne out by the researches of the late Dr. Schegg, Professor at the University of Munich. In his work (Biblische Archæologie, Part I, pp. 172-180), where the subject is well treated, nothing occurs to give rise to any doubt as to the nature of the wine used. (Published 1886.)

The idea of using any other wine for sacramental purposes, at least in the Catholic Church, cannot be discussed ; for juice of the grape only, arrested in fermentation by other means, cannot be called wine, and it is not the *materia* proper for preservation under the appellation of wine.

I do not see how the abettors of such a theory can overcome the arguments of Dr. Jewett's pamphlet, or any facts so well established in the researches of biblical archæology. I hope you will find such is the general opinion of all scholars and divines in the country.

Very sincerely yours,   P. SCHMITT,

Rector of St. Mary's Church, formerly Professor of Biblical Archæology.

[184]

Hillsdale, June 4, 1888.

DEAR BROTHER :—In the good cause of Bible Temperance, I am ever so much obliged to you for Dr. Jewett's pamphlet relating to Bible Wine.

He makes the matter as clear as a mathemathical demonstration to unprejudiced minds.   Yours truly,

JOHN MINOR.

[185]

Bath, N. Y., May 29, 1888.

REVEREND AND DEAR SIR :—My father, Rev. A. P. Brush, wishes me to write in answer to your letter of the 15th. He is suffering from an accident, being thrown from his carriage five weeks ago, and is still confined to his bed.

He has read Dr. Jewett's pamphlet, and begs to say that he knows of but *one* kind of wine—*that is Fermented Wine.*

Yours truly,   A. P. BRUSH.

[186]

Yates, N. Y., May 30, 1888.

REVEREND AND DEAR SIR :—I have read the pamphlet by Dr. Jewett on " Communion Wine," and am highly pleased with it.

He handles the question fairly, and leaves no room for doubt as to the matter of the wine of the Bible. In the face of such an amount of evidence, I do not see how any one can favor the idea of two kinds of wine. But if the object of the pamphlet is to convince its readers that this kind of wine is essential to the proper administering of the ordinance in our churches at the present time, it has in my case failed utterly.

With our different habits, and the impossibility of procuring wine like that in use at the time of our Saviour, I do not think that the use of unfermented juice of the grape detracts from the value of the ordinance in any degree. On the other hand, I know of brethren who have gone back to their cups, from which they believed themselves saved, because the taste of the wine at the Lord's Table brought back their old appetite with all its force. Is the principle expressed by Paul in 1 Cor. viii. inconsistent with our Lord's teaching, and may it not apply here ?

In my administration I use only the unfermented " fruit of the vine."

Fraternally yours,   F. R. HOLT.

[187]

90 Fleet St., Brooklyn, N. Y., May 30, 1888.

REVEREND AND DEAR SIR:—I have read Dr. Jewett's pamphlet with great benefit. My mind was unsettled on the wine question, but Dr. Jewett's articles have convinced me. It seems to me that his dictum is final, that there is no appeal from his facts and conclusions. I will be interested to see an attempt to break the force of his arguments and to deny the validity of his conclusion. Thanking you for calling the articles to my notice, I am,

Yours very truly,   WILLIAM V. TUNNELL.

[188]

430 West 35th St., New York, May 29, 1888.

DEAR BROTHER:—I desire to thank you for the pamphlet on "Communion Wine" sent me. I have read it, and acknowledge it to be a very able argument, and I trust will greatly help the settlement of a question on which abler minds than mine widely differ. Again thanking you, I am, yours, with respect,

W. C. SMITH.

[189]

House of the Paulist Fathers, 59th St. and 9th Ave., New York, May 30, 1888.

REVEREND AND DEAR SIR:—Allow me to express my thanks to you for sending me a copy of the article on "Communion Wine" by Rev. Edward H. Jewett. Every lover of Divine Truth ought to strenuously oppose those who distort the Sacred Scriptures to justify fanaticism. Your views on the Temperance Question are the best that I have ever read from the pen of any Protestant clergyman.

Respectfully yours,   H. M. WYMAN, C. S. P.

[190]

61 East 123d St., New York, May 30, 1888.

MY DEAR DR. CROSBY:—I have read Dr. Jewett's pamphlet, which you kindly sent me, with care and intense interest and satisfaction. Its spirit is admirable, and its argument seems to me conclusive. It has made clearer and stronger my conviction on the Scripture Wine controversy. Only unreasoning prejudice and judgment warped by enthusiasm ought to be expected to carry on the discussion, in the clear light which Dr. Jewett's paper casts upon the whole matter. Very sincerely yours,

I. ELMENDORF.

[191]

Nyack-on-the-Hudson, N. Y., May 19, 1888.

DR. HOWARD CROSBY.

DEAR SIR:—I thank you for calling my attention to Dr. Jewett's articles on Communion Wine. I have read every word with careful attention. I have held to Dr. Jewett's view tenaciously for a dozen years. The persons who adopt the two-wine theory must face the combined scholarship of a frowning world. Drs. Samson and Lee, in our day, and Drs. Nott and Stuart in the preceding decades, are the only writers I know much about who have taken what may be called HIGH GROUND on the question. But Drs. Jewett, Moore and I. P. Warren, together with Dr. A. Hovey, have settled the question forever. I regard Dr. Jewett's articles as a complete refutation of the two-wine theory. This hypothesis is a delusion so incoherent and baseless that it is almost a mental disgrace to urge it. If the person who reads Dr. Jewett's articles with attention is not overwhelmingly convinced of the truth of his position, it is because these persons are mentally disqualified to study Greek and Semitic philology. Dr. Jewett's articles, in my opinion, are unanswerable. The moral phases of the "two-wine" hypothesis can be argued *ad infinitum*, but the linguistic phase of the subject, not only can be demonstrated, but has been scientifically proved by Dr. Jewett. Very truly yours,

E. E. THOMAS, Pastor of the Baptist Church.

P. S.—To illustrate the position which thinking men will sometimes take when mentally convinced, let me call your attention to the following fact:

Some years ago I reviewed Wendell Phillips's reply to your "Calm View," before the Baptist ministers' conference in Providence, R. I. A good Doctor of Divinity, who was present, and who was naturally opposed to my defense of your position, acknowledged this much: " Yes," said he, " I suppose Christ did make fermented wine and drink it, but I AM SORRY HE DID IT."

If you have a copy of your " Calm View" at hand, or will tell me where I can conveniently procure a copy, I shall be grateful, as I lost my copy long ago.   E. E. T.

[192]

West Town, N. Y.

MY DEAR DR. CROSBY:—I know of no apology that can be rendered for what has been said by some notable divines in regard to the Bible account of the wines used in the Communion, except that some of the most learned and truthful men have sometimes said some of the most false and foolish things.

How any one that could read the Bible, even in the King's English, and note what is there said in regard to wine-drinking, could come to the conclusion that there was a peculiar kind of wine that all good people that loathed drunkenness were in the habit of only using, and which only was used in all their sacred rites and ceremonies, is to my mind one of the greatest marvels in all the wide range of this world's literature.

The Bible certainly does say much in favor of refraining from the excessive use of wine, and often expresses this sentiment in such strong terms that it would seem almost to amount to a prohibition, while no reference is made to any other kind of wine that might be used in its place, against the use of which there could be no such objections.

Besides, it is not to be denied there were cases in which the use of intoxicating wine was not only tolerated, but even recommended. There is no reason why a different wine should have been used in the Passover, as there was for the use of the unleavened bread.

But in the case of the wine used in the Sacrament of the Lord's Supper, the intoxicating properties had nothing to do with it as an appropriate symbol, but only its dietetic, as used in their principal meals.

A symbol, as has been well said of a parable, can not be made to go on all fours: its use is not responsible for every objectionable feature that may be pressed out of it.

Besides, it has been made patent by the Apostle himself that such wine was actually used in the Sacrament, by his rebuke of those who were represented as being drunken by the drinking of this very wine in connection with this sacred ordinance.

And yet it would be needlessly straining the matter to make this any impediment to the temperance cause. We learn from Christ's Sermon on the Mount that many things tolerated in the Old Testament were set aside by him for a higher and purer practice in the New, and there are many customs and duties enjoined in the New Testament that should not be tolerated in our age.

Laws can not well be made much better than the people they are made to govern.

It would have availed but little for a high-license law or a prohibitory law to have been enacted for the people of either the Old or the New Testament.

No laws ever encountered greater obstacles than those enacted to repress the evils of intemperance. The appetites are more ungovernable than the passions.

A hundred years have been spent in endeavoring by every means to induce people to abandon a practice that does no good, but infinite evil.

License laws, instead of restraining, seem rather to promote it. They seem but the throwing around the practice the sanction of law, that deadens the moral influence. The seller sells by right of purchase, and the drinker too often drinks from the temptation thus presented, so that gain and appetite by this means bear sway.

Would it not be better to give a free and open license to every one to make, sell and use intoxicating drinks, as one might please, but prohibit them as a public beverage within all saloons—the very recruiting stations for the great armies of the Prince of Darkness,—and leave to moral suasion to do the rest?

If any will use intoxicating drinks, let the bad practice be confined to their own castles, where public law cannot reach them, but be prevented from intruding upon the rights of others.

I think it must come to this, or the temperance cause and free government will prove a failure.

Well, now, Doctor, I have answered your request as briefly, if not as satisfactorily, as I could, and I would like very much to see what others may have said in answer to the same question. Mine has been too long delayed, owing to being put *hors de combat* by a severe cold, so that I was hardly able to read your pamphlet.

I have a couple of sermons on intemperance in poetry, entitled " The Drunkard's Funeral." I would like you to criticise, if I might take the liberty to trespass so much upon your time. It is not what I actually did preach at the time, but rather an account of it, improved by second thought, and I would like your criticism on the poetry as much as the sentiment; but I will not impose it upon you unless you have curiosity enough to request it.

I feel quite honored in what you have requested of me, and only wish what I have said might be more worthy of your consideration.

Yours truly, HORACE FRASER.

[193]

133 East 29th St., New York, June 9, 1888.

DEAR DR. CROSBY:—I have read carefully and with interest Dr. Jewett's pamphlet, " Communion Wine."

I agree with him in the position so ably maintained that the wine of the Bible, in both the Old and the New Testaments, was fermented and intoxicating. I have no sympathy with the attempt to twist and subvert the plain meaning of תִּירֹשׁ יַיִן and *οἶνος*. They should always be rendered wine, *i. e.*, the fermented juice of the grape.

I have no doubt our Saviour used WINE when he instituted the Communion.

At the same time, I do not think that his example is binding upon us in this respect.

We use leavened bread, and unfermented grape juice.

In a congregation like mine, which numbers many reformed men among its communicants, I should not be willing to give them any occasion to stumble by reviving former appetite through the smell and taste of alcoholic wine. I do not say they would fall thereby; the power of Christ might keep them; but I prefer to err, if it is an error, by withholding all temptation.

Thanking you for these able articles from the pen of Dr. Jewett, which I had not seen before, I remain,

Fraternally yours, JESSE F. FORBET.

[194]

60 Seventh Avenue, New York, June 10, 1888.

MY DEAR DR. CROSBY :—I have no doubt whatever that Dr. Jewett has the right of the question, in point of exegesis as well as historic testimony. Nor is he too severe on the tricky wine-musty critics.

At the same time, I'd like to know of a decent " juice."

Yours faithfully, C. S. HARROWER.

[195]

[*From Our Church, Vol. I, No. 2, July 1, 1888.*]

COMMUNION WINE, ETC.

Dr. Jewett has done a work of real merit in this pamphlet. The two articles formerly appeared in the *Church Review* of April and July, 1885. In a clear, critical, historical, truthful and scriptural way he has met the question of "Communion Wine" as no other scholar has ever done before. It is a delight to read such a work. Not one word of caviling, but pages of solid truth. It must do good. All who are interested in this subject should read this pamphlet.

[196]

Ithaca, N. Y., June 5, 1888.

MY DEAR DOCTOR :—I have read carefully, and with pleasure and profit, Dr. Jewett's pamphlet. Its argument is complete and conclusive. I did not read it for my own conviction on the subject, however, as I have for many years held the same views.

I am not enough of a literal formalist, however, to insist that the administration of the Sacrament in ordinary fermented bread and extraordinary unfermented grape juice is invalid and improper, both of which customs my own church follows, though none of its officers and very few of its members hold the views so ably controverted by Dr. Jewett. A few consciences we found troubled by the wine ; and, without controversy or public notice of any sort, the "juice" was substituted, and no damage appears from it. Are your own views opposed to that ? Yours sincerely, A. S. FISH,

Pastor First Presbyterian Church.

[197]

Flushing, L. I., June 6, 1888.

DEAR SIR AND BROTHER :—The pamphlet on Communion Wine by Dr. Jewett, which you so kindly sent me, came duly to hand, and I have read it with interest. As you asked for an opinion on it, I will say that I agree with the author in his conclusions and most of his arguments.

It has always seemed to me that the theory of two kinds of wine was not founded on any sound scholarship, and it is a dangerous and untenable ground from which to fight the battle against intemperance. Such extravagant and unfounded statements make it very hard to stand on any reasonable ground with the radical workers for Prohibition.

Hoping that this is the kind of statement you wished to obtain, and praying that you may have all success in your brave and good work for reasonable principles in the struggle against intemperance, I remain,

Yours very sincerely, JOHN ABBOTT FRENCH.

[198]

The Evangelical Alliance for the United States of America,
42 Bible House, New York, June 7, 1888.

DEAR SIR :—Agreeable to your request, I have read the paper on "Communion Wine," by Rev. Edward H. Jewett, S.T.D., and I consider that he has fully established the views presented. I feel that churches in the present state of temperance agitation and work do well to use a milder than an intoxicating liquid in the sacred ordinance. But I also feel certain that the cause of temperance has been injured by the attempt to establish untruthful positions by arguments themselves untenable because untrue. I believe this pamphlet will do great good in the clear establishment of the correct view on the "two-wine" question.

Permit me to say that a very worthy friend of mine (not a Christian), whose family were members of my church in Mansfield, Ohio, son of Gen. Brinkerhoff, a man of very high character, is a regular attendant upon your church. He is a lawyer, and a deputy in the Mutual Reserve Fund Life Insurance, Potter Building, 38 Park Row. I hope he may find goodly acquaintance in your church. With high regard, I am, dear sir,

Very truly yours, FRANK RUSSELL.

[199]

Tract Department, 805 Broadway, New York, June 6, 1888.

DEAR DOCTOR CROSBY:—I have carefully read Dr. Jewett's pamphlet on "Communion Wine." I consider it unanswerable. The "Two-Wine" theory seems to have no foundation in scholarship or common sense, and as a theory, I think, has spent its force.

I think, in our denomination, what is called "unfermented wine" is commonly used, to avoid difficulty with those who are scrupulous on this point.

Yours truly, GEO. H. GOODSELL.

[200]

Weedsport, N. Y., May 8, 1888.

MY DEAR BROTHER:—Your circular-letter and the pamphlet are at hand. I have read the latter with some care, as I have read many another work on both sides of the subject. Nothing absolutely convincing to my mind has yet appeared on either side of that vexed question.

If I thought the critical scholarship of the day could settle it, I know of no one to whom I could look with more confidence to do the work than to you. But I find in every argument I have read so many *exparte* statements, so much belittling of strong points, and magnifying of weak ones, that I am satisfied that the scholar has not yet risen with a sufficiently judicial mind to do justice to the subject.

In the meantime, not being a sufficiently exact and exhaustive scholar to make a satisfactory, independent examination in that line, I bring my judgment to bear upon it from another direction. The question arises to me, Did Christ cause the command in Proverbs which forbids to look upon the wine when it is fermented to be broken at Cana? or did he wish the breaking of that one in Matthew, which gives it as "Woe to the one who giveth his neighbor drink," by making a practically unlimited quantity of strong wine, after men had "well drunk?"

If he did not, I see no alternative but an unintoxicating wine.

Yours fraternally, A. R. HEWITT.

[201]

Ghent, Columbia County, N. Y., June 1, 1888.

REVEREND AND DEAR SIR:—In accordance with your request, I read Dr. Jewett's pamphlet, and send you now my opinion. It is a fair and logical discussion of the question.

I am at a loss to understand how any fair-minded man can build up a "two-wine" theory. An ardent temperance worker, desiring the day speedily to come when the wretched saloon, and its attendant vices shall be wiped out, I am, nevertheless, out of conceit with the methods and positions used and taken by overzealous advocates. We need in many cases seek deliverance from our friends.

Very kindly and truly yours, J. N. MORRIS.

[202]

Sackett's Harbor, N. Y., May 31, 1888.

DEAR BROTHER:—I have read the article on "Communion Wine" which you sent me. Of course, I could not verify the citations, etc.; but, assuming that they are correct, the argument seems conclusive.

I have never seen good proof for the "two-wine" theory.

Shall I return the pamphlet? I would be glad to know if you fully indorse the position taken therein.

Yours, etc., L. R. WEBBER, Pastor Presbyterian Church.

[203]

Mount Vernon, N. Y., May 31, 1888.

DEAR SIR AND BROTHER:—I received a copy of the articles of Prof. Jewett on the "two-wine" question, with your circular note, for which accept thanks.

Prof. Jewett's articles are exceedingly interesting, able, scholarly, clear and candid, and withal a little caustic at times, particularly at the expense of my old friend and brother, Dr. Samson.

I think Dr. Jewett makes out his case, manifestly, though I cannot say what reply to him may be made. Indeed, I think the case was already made out before this scholarly review of the subject appeared.

But, so far as the TEMPERANCE QUESTION of to-day is concerned, it makes not the least difference in the world whether the "TWO-WINE" theory be true or false. That may affect the ARGUMENTATION of the question, but not the moral principle involved, nor yet the practical bearing of it. Wine itself, *per se*, is not an evil, nor is the making of it, *per se*, a crime, nor is the use of it, *per se*, a sin, and yet—and yet, in the present state of society, with the unmeasured calamities produced by intoxicating drinks, I do not see how any Christian, or any lover of humanity, can by word or deed, by silence or example, encourage a habit fraught with such misfortunes, or hesitate to make any sacrifice of comfort or of personal liberty in connection with wine, so that he may help stem the tide of misery it causes. With great respect,

Yours truly,   E. T. HISCOX.

[204]

Trinity Parish, New York, Chapel of St. Augustine, June 1, 1888.

REVEREND AND DEAR SIR:—My opinion regarding the question of one or two wines is this: Dr. Jewett is on the side of the right.

Yours truly,   ARTHUR C. KIMBER.

P. S.—I am aware that the question is not fully answered above, but I hope what is said is satisfactory.

[205]

2182 Fifth Ave., New York, May 31, 1888.

REVEREND AND DEAR SIR:—I am glad that the opportunity of reading Dr. Jewett's pamphlet has been given me.

It ought to set at rest the question of two wines for this generation at least. Doubtless there will arise men now and then whose scholarship is always wrested into the support of an idea which dominates all their thought.

Their search is not after the truth, or what is, but they seek what—as it seems to them—ought to be. Unwittingly they fall into dishonesty, from which there never seems any escape.

I am very truly yours,   JOHN W. KRAMER.

[206]

Troy, N. Y., May 30, 1888.

DEAR SIR:—I heartily agree with Dr. Jewett's views on the subject of Communion Wine. My church uses wine at the Communion Table.

Please accept my thanks for the pamphlet; I am very glad to own it.

Yours very truly,   WM. H. SYBRANDT.

[207]

Summer Hill, N. Y., May 29, 1888.

DEAR SIR:—In reply to your circular letter of the 15th inst., concerning the pamphlet on "Communion Wine" by Rev. Edward H. Jewett, would say:—

As a pastor and Christian teacher, I have read nothing more conclusive against the notion of two wines mentioned in Scripture as fermented and "unfermented."

This is a matter that I have felt no need of inquiring into, particularly since nothing I have read in the Scripture has seemed to warrant the thought of two wines. When I read articles or books on the subject I find myself, *a priori*, in favor of WINE, simply and singly, from my Bible study—THOUGH NOT FOR ITS USE.

I don't like to throw a needle into a haystack and then shake up the whole stack to find it. Nor do I like to encourage others to do it. Life is too short, and there are too many necessary things for servants of Christ to do.

Respectfully,   CHAS. H. CURTIS,
Pastor Congregational Church.

[208]
Walton, N. Y., May 30, 1888.

DEAR BROTHER :—Your note of the 15th inst. was duly received, with the pamphlet accompanying it upon the wine question. I have read the document with much interest. Excluding the newly expressed grape juice, or WINE unfermented, the argument is unanswerable for the one kind of wine in Scripture use. But pure, unadulterated wine is hard to be found for Communion or medical purposes. Water is preferable which has no whiskey in it, to whiskey that has no wine in it.

Yours, etc.,   I. S. PETTENGILL.

[209]
Rector's Study, 16 West 126th St., New York, May 29, 1888.

REV. DR. HOWARD CROSBY :—I have traversed, for the second time, the greater portion of Dr. Jewett's exhaustive argument on the wine question.

It does seem to me to be cumulative and conclusive. I have not had the time to verify his many references, or his very scholarly criticisms, but so far as I am able to judge, he has treated his subject in a conservative and masterly manner, and his conclusion seems irresistible.

Respectfully,   J. NEWTON STANGER,
Rector of Holy Trinity Church.

[210]
Theological Seminary, Rochester, N. Y., May 23, 1888.

MY DEAR SIR :—I thank you for Dr. Jewett's pamphlet, with which I was already acquainted, and the argument of which seems to me to be irrefutable. No good can come from wresting Scripture to make it serve the best of causes.

In an English paper, just arrived, I find a reference to the Jewish use of wine at the Passover which seems worthy of notice. You will, I hope, forgive me for enclosing it. I may say that Dr. Chaffee is Chairman of the Baptist Union of Great Britain, and a scholarly, fair-minded man.

Faithfully yours,   G. HARWOOD PATTISON,
Prof. Rochester Theolog. Sem.

[211]
St. Vincent Abbey, Beatty P. O., Pa., May 31, 1888.

DR. HOWARD CROSBY (*Permissis reliquis titulis*).

DEAR SIR :—Owing to absence from this place, I read your letter and pamphlet, with Dr. Jewett's articles, only on May 28.

I read the pamphlet carefully, and my opinion is that Dr. Jewett's articles are very good and convincing, leaving no solid ground for his opponent, whether on the question of two wines (fermented and not fermented), or on the incidental question about the intrinsic evil of fermented wine, as such.

I could not, on account of illness, verify Dr. Jewett's quotations from the Standard Lexica, etc., but feel rather sure he would not misquote, as this would evidently ruin his cause. His logic is sound, and, to my mind, convincing.

Roman Catholic clergymen will very generally side with Dr. Jewett, as fermented wine is universally used by them for consecration.

I have already said more than your question called for.

Very respectfully yours, JAMES ZILLIOX, D.D.

(Abbot-resigned).

[212]

Montgomery, N. Y., June 9, 1888.

DEAR SIR :—I acknowledge my obligation to you for a copy of Dr. Jewett's pamphlet. I have given it a careful reading, and am happy to say that its position accords with my own convictions.

I have never been able to accept the two-wine theory. In fact, during my connection with the United Presbyterian Church, I wrote and published against it.

So also, in regard to the teaching that "leaven" is a "symbol" of evil or corruption, I endorse the views of the author; and in both *The United Presbyterian* and *The Evangelist* I have controverted it.

At the same time, I am a total abstainer in reference to the use of all kinds of spirituous liquors, and am in favor of the prohibition of the liquor traffic.

I can not accept the views or adopt the methods of extreme temperance men, and yet I concede their sincerity and recognize their efficiency. As I conceive that the standard of morals must always be in advance of the requirements of statutes, hence I regard the rejection of legislation that fails fully to embody our morality to be unwise, and the denunciation of it as sinful to be unjust.

But I do not wish to enlarge. With thanks for the pamphlet,

I am truly yours, D. F. BONNER.

[213]

The Rectory, St. Paul's Church, Flatbush, N. Y., June 11, 1888.

REVEREND AND DEAR SIR:—Many thanks for your kindness in sending me Dr. Jewett's admirable pamphlet.

He has worked out his results with wonderful patience and clearness, and I agree with him in toto.

Very sincerely yours, SUMMERFIELD E. SNIVELY.

[214]

Sackett's Harbor, N. Y., June 9, 1888.

DEAR BROTHER:—My opinion of the pamphlet sent me is one thing, and my practice in using unfermented wine at Communion is another. This may not seem to you consistent, but I find my reason in this law : "If meat make my brother to offend," etc.

I am well assured that some find a former appetite for strong drink revived by alcohol at the Lord's Table ; I can not think that he would have it so.

Moreover, Jesus, using the expressions "The Cup" and "Fruit of the vine," seems to me to give abundant liberty for so doing.

Very respectfully and fraternally,

L. R. WEBBER, Pastor Presbyterian Church.

[215]

Glens Falls, N. Y., June 1, 1888.

REVEREND AND DEAR SIR:—I thank you for Dr. Jewett's pamphlet on Communion Wine.

The fanaticism of the average Prohibitionist has always been with little regard for the truth, or for the rights and the conscience of those who do not go all lengths with them.

Dr. Jewett's article, unanswerable as it is in its proofs, will not convince the typical Prohibitionist any more than proofs of fraud open the eyes of the average spiritualist.

Yours faithfully   FENWICK M. COOKSON.

[216]

Poughkeepsie, N. Y., June 1, 1888.

REVEREND AND DEAR SIR:—Your circular of the 15th ult., asking for opinions as to the merits of Dr. Jewett's pamphlet on the question of two wines, would have received a more prompt answer but for absence from home for several weeks. I sent for a copy of Dr. Jewett's pamphlet soon after its appearance, and read it with great interest and care, and the impression left on my mind was that the proofs adduced by him in favor of his position are unanswerable ; at any rate, I have not seen them met and fairly and squarely answered ; I do not think they can be. I have read a good deal on the wine question, but the two-wine theory, so-called, I have long regarded as unwarranted and untenable.

Very truly yours,   ISAAC BRAYTON.

[217]

Arkport, N. Y., June 8, 1888.

DEAR SIR:—Permit me to express my thanks for the privilege of reading Dr. Jewett's pamphlet on "Communion Wine." To my mind, it adds new emphasis to the correct theory that the Bible recognizes but one kind of wine.

Very truly yours,   E. C. HULL.

[218]

June 12, 1888.

DEAR SIR:—The pamphlet has been very carefully read, hence delay. Though some points made (in the very mooting of a question which is entirely pacific among Catholics) seem irrelevant and absurd, yet the writer's argument from the parts taken out of the New and Old Testaments, and from tradition, is simply quite unanswerable. Such prohibition is wicked and heretical, but doubtless is a logical outcome of private judgment, &c.

Very truly yours, &c.,   THOMAS A. BECKER, Bishop of Savannah, Ga.

[219]

Cooperstown, N. Y., June 12, 1888.

MY DEAR DR. CROSBY:—I am obliged to you for Dr. Jewett's pamphlet on "Communion Wine," which I have read with much profit. It seems quite impossible for a candid mind to escape his conclusions that but one kind of wine was known to the ancients. The old wine and the new were both the same wine at different stages of fermentation.

Thanking you for your kindness, I am, sincerely yours,

CHARLES S. OLMSTED.

[220]

Jamaica, N. Y., June 13, 1888.

REVEREND AND DEAR SIR:—I regret very much that I have been so busy since your polite letter of May 15th came in, that I have not had time till within a day or two to re-examine Dr. Jewett's pamphlet. I remember very well reading the article when it came out in the *Church Review,* and being satisfied that he had proved his point; and, looking over it again, I find myself confirmed in that opinion.

Yours respectfully,   BEVERLY R. BETTS.

(221)

130½ Hayward Street, Brooklyn, N. Y., June 14, 1888.

REVEREND AND DEAR SIR:—Absence from the city and other pressing engagements prevented me from replying to your letter of May 15th, in regard to the pamphlet sent to me.

I happened to find an article,* in the *American Israelite*, which I herewith send you. This will relieve me of dilating upon the subject, as I concur in the opinion of Dr. Wise of Cincinnati, the editor who writes the article ("It Is Fermented Wine") which I marked for your perusal.

יין *Yayin* in the Bible means, beyond doubt, fermented wine, which was used by the ancient Hebrews, and also by modern Jews, on many festive-religious occasions. Hoping this will answer your purpose, I am,

Your respectfully, DR. L. WINTNER, Temple Beth Elohim.

[222

Albion, N. Y., June 11, 1888.

MY DEAR SIR :—Your favor of recent date, accompanied by Dr. Jewett's papers on "Communion Wine," was received in due time.

I prefer to write you than to our village newspapers. The minds of some good people are not ready nor willing to receive what I believe to be the scriptural teaching on this subject. I have read with great pleasure Dr. J.'s papers. It is needless to say that they are scholarly. He has given what I believe to be the scriptural doctrine concerning wine—Communion Wine. It is simply unanswerable. Truly yours, L. B. ROGERS.

[223]

Peekskill, N. Y., June 12, 1888.

MY DEAR DR. CROSBY:—I have read the book which you kindly sent, and entirely agree with the conclusion reached. I have been familiar with the controversy about Bible wines for years, and I am unable to see how any biblical scholar can hold the theory of unfermented grape juice being wine.

Very truly yours, D. MURDOCK.

[224]

New York, June 15, 1888.

MY DEAR DR. CROSBY :—I beg to thank you for the opportunity of reading Dr. Jewett's pamphlet on "Communion Wine." It is a very happy illustration of Prov. xviii. 17: "He that is first in his own cause seemeth just ; but his neighbor cometh and searcheth him." His strictures recall a bit of wisdom from one of our own philosophers : "It is better not to know so many things than to know a lot of things that ain't so."

While I believe it is neither wise for me nor profitable for my brother that I drink wine or strong drink, and could wish that more of my Christian brethren were of the same mind, I am, nevertheless, glad to see frustrated all attempts to restrain personal liberty, which are based on the false interpretation of Scripture or a misapprehension of facts. May it not be well-nigh as sad to be so intoxicated with zeal that one sees facts upside down, as it is to be so drunk with wine that the whole breadth of the avenue does not suffice for a way ? Yours truly, J. F. ELDER.

[225]

Buffalo, N. Y., June 13, 1888.

MY DEAR DR. CROSBY :—I have read the pamphlet of Dr. Jewett, and agree in the main with his conclusions.

There may have been some ancient prehistoric wine of a non-intoxicating nature.

*Article referred to not received.

But no sample has survived, and, if it had, the ordinary use of language would prevent the name of WINE from applying to such a mixture.

Hundreds of persons would be glad to accept the two-wine theory as a refuge from embarrassment in reconciling Scripture with Scripture. Many such persons prefer to sail in smooth waters under a dubious flag, rather than brave the billows for Truth's sake. But I have always felt that the "two-kinds-of-wine" theory was an ignominious refuge for defenders of the faith. A theory of Bible wine, which cannot be stated in the land of the Bible without exciting amazement and ridicule, is surely open to suspicion.

Yours, with sincere regard,   WM. S. HUBBELL.

[226]

New York, June 15, 1888.

DEAR SIR :—Thanks for your kindness in turning my attention to Rev. Dr. E. H. Jewett's pamphlet on Communion Wine.

It is a lucid, comprehensive, accurate statement of the teaching of the Bible on wine, the pure juice of the grape. It proves, by an exegesis which can not be invalidated, the divine sanction of its moderate use in its fermented state, and the divine condemnation only of its abuse.

It shows the Bible doctrine on the subject to be temperance, not total abstinence ; and exalts temperance therein to the virtue of SELF-CONTROL, as in the use of all divine blessings.

The exposition is valuable aid to all inquirers after Bible truth on the subject. And it will serve a noble purpose if it induces the champions of temperance, in their warfare against the evils of intemperance, to arm themselves with the "Sword of the Spirit" instead of the mock weapons of human sophistry.

Yours truly,   J. A. SAXTON.

[227]

Woodside Church, Troy, N. Y., June 14, 1888.

REVEREND AND DEAR SIR :—Your circular letter of the 15th ult. was forwarded to Philadelphia, while I was at the Assembly, and on returning home Dr. Jewett's pamphlet was in my accumulated mail. After some delay I give as condensedly as possible my opinion as to its merits.

The argument seems conclusive and irrefutable. Without being able to verify many of Dr. Jewett's references, they seem genuine, and not garbled, as some have been by the two wine advocates. He effectually disposes of the figment that תירוש *must* be kept unfermented. It is hard to see how a scholar can longer entertain that position.

It seems absurd that it should be necessary for a learned man to spend so much strength on a "man of straw," as this whole theory surely is. Dr. Jewett does his work thoroughly and *finally*. It has long been my conviction that the matter of two wines was a mere modern speculation. Dr. Moore's articles in the *Presbyterian Review* for 1881 and 1882 (and Dr. Lawrie's in the *New Englander* for 1881) confirmed that conviction, and this pamphlet clinches it.

I thank you for the pamphlet, which is a valuable possession. It is kindly, yet keen, and some bits (*e. g.*, on page 11) are very amusing, and the descriptions of the Paschal rites are graphic and valuable.

Regretting that I can do no more for you in the way of a criticism, and thanking you for all your tokens of kindness and good will, believe me, my dear Dr. Crosby, very respectfully, your obedient servant,

ARTHUR H. ALLEN.

[228]

Marcy Avenue Baptist Church, Brooklyn, N. Y., June 14, 1888.

MY DEAR DR. CROSBY:—I have read with care Dr. Jewett's pamphlet. It is in almost exact accordance with my own views on the question of two wines.

It seems to me to be a careful, conscientious, fair discussion of the subject, and I believe it will do much good.

Yours very truly,   W. C. P. RHOADES.

[229]

Brooklyn, June 14, 1888.

MY DEAR SIR:—I have very carefully read the pamphlet, which you kindly sent me, of the Rev. Edward H. Jewett, S.T.D., on "Communion Wine," reprinted from the *Church Review* of April and July, 1885. I fully concur with him in his conclusions, as expressed on pages 12 and 13, at the middle of the page, and elsewhere.

Regretting that I could not sooner reply to your letter,

I am, my dear sir, very truly yours,   T. J. CONANT.

[230]

109 East 73d Street, New York, June 12, 1883.

MY DEAR BROTHER:—I am indebted to you for the pleasure and satisfaction of reading Dr. Jewett's excellent articles on "Communion Wine." In response to your desire for the opinion of readers of the pamphlet on the question of the two wines, I have only to state that, so far as my information goes, I thoroughly agree with Dr. Jewett's view. Without having given the subject exhaustive study, I have read considerable upon it, and have had for years the clear conviction that the wines in common use in Eastern countries in Bible times were essentially what they are now. It requires a deal of special pleading to make from Scripture or the facts of history a kind of wine which was not wine, but which was called wine, though it had neither the qualities nor effects of wine. It will take a stronger than Samson to carry away the gates of the wall of proof erected by Dr. Jewett about the Bible fact in the case.

Again thanking you for the pamphlet, I am, yours fraternally,

JOHN H. EDWARDS.

It may be presuming on my privilege, but I would like to add that I have a strong sentiment, if not conviction, against the use of any wine at the Lord's Table, which, by its alcoholic odor or tang, could overthrow a weak brother, or give the children and young men who are communicants a familiarity with it which might lead to playing with the adder in places where they would not be surrounded by the sacred associations of the Sacrament. I cannot think that our Saviour, in our day and circumstances, would make use of the FORTIFIED wines of commerce for sacramental purposes. If wine—that is, wine in the proper sense of the word—be insisted on, though I cannot see why the Supper may not be as profitably observed with the unfermented juice of the grape, I am persuaded that we should IMITATE THE SAVIOUR'S EXAMPLE TO THE LETTER, and remove the greater part of danger by drinking the Communion Wine ONLY WHEN DILUTED WITH WATER in considerable quantity. This was the custom at the Passover Supper (Dr. Jewett, p. 44), it being forbidden that grace should be said over the cup of blessing until it had been so diluted. The same custom prevailed in the early Christian Church (Just. Mar., Apol. i. 65).

To drink wine unmixed with water was deemed, among the civilized nations of the old time, drinking "like a Scythian." It surely can not be Christian-like to insist on the use of strong, undiluted wine at the Lord's Table, contrary to our Saviour's own act and the custom of the better civilization of that wine-drinking age.

Pardon my long postscript. The point is of too little importance, in my view.   J. H. E.

[231]

302 East Broadway, New York City, June 15, 1888

DEAR DR. CROSBY:—In reply to your note requesting my opinion of Dr. Jewett's pamphlet, I would say :—

To me the exegetical proof and historic testimony which he brings out strengthen my early, later, and now probably matured, conclusion in regard to the "two-wine theory." I never had occasion to differ from Dr. A. A. Hodge's teachings. I am Princeton *ad ossa*, and therefore thoroughly in accord with the view that the wine referred to in the Bible was fermented. I am, very sincerely yours,

JNO. T. WILDS, 7th Presbyterian Church.

[232]

103 East 40th Street, New York, June 15, 1888.

MY DEAR DR. CROSBY:—I have read Dr. Jewett's pamphlet on the "two-wine" question with much interest.

It is *unanswerable* and CONCLUSIVE. I have held to this view during all my ministry, whilst all my life long I have been a total abstainer for example's sake. With best wishes, ever yours, J. FORD SUTTON.

[233]

DEAR SIR :—I have read very carefully Dr. Jewett's pamphlet. I have long thought the "two-wine" theory ought to go ; I am now satisfied it has gone. Rev. Dr. Pettengill, an old minister residing here, wants me to tell you that, in his opinion, if anything was needed to lay the "two-wine" ghost, Dr. Jewett has supplied the need. Very truly,

J. S. BACON, Pas. Pres. Ch., Corning, N. Y.

[234]

Windham, Greene Co., N. Y., June 16, 1888.

REV. HOWARD CROSBY, D. D.

DEAR SIR :—In compliance with your request, I have read carefully Rev. E. H. Jewett's treatise on "Communion Wine." In the January number for 1882 of the *Presbyterian Review* is a similarly able discussion by Rev. Dunlop Moore, D. D., on " Sacramental Wine."

Of the making of books on this question there is no end, and probably there will be no end so long as radicalism runs ranting amuck against the dicta of pure, profound, disinterested scholarship and conservatism is in the attitude of timid, shrinking self-defense.

I made up my mind many years ago, as the result of personal study of the Bible in the Hebrew, the Greek, and the Latin, on this wine question ; and the conclusion at which I thus arrived, and which has been confirmed by my missionary life of six years in the heart of Asia Minor, is identical with that of Dr. Jewett. The very word wine, as found in the languages which I have access to, is itself conclusive as witness.

I have before me a Bible in HOLLAND DUTCH, published in Dordrechat, "Anno 1741," giving in the word 𝔚𝔶𝔫 the name of an article which the dwellers in that well-watered country could not use very freely without bringing on drunkenness.

I turn next to my ARMENO-TURKISH Bible, and I find " SHARRAHB," the TURKISH for WINE, and wine which I know, from abundant observation, was capable of making the Moslems drunk.

I turn next to my Bible in the Armenian, and I find " *Keenée*," the ARMENIAN for WINE, and wine, too, which, if signs after feasts held by Armenian Christians (of the old Church) do not mislead, makes people drunk, producing the same effects in the interior of Asia Minor as are produced in the streets of New York.

But I need not argue the matter. So far as Exegesis is concerned, it seems to me that Dr. Jewett's elaborate and learned argument is absolutely invincible.

Fraternally yours, BENJAMIN PARSONS.

[235]

Wampsville, N. Y., June 16, 1888.

REV. HOWARD CROSBY.

DEAR BROTHER :—I have read the pamphlet you sent me with great interest, and think the argument conclusive.

I have read quite a little on the wine question, and I believe that when the Bible speaks of wine IT MEANS WINE, and not grape juice.

Yours most respectfully,   DANIEL C. TYLER.

[236]

Watertown, N. Y., June 18, 1888.

DEAR SIR:—Some time since, I received from you the two articles by Dr. Jewett upon the subject of "Communion Wine," with a request that I communicate to you my personal conviction upon the question so ably treated in them.

I fully endorse Dr. Jewett's position as, in my belief, the only tenable one.

Years ago I conducted in a local discussion with a Baptist minister upon the question of two kinds—fermented and unfermented—of Bible wines. To secure the opinions of those presumably best qualified to judge, I wrote to the Hebrew Professors in all the more prominent theological schools in the country.

Without exception, they confirmed my position. I then published their names and some of their replies.

Being aware of your own able efforts in withstanding the current of false teaching in regard to temperance in the use of alcoholic drinks, permit me to express to you my personal thanks, and to assure you of my sympathy and co-operation.   Very truly yours,

RUSSELL A. OLIN, Rector of Trinity P. E. Church.

[237]

Saratoga, June 19, 1888.

DEAR SIR:—In response to your inquiry concerning a paper by Dr. Jewett on Communion Wine, I would say that it is one of the most lucid and logical presentations of the truth.

I have read the article with a great deal of interest, and am satisfied that it is the only view that will bear the light on the question of "two wines."

Respectfully,   R. F. McMICHAEL, Pastor Regent St. Bap. Church.

[238]

59 Hawley St., Syracuse, N. Y., June 15, 1888.

DEAR SIR:—I have read with great care the pamphlet sent to me by you, entitled "Communion Wine." I am thoroughly convinced of the truth of its position. Any other view, I think, is plainly inconsistent with the teachings of Holy Scripture. It is strange that Christian men, to sustain a "Theory," can so wrest its meaning.

Very respectfully yours,   T. L. RANDOLPH.

[239]

DEAR SIR :—I have read with great interest and satisfaction the pamphlet you were so kind as to send me. It seems to me to be a conclusive refutation of the "unfermented wine" theory, which is the cause of discussion and disturbance and division in the administration of the Holy Supper that I cannot but regard as harmful in many ways.

I am, yours respectfully,

Brooklyn, May 28, 1888.   J. C. AGER.

[240]

St. George's Clergy House, 208 East 17th St.,
New York, June 20, 1888.

DEAR DR. CROSBY:—I have read with some care the able pamphlet (Dr. Jewett's) sent some time ago by you, and will simply say it confirms very strongly the views I have had (as a total abstainer) for many years, that there is no solid ground in Holy Scripture for the distinction said to exist therein between intoxicating and non-intoxicating wine. One can only regret that a good cause should be upheld by so poor an argument.

Believe me, yours faithfully,   HENRY WILSON.

[241]

329 West 34th St., New York.

MY DEAR DR. CROSBY:—I have just found leisure to look over the pamphlet of Dr. Jewett on "Communion Wine." I thank you for calling my attention to such a masterly presentation of the subject. The analysis is calm and critical, and the conclusion irresistible. Although it may not be properly appreciated by the radical temperance people, it is certainly a contribution of strength to the cause of true reform. Only when this great cause is pushed scripturally and consistently may we hope for its enduring triumph. Just as in our civil war there was a black brother to be considered, so in this war with the liquor curse there is a weak brother to be considered, and for his sake should the bugle blow and the battle be joined. This will save us from wresting the Word and help us to save the man.

Yours, with great regard,   JOSEPH R. KERR.

[242]

June 28, 1888.

DEAR SIR:—Having read the Rev. Dr. Jewett's discussion on Communion Wine when it appeared as two articles in the *Church Review*, I afterwards read it again on receiving it in pamphlet form, accompanied by your printed request that readers would send you their opinion of its merits on the question of two wines.

Dr. Jewett seems to have handled the question with great ability, discussed it fairly and thoroughly, and reached the right conclusion. In this matter the obvious meaning of Scripture is the real meaning. The theory of two kinds of wine was born of teetotalism, not suggested by anything in the Bible; and teetotalers do always wrest the Scriptures; for instance, in pretending that the Rechabites are set forth as commendable examples of ABSTINENCE, who, in fact, are commended for OBEDIENCE, and whose abstinence was from grapes and raisins and from dwelling-houses as much as from wine.

No doubt, our Lord, in his institution of the Holy Communion, made use of WINE, in the ordinary sense of that word, and his Church must observe his institution, to have the Sacrament of his appointing ; yet many presume to better his institution. I think it would shock men who have any idea of what a divine institution is, to know how far and wide the use of raisin water and other sloppy substitutes has spread among those who profess to be Christians, dutifully keeping the ordinances of the Lord's Name. In my own church (Episcopal), I never knew or suspected the substitution of anything for wine in the Communion ; and I believe the Presbyterian churches, generally, are free from the CRAZE that affects almost all the others. Some persons say, with amazing complacency, that "fermented wine." or "alcoholic wine," is not used in their Communion. If it were, there are church members who would either refrain from the Sacrament altogether, or take a half-Communion with the bread only. I think that the opinion is extending that this "solemn and interesting ordinance" is not by any means "essential," that we can have just as good Christians without it, and better, if it is to be an ecclesiastical refuge for "rum sympathizers."

Thus Christ is not treated as Master of the Feast, and his Sacrament is modified or destroyed by the overmuch righteousness of meddlesome men.

With Christian regard,   JAS. H. KIDDER,

Rector St. Paul's Church, Owego, N. Y.

[243]

Oneonta, N. Y., June 22, 1888.

DEAR BROTHER :—When your letter asking my view of the pamphlet on Communion Wine reached me, I was sitting behind you at the General Assembly. On my return, I found the document, and only succeeded the last week in looking it over. I have never given the subject any serious study, but have always held the view, and still do, advocated by Dr. Jewett. And I have been led to it both by my common sense and by a cursory examination of the respective Hebrew terms translated wine and strong drink. I have never had any patience with those who hold up Daniel as the model temperance man, since the plain inference of Dan. x. 3 is that he was accustomed to use wine. My views in the matter are not entitled to much weight, but I have no sympathy with the two-wine theory, and I am of the opinion that the wine made by our Saviour was first class, and used to excess would intoxicate like the common wines of the age in which he lived, just as the bread and fish he multiplied would have been bad for the stomach of the glutton.

Sincerely yours,   H. H. ALLEN.

[244]

Church of Good Shepherd, Canajoharie, N. Y., June 26, 1888.

REVEREND AND DEAR SIR:—The pamphlet of Dr. Jewett was duly received. I read it before when running in the *Church Review*, and fully endorse its views regarding the Wines of Scripture. Very truly,   J. N. MARVIN.

[245]

S. S. Harbor, Staten Island, N. Y., May 30, 1888.

MY DEAR BROTHER:—Your note of the 15th inst., with accompanying pamphlet on Communion Wine, by Rev. Edward H. Jewett, S.T.D., came duly to hand. I have read the discussion with great interest, and consider his position impregnable.

As to the merits of the pamphlet: One can only admire the patient industry of Dr. Jewett in searching the originals and securing with literary accuracy the quotations of the writers on the other side, as well as the logical acumen with which—by his careful and scholarly exegesis and his keen analysis of the expert and historical testimony—he has so thoroughly dissected and exposed their sophisms and the garbled use made of their quotations.

I hope the pamphlet may have the large publicity of which it is most worthy.

For myself, I may add, I have never been able to accept the two-wines theory, from the standpoint of the sacred Scriptures. Nor have I ever met with an argument on that subject that carried my judgment, or that has in the least shaken my confidence in what I believe to be the biblical view, viz., that the wine referred to in the Word of God is a fermented wine, the USE of which is—under certain circumstances—rendered necessary, as a religious duty, as in the drink offerings (Lev. XV. 3, 5, 7 and 10), and the ABUSE of which is everywhere forbidden and condemned.

That the wine used in the Passover feast by the Jews, and that in the institution of the "Last Supper" by our Lord, was the wine commonly used by the people in their social entertainments and in their religious festivals was a fermented wine, I have never for a moment doubted. The Jews would scarcely have stultified themselves by calling Jesus a "wine-bibber" if he had used only the MUST.

Sincerely yours,   CHAS. J. JONES.

[246]

Avon, N. Y., July 5, 1888.

DEAR SIR:—I have read Dr. Jewett's articles on Communion Wine with pleasure and profit. His arguments seem unanswerable. I have no doubt at all that the wines of the Bible are just what they purport to be.

While in my own church, in the spirit of charity for weak consciences, the unfermented juice of the grape is used, as satisfying the essential requirements of the ordinance, yet it is not because we believe that such may be the nature of the wine with which Christ established the Sacrament.

In my judgment, those people who are fighting for the temperance cause by fighting against the plain statements of Scripture, and even going so far as to assert that God did not make alcohol, thus necessitating a second Creator, are wielding a double-edged sword, which will surely pierce them through to their ruin. A good cause does not need the support of falsehood.

Yours sincerely,   H. P. S. BOGUE.

[247]

The International Committee of Young Men's Christian Associations, 23d St. and 4th Ave.,
Office of Gen'l Sec'y, 139 E. 18th St., New York, July 6, 1888.

DEAR DR. CROSBY:—In the press of other things I had nearly neglected to acknowledge the pamphlet of Dr. Jewett, to thank you for the pleasure of its perusal, and to express my hearty concurrence in the views he expresses and the sound exegesis which characterizes his treatise.

With affectionate regard, fraternally yours,   RICHARD C. MORSE.

[248]

Amagansett, N. Y., June 1, 1888.

MY DEAR DR. CROSBY:—I thank you for sending me the little brochure on "Communion Wine" by Dr. Jewett. I have read it carefully, reviewed it concisely* and applied it practically. I have appended to my review of it— which I herewith enclose—two original notes. The light that comes from Tacitus, as to Jewish bread, I think I am the first one to discover and apply to the temperance question. Please observe particularly my four suggestions, and the final note. After you have read them, please write me your impressions in regard to them. I am glad, my dear Doctor, that you stand so strenuously for conservative biblical scholarship. You are somewhat older than I am, and you are backed, as I am not, by a strong city church; but what influence I can exert, either through pulpit or press, to support your advocacy of biblical ethics or biblical theology, I shall be glad to exert.

Fraternally,   JAMES B. FINCH.

[249]

Rome, N. Y., June 27, 1888.

DR. H. CROSBY, 116 E. NINETEENTH ST., NEW YORK.

DEAR SIR:—According to your special desire, I have ordered a short review or *critique* of Mr. Jewett's book on C. W. to be printed in one of our daily papers.

Concerning the said pamphlet itself, I can only state that it is a real desideratum in this our newly adopted Fatherland, where superficial flatness and arrogance seem to flourish equally with mystic stubbornness and stupidity, while in our European schools such questions as this prohibition matter would be referred to lunatic asylums rather than to any learned faculty by men like Gesenius or Rödiger, the former a teacher in my father's time when at Berlin, the latter my own Prof. of Hebrew and Arab, at Halle.

Concerning orthography in Latin quotations, Dr. Jewett will mark the following in a second edition: p. 44, 1, 4 and 5, adeo—severi, instead of ades—

---

* See next page.

servari, 1, 23; ad potationem, instead, et p. 56 v. 1, 7 and 10, admonitos—commemoration*em*.

There is also a slight error in the Arab. foot-note on p. 16.

The few errata in the Eng. text on p. 46 and p. 50 will be easily found out by any well-versed reader, while such *lapsus calami* as f. i. on p. 54, 1, 9 from below: *omne stomacho* ought to be avoided, and changed into *omni stom* . .   Yours truly and sincerely,   O. F. EBERT.

•   [250]

COMMUNION WINE.*

BY THE REV. JAMES B. FINCH, M.A.

We were recently presented with this little brochure on Communion Wine, asked to read it, and give our opinion upon it. We have read it with care, pleasure and profit. It is a keen and scholarly production from the pen of Dr. Edward H. Jewett. From a critical examination of Scripture words and historic testimony, he shows that there is no proper basis whatever for "two classes of wine," fermented and unfermented, as maintained by some modern scholars. The Hebrew words that the Doctor critically examines are *Yayin, Tirosh, Sove, Shekar, Meseg* and *Asis*. From the light that comes from this examination, it is very evident that no thorough Hebrew scholar, without some pet temperance theory to buttress, would question that they all, from their etymology or use, denote wine as a fermented liquor. Dr. Samson, however, the Rev. Mr. Thayer, and others, maintain that "all the direct endorsements of wine in the Bible are connected with the word *Tirosh*." But this is shown to be a mistake: it is *Yayin* which the Psalmist declares "maketh glad the heart of man;" it is *Yayin* that Isaiah exhorts thirsty souls to buy without money and without price; but it is this same *Yayin* which, by abuse, becomes a "mocker." *Tirosh*, also, though more commonly spoken of as a blessing, yet, as seen from its etymology, *Yarash*, to seize, *i. e.*, the brain, to inebriate, denotes intoxicating wine.

The Doctor, in the next place, examines the literature of the Jews subsequent to the close of the Old Testament canon, viz., the Apocrypha, the Targums, the writings of Philo and Josephus, and finds from these sources no testimony to "two kinds of wine, evil and good, *per se*." In refuting the opinion of Dr. Samson that *Tirosh* is *Must*, or unfermented wine, Dr. Jewett, while conceding that the Greeks and Romans understood the process by which *Must* could be preserved in an unfermented state for at least a year, denies that *Must* is wine, and quotes the opinion of Father Gavazzi: "To me," said Father Gavazzi, "as an Italian, the expression, unfermented wine, imports downright nonsense. In fact, wine is only wine by fermentation, and to speak of unfermented wine is to speak of dry water, of nightly sun, of unelectric lightning." But though in making this concession as to the Greeks and Romans, Dr. Jewett denies that there is any evidence that the Jews knew anything whatever about the article which the Greeks called *Aigleukos*, or the Latins *Semper mustum*. "Neither in the Apocrypha nor in the Targums, in the writings of Philo or Josephus, can one word or sentence be found that the custom was either known or practiced in Judea."

To show that there is not now, nor ever has been, anything like unfermented wine known in Syria and the East, the Doctor adds the following testimony from missionaries resident either now or recently in Syria:—

"We, the undersigned, missionaries and residents in Syria, having been repeatedly requested to make a distinct statement on the subject, hereby declare that during the whole time of our residence and traveling in Syria and the Holy

---

* Communion Wine: A Critical Examination of Scripture Words and Historic Testimony. By the Rev. Edward H. Jewett, S.T.D. The Church Review Association, New York.

Land, we have never seen or heard of an unfermented wine; nor have we found among Jews, Christians or Mohammedans any tradition of such a wine having ever existed in the country.—Rev. S. H. Calhoun; C. V. A. Van Dyke, D.D.; Rev. James Robertson; Rev. H. H. Jessup; Rev. John Wortabel, M.D.; James Black, Esq.; Michael Meshaka, doctor; Rev. John Crawford; R. W. Brigstocke. M.D., F.R.C.S.; Rev. Wm. Wright, B.A.—May, 1875."

In the second half of the brochure the use of the Greek word *Oinos* is carefully considered: it is shown by classic and Aramaic vouchers to mean always the fermented juice of the grape. Dr. Jewett thinks that *Oinos* is never, in use, the equivalent of *Gleukos*, though the latter may, in the lapse of time, become intoxicating.*

The Doctor goes on to point out the fallacy of the argument that because fermented bread was interdicted, consistency requires the interdiction of fermented grape juice also, by showing that wine was not originally used at the Passover. Besides, "the words used to describe the fermentation of liquors differ etymologically from those used for the leavening of bread."

Moreover, as to the assumption that the leavening process is one of corruption, and hence symbolical of evil, the hint is given to logicians that chemistry is a very modern science, and that it is absurd to suppose that the ancient Jews knew that the leavening of bread and the fermentation of wine were chemically identical processes.†

In concluding this little treatise, Dr. Jewett shows from historic sources, past and present, that the Jews have not discontinued the use of fermented wine at the celebration of the Passover, though concessions were sometimes made to circumstances; and that Christians have ordinarily celebrated the Eucharist with fermented wine, though in cases of necessity the fresh juice of the grape has been, on rare occasions, used in the Sacrament, and even water has been used by such heretics as Tatian and his disciples. The Doctor also shows from the Talmud, through the testimony of Dr. Lightfoot, two centuries ago, that though Mosaic legislation enjoined the eating of unleavened bread, yet the drinking of wine was an ecclesiastical regulation of late date, introduced for the purpose of bringing cheer into the entire Jewish household, that the wine thus used was mixed with water that it might not intoxicate, and that only leavened bread was ordered to be removed from the house, while both *Yayin* and *Chometz* (vinegar) were rubrically allowed. He shows, moreover, from the testimony of modern scholars, either Jews or of Jewish extraction, that "unfermented wine (must) is not regarded as wine, and would not suffice for the fulfillment of the duty to drink wine on the Passover eve.—Rev. D. Edward, of Breslau. The testimony of Dr. F. Delitzsch, a Hebrew scholar of world-wide reputation, is added, as follows: "What Moses Stuart affirms in Bib. Sac. 1843, p. 508, is incorrect. The wine of the Passover has at all times been fermented wine, which, according to prevalent custom, was mixed with water."

We have barely sketched the salient points of this little treatise of sixty pages. We advise every one who wishes to make a thorough study of the subject to send to "The Church Review Association," New York, for a copy. It is very cheap at twenty-five cents.

---

* The reviewer adds in this note that *Gleukos* is certainly intoxicating, as seen by its use in Acts ii. 13: it is probably equivalent, sometimes, to *Tirosh ; i. e.*, denotes sometimes the product of the vintage for the season, although it is used in the Septuagint for *Yayin* in Job xxxii. 19.

† Item by the reviewer.—From a Leaflet of Woman's Temperance Publication Association we are informed that "where the Passover is celebrated by the Jews to-day it is celebrated with unleavened bread and unfermented wine." Comment: There is no good Jewish or other good authority for the above statement. Dr. Delitzsch, the very best authority, denies it; and we may add that Tacitus shows that unleavened bread was used in the celebration of the Passover, not because fermentation implies corruption, but because the Jews wished to represent vividly the haste of the Israelites' departure from Egypt. Cf. Deut. xvi. 3. Tacitus says: "The Jewish bread made without leaven is retained as a sign of the sudden seizure of corn." We quote the Latin: *Et raptarum frugum argumentum panis Judaicus nullo fermento relinetur.*—Histories, Lib. 5, Chap. IV., in med. Tacitus was born about 50 A. D., and hence is a little better authority on Jewish archæological questions than any hobbyist of the nineteenth century.—J. B. F.

We wish to say, as we dismiss this little brochure on Communion Wine:—

1. That it accords, in the main, with the views which we adopted twenty-five years ago, after giving the subject careful study. We were then convinced, by a critical examination of the words used in Scripture to designate wine, that wine has always and everywhere a fermentative nature; that the wine spoken of with approbation in Scripture was in greater or less degree fermented wine; that the wine our Lord miraculously made at Cana was no different, in respect to fermentative properties, from that which he used at the institution of the Supper; and that, in either case, it was like the wine in common use at the time. But we were not then, nor are we now, quite sure but that *Yayin* and *Oinos*—the Hebrew and the Greek terms for wine—may not have been originally used to designate, at times, the expressed juice of the grape, having in the product, of course, always the elements of fermentation, yet covering the product in all stages, from the time that product left the wine vat until drank by man, whether the product were a day or a century old. In favor of this view is the fact that new wine, or wine not fully fermented, is designated in various places in the Gospels by *Oinos*, with the adjective *neos*.* The adjective is used, of course, when the contrast is sharply drawn, as in Luke v. 38. 39, where new wine (*Oinos neos*) is contrasted with old wine—*Oinos* (*palaios*). When no such contrast is intended, the generic product might be readily designated by *Oinos*, with the adjective omitted. On the other hand, the Latin *Mustum vinum* is from the Latin adjective *mustus*. The complete expression was *mustum vinum*, but in common use the noun *vinum* was omitted, and the adjective was retained, or became the noun; originally the expression was *must-wine.* Thus we see that it is not far-fetched to claim that the word wine may have been used generically by the ancients, as we moderns use the word cider.

2. That as rigid temperance views have, unquestionably, led to the unscriptural two-wine theory, may we not ease conscientious souls by permitting the use, at Communions, of the recently expressed juice of the grape? May we not give them the benefit of the suggestion contained in 1?

3. That in case reformed drunkards are members of our churches, may not the cup be omitted in respect to them? Is not the whole sacrifice, in fact, typed in the bread? Does not the bread really represent Christ's body, *i. e.*, both flesh and blood? Dr. Gottheil, the Jewish rabbi, tells us that, among the Jews, "concessions are made to the force of circumstances;" that unfermented wine is permitted in case fermented cannot be obtained, or is forbidden for sanitary reasons, *i. e.*, because a brother is weak, is diseased by former use of intoxicants.

4. That though in ancient times the use of fermented wines was commended to God's ancient people, we are not to suppose that the moderns, living in different lands and with different nervous constitutions from the ancients, may plead ancient precedent in favor of the wine-cup. The moderns do not need heart-stimulants, but nerve-tonics. Besides, it may be necessary to-day to practice self-denial for the sake of the weak. Wine, or whatever stimulant the term in modern usage may represent, is a "mocker" as never before. The Pauline principle as to eating meat offered to idols is that by which we should be governed in our use of intoxicants. "It is good neither to eat flesh, nor to drink wine, nor to do anything whereby thy brother stumbleth."—Rom. xiv. 21, R. V. But beyond the insistence of the practice of these general principles we may not go in our judgment of another man's liberty.

AMAGANSETT, N. Y., May 24, 1888.

[251]

Buffalo, N. Y., June 12, 1888.

DR. HOWARD CROSBY :—Dr. Jewett's pamphlet on "Two Wines" is a strong and impartial paper. Had I not held his views before, I certainly should now. Please pardon me for expressing my high appreciation for your courageous stand-

---

* Vid. Matt. ix. 17; Mark ii. 22; Luke v. 37.

ing on Bible ground, though often so malignantly misrepresented by those who would be defenders of God's truth, and who frequently sit, unconsciously perhaps, in judgment upon the Holy One.

W. C. RABE, Pastor German Baptist Church.

[252]

Schoharie, N. Y., May 28, 1888.

DEAR SIR AND BROTHER :—Dr. Jewett's pamphlet is convincing. I welcome it all the more gladly as it fully establishes my prior belief.

Yours, etc.,   C. E. KELLER.

[253]

Bath, N. Y.

REVEREND AND DEAR SIR :—Dr. Beardsley and the bishops have expressed my thoughts on the whole subject of "Communion Wine" far better than I could express them myself. I feel that I am in most perfect accord with them all, and yourself in particular.   Very sincerely yours,

O. R. HOWARD, Rector (*Emeritus*) of St. Thomas.

[254]

Governor's Island, N. Y., May 18, 1888.

DEAR SIR :—I read Dr. Jewett's paper at the time of its first publication, and entirely agree with its conclusions.   E. H. GOODWIN.

[255]

115 Fifteenth St., Buffalo, N. Y., May 25, 1888.

DEAR DOCTOR :—As I have read Dr. Jewett's pamphlet somewhat prepossessed in favor of his position, I naturally regard it as tenable.

As a practical matter, I have never known the faithful turned to drunkenness by the use of wine at the Communion, even when undiluted. But the mixed Chalice, it seems to me, may be so used as in great measure to allay conscientious scruples. Besides, the Doctor himself admits that "in case of necessity the fresh juice of the grape" may be used.

Yours truly,   F. GRANGER.

[256]

Bergen, N. Y., June 1, 1888.

DEAR SIR :—My views on "Two Wines" are those of Dr. Edward Robinson, under whose instruction I sat from 1845 to 1848 in N. O. Seminary. My hand's too lame and sore from rheumatism to write more.

Fraternally yours,   HAMILTON W. PIERSON.

[257]

Shelter Island, Suffolk Co., N. Y., July 13, 1888.

DEAR SIR :—The pamphlet by the Rev. Dr. Jewett on Communion Wine was sent me, with your request that I read it, and give my opinion as to its merits on the question of two wines. Absence from home, and some necessary engagements, have prevented my giving it the prompt attention I would have liked to bestow.

I have read the pamphlet with care, and so far as the authorities cited are at my hand, have examined them anew, both to verify the author's statements and to review my own study of the matter, so far as concerns the Bible testimony, made several years ago, and I see no reason to change the conclusions to which I was then led, and which agree with the positions taken by Dr. Jewett.

I do not think the Bible gives any support to the theory of two wines, one of which was an intoxicant, while the other was non-intoxicating. The Bible wine is alcoholic and intoxicating. Here etymology (according to its admitted masters) and the use of the words, as determined by the context, have but one voice.

I have no acquaintance with the "Temperance Bible Commentary," which is supposed to furnish the etymological foundation for the writers whose opinions Dr.

Jewett opposes. I cannot pronounce upon the fitness of the authors of this commentary to direct opinion in this sphere. But I presume it is admitted that Gesenius easily holds the first place among Hebrew scholars in the department of etymology. The opposition of Assyriologists to Gesenius, or more correctly, to the recent *editors* of the new editions of his "Handwoerterbuch," is concerned more especially with the preference given to *Arabic* etymologies, where it is claimed better results could be reached through the Assyrian.

I do not know whether the Assyrian has any new derivation to present for the words concerned in this argument of Dr. Jewett, but the presumption is against this. It is still safe to respect the authority of Gesenius. I have at hand the eighth *German* edition, much later, of course, than the one from which Dr. Robinson made his translation. No change has been made in the definitions of the words concerned in this discussion.

Under "Tirosh" I find "Most, ungegohrener Wein : der Most ist von der den Kopf einnehmenden Wirkung benarint (vgl. Hos. iv. 11.) יָקַח לֵב er benimmt den Verstand." This is proof that present German scholarship has no opinion at variance with that of Gesenius when he wrote.

Young, in his "Analytical Concord," translates *Yayin* "what is pressed out grape juice," and *Tirosh* "what is possessed, mead, new wine." In his Preface he mentions as his authorities in lexicography, "Fuerst, Robinson, etc." In these definitions he has manifestly followed *Fuerst*, who cannot rank with Gesenius in this sphere.

The position gained on the ground of etymology and biblical use and context Dr. Jewett supports by extra biblical testimony, that would seem sufficient to put the matter at rest. The larger part of the authorities thus cited are out of my reach at the present, but the general candor and fairness of Dr. Jewett's treatise give reason to presume that he has not distorted the testimony.

Dr. C. V. A. van Dyke was my teacher in Hebrew and cognate languages, and I heard from him several times, and with emphasis, the same statements as Dr. Jewett quotes from him and from others who are personally familiar with modern customs of the East. I see no reason to think that Christ used, at the institution of the Supper, any other wine than that used ordinarily at the Passover, or to suppose that this was unfermented and non-intoxicating. It seems to me evident that at Cana Jesus produced a wine with inebriating quality.

I am myself a total abstainer from intoxicating liquors as a beverage ; but the foundation on which I stand, in this matter, is that of Paul in abstaining from meat I think the temperance cause is injured and hindered by attempts to press the Bible into giving testimony not clearly in it. On the Communion question Jesus' example does not, to my mind, oppose the use of freshly expressed grape juice, if any congregation desires so to do, any more than Jesus' use of unleavened bread compels the use of the same now. The churches I have served have always used ordinary wine, taking care to procure a pure article, as far as possible. But I should not oppose the other course, if the church I was serving thought it advisable. These last statements, outside of any discussion of Dr. Jewett's article, are given as a definition of my own position.

I am glad to put any weight that my opinion may carry on the side which I feel constrained to regard as the side of truth.

Yours sincerely,   A. P. BISSELL.

[258]

Hudson, N. Y., July 16, 1888.

REV. DR. CROSBY.

MY DEAR BROTHER :—I thank you for the copies of Dr. Jewett's pamphlets sent me. I have read the article with interest, though I never had any doubts of the fact that Bible wine was *wine*, and not vegetable soup or grape jelly. As a concession to weak brethren, however, I can see how "the fruit of the vine," which is not fermented, may be used on sacramental occasions, and the administration still be valid. Charity covers a multitude of alcoholic omissions. I am enough of a Presbyterian to feel that the character of the bread and the wine need not affect the benefit which the devout and spiritual communicant may receive. I do not object to the use of unfermented grape juice where weak consciences and former inebriates feel they can commune more comfortably.

I would not, however, yield to the demand for such use if made on any other ground than charity.   Very truly yours,   GEO. C. YEISLEY

[259]

152 South West Street, Syracuse, July 11, 1888.
REV. DR. HOWARD CROSBY, LL.D., New York.

REVEREND AND DEAR SIR :—I know that a *necessarily* tardy acknowledgment of the receipt of your letter of inquiry and of Dr. Jewett's pamphlet has your pardon. To me Dr. Jewett's arguments are conclusive. While this is so, with many others, I would suggest that the question of the *modern* use of intoxicating sacramental wine, and of the use of intoxicating wine in general, is not to be settled either by ancient custom or critical etymology. It is now a question of *moral expediency*, as viewed in the light of history, and tested by its relation to *modern* customs and *modern* society. So viewed, and thus related, I think that the principles of the New Testament would counsel the disuse of fermented wine in the Communion, and would *condemn* its use as a beverage.

Respectfully,   THERON R. GREEN,
Pastor of Centenary Methodist Episcopal Church, Syracuse, N. Y.

[260]

MR. HOWARD CROSBY.   Cazenovia, N. Y., July 17, 1888.

DEAR SIR:—The pamphlet by Dr. Jewett, which you sent me some time since, I have glanced over. As far as I have examined it I agree with his views. There is in my mind no question as to the matter. Wine is wine, and that is the end of it.   Sincerely yours,

DOUGLAS PUTNAM BIRNIE, Pastor of First Presbyterian Church.

[261]

TO THE EDITOR OF THE "BROOKLYN TIMES."

SIR:—I have carefully examined Dr. Jewett's pamphlet on "Communion Wine," and would like to lay its conclusions before your readers. I am fully persuaded that it is amply sufficient to satisfy any mind, not biased by prejudice, that the wines of the Bible are all reducible to one, of different grades, such as old and new, good and better and best, and wine mixed with water, and that all such wines are intoxicating to a greater or less degree, and all were indulged in by Divine approbation under certain limitations and condemned in others. Aaron and his sons "were not to drink wine nor any strong drink when they went into the tabernacle of the congregation" (Lev. x. 9), implying a permission to drink at other times. This drinking of wine formed a ceremonial obligation in many of the offerings presented unto the Lord. The morning and evening sacrifices were accompanied with drink offerings of wine (Ex. xxix. 40; Num. xv. 5, 7, 10). The wines used on these occasions were always the wines of commerce, or wine in the proper acceptation of the term *yayin*, which was fermented.

"Kings were not to drink wine nor princes strong drink, lest they drink and forget the law" (Prov. xxxi. 4). But in the sixth verse of said chapter "strong drink was to be given unto him that was ready to perish, and wine unto those that were of heavy hearts," indicating beyond a peradventure that the same word is used commendingly and disparagingly at different times and under different circumstances. Of this wine David says, "It maketh glad the heart of man." With this wine Melchizedek refreshed Abraham and his men when returning from the slaughter of Chedorlaomer and his allies. In Deut. xiv. 26 there is express authority given to those Jews who lived at a great distance from the house of the Lord "to sell their offerings, and with the money to purchase whatever their soul lusteth after—for oxen, or for sheep, or for wine, or for strong drink," etc. In other circumstances Solomon tells us that "wine is a mocker, strong drink is raging," and is the cause of woe and sorrow when liberally indulged in.

Now, that one of the ancient symbols of the Sacrament of the Supper of our Lord is on trial at the bar of public opinion, the friends of the institution should not be backward in giving their views on the teaching of Scripture and the usages of antiquity. One grand object of some temperance people is to banish fermented wine from the Lord's Supper, and they chronicle from year to year the number of congregations they have brought over to their way of thinking. This agitation, if persisted in, will disturb the harmony of the Church and sow seeds of discord where peace and unanimity now prevail. The efforts of these people to guard reformed drunkards from the danger they suppose lies in the Communion cup naturally secures the co-operation of those who are in sympathy with them in the good cause of temperance, and the strong current of temperance agitation that now prevails in the land favors this assumption. Is it wise for the Christian Church to follow the stream, and to "forsake the old paths" in which their fathers walked, and, for the sake of peace, substitute some decoction of grape juice or other compound for the wine of the Sacrament which has been so long in use and neve. called in question until now? The changed state of public opinion regarding alcoholic drinks, and the present excitement, imperatively call upon the leaders of thought to give an intelligent opinion of the Church's historic action. Reform movements should be watched with jealous eye. Innovations are full of warning. The Roman Catholic Church, from one lapse to another, has taken away the cup of the Sacrament from the laity altogether, and it is not uncommon for some weak-minded, conscientious people to refuse the cup, even in orthodox churches.

The question at issue is not that adulterated compounds and spurious wines that are frequently used at the Lord's table should be abandoned (this is admitted, and is equally offensive to all conscientious Christians and greatly mars the symbolism of the ordinance). But should the wine of the Sacrament commonly used be laid aside?

The objections raised against fermented wine at the Lord's table are of two kinds. The one is in the interest of humanity, and the other in a misinterpretation of the word wine. If it can be shown that the wine used by our Lord at the first Supper, and employed by his immediate followers, was not fermented, that should settle the question finally and forever. But should it not be clearly established, intelligent Christians will hesitate before adopting a new view in consideration of weak minds, implying, as it does, a want of forethought on the part of Christ when he instituted this memorial, and a reflection on his judgment, that were he on earth now he would guard his followers against the danger to which he has inadvertently exposed them.

But as regards the danger of reformed drunkards being led away back to their old habits by the wine of the Lord's Supper, we think that is exaggerated. It will not be denied that reclaimed drunkards have fallen away from their profession and have given loose rein to their former appetites; but it will be difficult to produce examples where this occurred by or through the means of the Lord's Supper. It is not the wine cup of the Lord's Supper that reformed drunkards are to be guarded against so much as the company of former associates, and the old haunts of seduction, and the foul odors of the gin shops, as they pass them by in their daily walks of life. I know of no instance of a reformed drunkard being led away by the wine of the Sacrament; but I know of many most notorious inebriates, now clothed and in their right minds, who have been for years sitting at the Lord's table without any inclination at any time to return to their former habits.

If danger lie in this direction, I do not think that an unfermented wine would remedy the evil. In this unfermented wine there is still the sight, the smell and the taste, appealing to the old appetite and reawakening former indulgences.

Turning now to the scriptural arguments respecting the wine of the Sacrament, it is argued that Christ did not so much as mention wine at the institution of the Supper, but used the terms "the cup" and "the fruit of the vine." Christ always spoke in language and used figures that could be understood by the people, and on this occasion would evidently use the language by which the Jews designated the wine of the Passover.

The term "fruit of the vine" was the common liturgical expression for the wine used by the Jews in their sacred ceremonials; and the natural assumption is that the wine used at the Passover would be the wine most esteemed, and which Christ himself would sanction as an appropriate symbol of his blood. Many of the ablest writers in behalf of unfermented wine at the Lord's table admit that the early Christian Church made use of the wine of commerce. They admit also that the wine used in the Corinthian Church by apostolic sanction was fermented, which is too plainly shown in 1 Cor. xi. 20, 21. They admit also that grape juice is not, properly speaking, wine until it has gone through a process of fermentation; and that "the early Church made use of common wine, stands unquestioned and unquestionable."

The question naturally arises, What is wine? What is cider? Is the fresh pressed juice of the apple cider? or does it require time to ferment in order to make it cider? If so, the fresh pressed juice of the grape must have time to ferment before it can be properly called wine.

The wine of the New Testament, universally esteemed, was the wine of fermentation. Christ says, "No man having drunk old wine straightway desireth new, for he saith the old is better." The governor at the marriage feast in Cana of Galilee admitted that "good wine" was intoxicating, and that the wine made by Christ on that occasion was "good wine."

It is worthy of note, also, that the reproof administered to the Corinthians by the apostle for their unseemly conduct at that symbolical feast was not founded on the nature of the wine used, but the quantity of it. Had the intoxicating wine which was used on that occasion been contrary to apostolic law and the original institution, Paul could not have passed it by in silence, but would certainly turn the point of his reproof upon the scandal of using an alcoholic production instead of an unfermented liquid. There is no authority to show that the wine used by the early Christian Church in the Lord's Supper or at the Passover, called "fruit of the vine," was anything else than pure fermented wine. That the wine of the Passover was intoxicating is clearly shown from the fact that those who partook thereof were obliged to mix it with water to prevent intoxication.

The wine of the Passover was originally " red." An unfermented wine cannot be red, inasmuch as the juice of the grape is not red. The coloring matter of the grape is in the husk, and can only be extracted by fermentation.

The argument used for an unfermented wine at the Lord's Supper, arising from the proscription of things leavened at the time of the Passover, is found in the common mistake made in confounding fermented liquors with malt liquors. It is true that all leaven was forbidden at the time of the Passover. Leaven is a sign of moral corruption, and would have been regarded as a defiling offering rather than of purification; but there is no identity between leaven and ferment. The one is ever the symbol of evil; the other is never so employed.

So radical were the Jews in their observance of the ancient rite, in putting all leaven out of their house during the time of the Passover, that they would not touch or taste any wine into which grain had entered, no matter by whom prepared or how. But the pure fermented juice of the grape was never objected to.

W. J. MacDOWELL.

[262]

DEAR SIR :—Referring to Dr. Jewett's "Historic Testimony on Communion Wine," as you request, I would say that, as a missionary to Greece residing in the vintage country of the Peloponnesus and the adjacent Ionian Islands, I became somewhat acquainted with the manufacture and character of wine and its use by the natives. The juice of the grape as it flows from the trodden winepress is, in Greek, γλεῦκος, in English, MUST. When it has fermented, it is in Greek, OINOS, in English, WINE. It becomes οἶνος, WINE, by fermentation; then, and not before. By the fermenting an equivalent of a constituent, the grape sugar in the juice is converted into alcohol. Fermenting, therefore, is the process of generating alcohol, and the presence of this alcohol, and not otherwise, is what constitutes it οἶνος, wine. To call it UNFERMENTED wine is a solecism as absolute as to say HOT ICE-CREAM. I know of but one process whereby grape juice can be prevented from immediate fermentation, and that is, to boil it down into grape molasses. This we were accustomed to do for our table, and in order to be able to do so, we had to have the γλεῦκος brought to us early in the morning after the wine-press had been trodden during the cool of the night previous, else the fermentation commenced would have destroyed the sugar in it, so as to render it unfit to make the molasses. In the heat of the vintage season, which is about the middle of September, fermentation commences immediately. It were impossible to keep grape-juice in an unfermented state six months after the vintage, to the date when our Saviour instituted the Lord's Supper, so that "the fruit of the vine" then had become οἶνος = wine. It could not have been γλεῦκος, MUST. The charge against the disciples at the Pentecost (Acts ii. 13) was sarcastic ridicule. In Greek idiom it is literally thus : "THESE MEN ARE HAVING FILLED THEMSELVES FULL OF MUST," meaning, ABSURDLY drunk. But Peter said in effect, "No ! we could not get drunk in this early morning hour." Wine in Palestine then was doubtless what wine in Greece is now—the common drink of the people at the table. It is called in the people's patois, in Greek, κρασὶ, a word derived from ἐκράθην, the Aorist Passive of the Greek verb, κεράννυμι, which means "wine mixed with water," as Scarlatos, a native Greek, says in his Lexicon that this verb means "THE MIXING OF TWO LIQUIDS TOGETHER, AS WINE AND WATER." Κρασὶ is too weak to produce drunkenness, unless the drinking is kept up all day and most immoderately. I never saw a Greek stupidly drunk on wine.

Wine imported to this country is wine mixed with rum, or with some extra form of alcohol to strengthen it, in order to prevent its acetic or second fermentation, whereby its natural equivalent of alcohol is converted into vinegar. The Greek Captain Alexandros, in whose ship I crossed the Atlantic to Greece, told me that his cargo of Crete wine which he had brought into Boston had, by its agitation on the passage, become vinegar, himself having neglected, before leaving Crete, the precaution to adulterate with rum. I have occasion to know that vessels to the Levant were usually well laden with "spirits" for strengthening wine to be exported. It is wine, not mixed with water, but with rum, which makes the imported wine of commerce unfit for the Communion service. But wine such as the Saviour used and drank and commands to be had for the Communion table, can be made in this country without difficulty. We, for our own Church, so make it from our own garden, with no alcohol in it other than what is generated therein by its own fermenting. The temperance cause must, to succeed, be content to deal with the drink-evil as the Bible does. Can we expect to promote it by calling it sin to drink such as the Son of God drank while on earth ?

I believe that drunkenness is the MOLOCH of this Earth, and that its temple must be broken down, and its altar utterly destroyed, by both law and gospel ; that its sin should be thundered from the pulpit, and that it should be made by law a crime to get drunk, or make drunk, to be punished by fine and imprisonment. And because alcoholic commodities must be (and rightly, as all admit) produced, manufactured, imported, exported, transported, bought and sold for the arts and sciences, and for medicinal and sacramental purposes, and because the same is dangerous to depravity in relation to the peace and welfare of society, he who handles it should pay license for the business sufficiently large to adequately compensate society and tax-payers in full for all the pecuniary evils and damages, direct and indirect, which result from its depraved abuse. Its sin must be left to the retribution of God. But I confess I am not quite able to see the logic of what is called Modern or Political Prohibition. I can never call Truth a Lie, to enforce what is right. Even Paul's doctrine (1st Cor. viii. 13) to prevent a brother man from sinning does not make it wrong for society to permit a meat-market, nor to license druggists or others to deal in alcoholic commodities, so only that such be properly punished for making drunk.   Yours very truly,   H. T. LOVE.
Babylon, July 17, 1888.

P. S.—Above please find answer to your request of May 15. Sickness has prevented it earlier. And lest I might be thought to apologize for intemperance, I have ventured to add a word in relation to the great evil of drunkenness.   Yours, etc.,   H. T. LOVE.

[263]

[From the Rome (N. Y.) Republican.]

A NEW BOOK.

No better and more exhaustive dissertation has ever appeared in our days than the pamphlet by Rev. E. H. Jewett on "Communion Wine" (containing 60 pages), New York Church Review Association. It gives a critical examination of the original Scripture words concerning the much ventilated question about two sorts of wine in ancient times and for church use, and proves in a classical style and scholarly way what the Rabbies, Church Fathers, and the most glorious and learned Reformers were teaching about *Yayin, Oinos, Tirosh* and *Mustum.* Also what the Saviour and his apostles professed in this direction is clearly stated, and not even the Apocrypha, the Jewish Targums, nor the writings of Philo and Josephus, are omitted.

If our modern temperance fanatics can digest the above-mentioned book, and understand the author's learned, pious and sober-minded ways, they will only profit by the same. Truth will prevail.

In reference to this word fanatics, we just quote part of Dr. Jewett's essay (page 8), which was published as a direct and rather crushing answer to the following one-sided, party-influenced legerdemain scribblings of Thayer on Communion Wine and Bible Temperance ; N. Kerr, on Wines (Scripture and Ecclesiastical) ; G. Samson, on the Divine Law as to Wines. The words in Dr. Jewett's pamphlet (page 8) are these : The Rev. W. M. Thayer affirms, nevertheless, "that the Bible speaks of two kinds of wine, there can be no doubt. It pronounces one of them a blessing and the other a curse." And in this, equally with Drs. Kerr and Samson, he follows the guidance of Dr. Lees, M. Stuart, and other early agitators of the question.

President Nott innocently asks, "Can the same thing, in the same state, be good and bad—a thing to be sought after, and a thing to be avoided?" as though the same could not equally be said of fire and water, and a multitude of things in daily use, which are a blessing or a curse, according as they are used.

O. F. EBERT, Pastor (Lutheran) Trinity Church.

[264]

[Letter Preceded by Dr. Crosby's Query.]

In compliance with the above request, I desire the favor of the *Republican* to state my judgment and conviction that Dr. Jewett has utterly and forever exploded the so-called "two-wine theory" by which the statements of Scripture, and the action and ordinance of Jesus Christ, as recorded in the New Testament, have been conformed to extreme and untenable positions as to the use of wine in the sacrament.

For popular readers, the testimony of an eminent authority in the *Century* for May, 1888, will be sufficient, unless they be prejudiced, or partisans who mingle policy with principle. ROLLIN A. SAWYER.

LETTERS ADDRESSED TO REV. E. H. JEWETT, PREVIOUS TO DR. HOWARD CROSBY'S INQUIRY.

[From Bishop Williams.]

Middletown, Conn., January 11, 1886.

MY DEAR DR. JEWETT :—I have read your admirable articles on "Communion Wine" with great pleasure and instruction. You have, it seems to me, settled the question beyond possibility of further argument.

The labor of preparing two such articles must have been enormous ; and there are not many among us capable of undertaking it.

I am sure you will receive, as you assuredly deserve, the thanks of all persons who desire to learn the meaning and teaching of Holy Scripture fairly brought out *from* it, and not any kind of notion imported *into* it. JOHN WILLIAMS.

Affectionately yours,

[From Bishop Seymour.]

Springfield, Ill., May 9, 1885.

MY DEAR BROTHER:—From the fact that I have an article in the *Church Review* for April, I have looked into the number, and in consequence I have seen and read your article on "Communion Wine." I beg to thank you for it. It is *convincing* and *crushing*. The principle involved is of very grave importance. This so-called "temperance movement" is in the line of doing an immense amount of mischief—it is confusing men's minds, and good men's too, in the distinction between good and evil. Your article is capital.

Affectionately yours,   GEORGE F. SEYMOUR.

[From Bishop Paddock.]

Boston, May 16, 1885.

REVEREND AND DEAR SIR:—I cannot help thanking you heartily for the pleasure and profit I have had in reading your article in the *Church Review.* When I saw the announcement, I feared you were threshing well-beaten straw; but you have done a good and needed work. Few of us could have done it as you have, but many of us know a good thing when we see it. Your ability, scholarship, and good temper have laid the Church under a debt of obligation to you.

Yours sincerely,   BENJAMIN H. PADDOCK.

[From the Rev. E. E. Beardsley, D.D.]

New Haven, Conn., September 14, 1885.

MY DEAR DR. JEWETT:—I have read with very great satisfaction your articles in the *Church Review* on "Communion Wine," and I write this note to thank you for them, and to express the hope that they will speedily be reprinted in book form. Such a critical, careful, and scholarly examination of Scripture words should have a wide circulation, and be accessible in these times to all clergymen and laymen who would have a correct knowledge of a subject which is in danger of being abused in the hands of misguided zealots.

Very truly yours,   E. E. BEARDSLEY.

[From the Pacific Churchman, December 1, 1885.]

It is, therefore, a pleasure to us to draw renewed attention to the remarkable articles on "Communion Wine," which appeared in the *Church Review* for April and July, and which we noticed briefly on their first appearance. We are glad to learn that they are to be republished in pamphlet form at the lowest possible cost, so as to permit the widest circulation.

The articles are full of learning and full of good-tempered humor, which make their refutation of fallacy and misstatement all the more telling. The "unfermented wine" theorists base their whole case upon an alleged distinction said to exist in Scripture between two kinds of wine—one fermented, the other unfermented; the latter, according to them, being referred to in passages where the use of wine is spoken of allowably, the former being always and everywhere spoken of with reprobation. Dr. Jewett examines the grounds of this theory historically and etymologically, tracing, with great care, not only the Hebrew usages, but also the history of wine among the Greeks and Romans, and he shows conclusively that it is a baseless assumption. In the case of the Old Testament, his array of evidence far more than substantiates his assertion, "No such distinction exists." In regard to Greek and Roman usage, his conclusion is: "Unfermented wine, in fact, would have been as much 'downright nonsense' to Cato, Columella, and Pliny as 'dry water' or 'unelectric lightning.'"

We had marked several passages for quotation from the second article, which views the question in the light of the New Testament, but space forbids. The irreverent juggling with our Lord's words and deeds, of which the advocates of the two-classes-of-wine theory are not ashamed, is such as to cause shame and violence to the feelings of any who have not a preconceived theory to justify.

How they can so light-heartedly kick against the facts of history has always been an unsolved riddle to us. Dr. Jewett conclusively disproves their contention by the mass of evidence which he adduces to prove that the wine used at the Passover Supper must have been ordinary fermented wine. This was ordered to be mixed with water, and the reason given in the Talmud shows, beyond a doubt, its fermented and intoxicating quality. " It was too strong, and hence unfit, without dilution, to be drank in so large a quantity. Also, when mixed with water, it was considered to be more wholesome and gave less occasion for intoxication."

The publication of these articles as a cheap pamphlet will enable any clergyman who has to touch this question in his parochial visitations to do it solidly and conclusively.

[1]

643 Monroe St., Brooklyn, N. Y., May 25, 1888.

DEAR DR. CROSBY :—I have read most of the Doctor's pamphlet you sent me, and I must say that the Doctor and the advocates of the one-wine theory make out as clear a case, to their minds, as did the advocates of slavery before the war, demonstrating the divine right of keeping slaves; but no one defends the divine right now. So I hope the time will come when ministers and all good people will be more concerned how to keep the multitude from looking upon the wine when it is red and when it giveth color in the cup than spend their precious time in trying to prove all kinds of wine are a blessing, when they know it is otherwise, even a curse.

I must, therefore, adhere to the theory of the two kinds of wine, because the juice of the grape is called wine pressed from the cluster, and certainly that does not intoxicate.

Dear Doctor, while I admire your course and zeal and perseverance in trying to lessen the evils of drinking, I often weep and feel sad to think such talent, power, and influence could not be given wholly and entirely to the cause of true temperance and a thorough reformation of the drinking evil. I have, however, always given you the credit of honesty; but with my views of the subject, I am ready and willing to appear in the presence of my Master and Judge.

Ever believe me, yours sincerely,   P. M. RIGHTMYER.

[2]

Pastor's Study, M. E. Parsonage, Ogdensburg, May 23, 1888.

DEAR SIR :—Your circular letter of the 15th inst. is at hand, and also Dr. Jewett's pamphlet. Contents of both carefully noted and considered.

I answer that I think the argument is against Dr. Jewett. And also, I think that experience, observation, and common sense are all against the use of fermented wine or other intoxicants as a beverage, and especially against the use of fermented wine to represent the blood of the Son of God. I believe it is blasphemous to charge the Lord Jesus Christ with making, recommending to others, and himself drinking intoxicating wines or liquors.

You will pardon me, dear sir ; I think your letter and the pamphlet, with their evident trend, give me the right to say one or two plain things. After twenty years in the active ministry and mingling with the people in cities, towns, and country, of all classes and conditions, to the extent of from twelve to eighteen hundred pastoral calls a year, I believe it susceptible of fair proof that your position and utterances in favor of the moderate use of alcholic wines and liquors, as a minister of God and one of the foremost educators in the land, are making more drunkards of the young men and young women of our country than any *five saloons on the continent.*

You may think this very severe, or you may throw it aside in contempt, but your position and utterances are simply *appalling*—as they are arrayed against our efforts to save men from the drink curse and get them to God.

Yours truly,   A. S. COWLES.

[3]

Argyle, N. Y., May 21, 1888.

REV. HOWARD CROSBY, D.D., LL.D.

REVEREND AND DEAR SIR :—Your inquiry received, and I reply:

1st. In the institution of the Lord's Supper, I do not find the word wine used, but the words "fruit of the vine" and "cup ;" hence, I believe at the Lord's table the use of the unfermented juice of the grape, or the "cup," or "fruit of the vine," satisfies the requirements.

2d. The Bible is a book for the common people—not meant only for the scholar, as you well know.

An "unlettered man" reading Prov. xxiii. 29–35 would conclude that the *wine* referred to there is bad, to be let alone—or treated as we would naturally

treat the "adder," to which it is compared. The same man reading John ii.
would conclude that Jesus could not make the same wine *condemned* in Prov. xxiii.,
and make it in such quantities that drunkenness would be apt to follow which he
himself had encouraged, perhaps by his own example.

3d. As you know, some eight or nine different Hebrew words are translated
"wine" in our English Bible. The natural inference is that they cannot all refer
to the same kind of wine. I have looked over the pamphlet you sent me; I have
also read a much abler work on the same subject by Dr. Eliphalet Nott, who was
a scholar equal to Dr. Jewett. Dr. Nott's views meet what I regard the demands of conscience, common sense and morality—and Dr. Jewett's do not.

I have read many arguments like that of Dr. Jewett, notably Dr. Atwater's,
but I am still convinced that the Bible can in no way even tolerate the use of
that, either as a beverage or at the Communion Table, whose poison is doing so
much to ruin the souls and bodies of men. Most assuredly I deprecate the use
of that at the Communion Table which is the symbol and suggestion of "woe,"
"sorrow" and "redness of the eyes" to symbolize the precious life-giving blood
of the Redeemer of the world.

Dr. Crosby, I respect your scholarship, but deplore your influence on this
"wine question." Yours truly,

THOS. A. SANSON.

[4]

Ogdensburg, N. Y., May 23, 1888.

DEAR BROTHER :—Your letter and Dr. Jewett's discussion of "Communion
Wine" are both received. I have read enough of the article to get the drift of it.
I do not perceive that Dr. Jewett has established his propositions.

But, it seems to me, that is a matter of *small importance*. Even if he should
prove, by argument, that fermented wine was used by the disciples of our Lord
without injury, and without danger of injury to themselves and others of their
time, how, pray, is that going to justify the use of fermented wine by us in
America, in these times, when such liquors are a temptation and cause of
stumbling to our brethren?

This is a *fact* of positive experience. There are men in my church, formerly
addicted to drink, who did not dare, and would not taste fermented wine, when
we used it about four years ago ; but they can take the unfermented wine with
safety.

In the Presbyterian Church in this city the fermented wine is still used at
Communion, and time and again it has led certain members into open debauch :
after having tasted liquor then, they rushed to get more and stronger elsewhere.
These samples could be multiplied almost indefinitely. Now, dear sir, we hold
it to be transparently clear, and a primary principle of Scripture teaching, that to
persist to use fermented wine at Communion service in the face of these facts, is a
gross sin against our Redeemer and his Church, and against our brethren about us.

I am *amazed* that any true preacher of the Gospel can, in the slightest way,
encourage the use of fermented liquors at the Lord's Supper in these days.

Very respectfully yours, JAMES STUART AINSLIE,
Pastor First Congregational Church.

[5]

Oswego, N. Y., May 29, 1888.

MY DEAR SIR :—I have read carefully Dr. Jewett's pamphlet, and do not
consider that he has proved his point. Why the pamphlet was written I cannot
tell. If it were possible to prove that the Jews used only fermented wine, it
would amount to nothing, unless it could be shown that the fermentation of wine,
and the presence or absence of leaven in the bread, are essential to the validity of
the Sacrament of the Lord's Supper. In my opinion, we are at perfect liberty to
use unfermented wine, and the great temptations which exist at the present time
in the use of alcoholic drinks make it very desirable for the churches to be doubly
careful as to what they teach and recommend in this respect.

I remain, yours truly, J. L. BURROWS.

[6]

512 Swan St., Buffalo, May 19, 1888.

REVEREND AND DEAR SIR:—Pamphlet, with request to read, received with thanks. Have read with care. You ask opinion.

For those who have not read the books which the writer assumes to review, and for those who have prejudged the whole case with the writer, the pamphlet is very convincing.

Otherwise, it is an argument that does not argue. To my view, the main contention of Thayer, Kerr, Samson and others is strengthened by this pamphlet, and I am thankful for the privilege of seeing it.

Permit me to add the confession of my inability to appreciate either the piety or the sense in the labor to prove the falsehood charged against the Lord Jesus that he was a wine-bibber. The attempt to furnish a religious excuse for a vicious and criminal indulgence is pitiful. You say "for the general good." A club in the hands of infidels, to break the heads of the feeble in faith, "for the general good." "What will the harvest be?" Yours, etc.,

HENRY WARD.

[7]

Fairville, May 22, 1888.

REV. HOWARD CROSBY, D.D. :—Your letter is received, also Dr. Jewett's pamphlet, which I have read.

The pamphlet is learned and able, but has not changed my views in regard to "Communion Wine."

I believe for the "Lord's Table" we should have "unfermented wine," or wine free from alcohol. I have not time or space to give my reasons, nor is it necessary. You ask for a reply, which I am pleased to give as above.

Yours, with respect. S. NELSON.

[8]

Howard, May 19, 1888.

REVEREND AND DEAR BROTHER :—I have read, with a good degree of care and interest, Dr. Jewett's pamphlet on the wine subject, and as you request, will give my opinion.

I have no doubt of the correctness of his statement concerning the wine used by the Jews and by our Saviour at the institution of the Eucharist—pure (fermented) wine, mingled with water. But why all this contention for wine (fermented), even if it was then used? He used, we are sure, "unleavened bread," but no one now contends for its use. They also reclined at the table, but no one deems that position essential. It seems to me that the sticklers for (fermented) wine, not only have a "hobby" to ride (as is charged to the other side), but also some taste or desire to gratify. "The fruit of the vine" in "the cup," pure and unadulterated, whether it be must or extract of raisins, etc., consecrated and received in the right spirit, is all-sufficient.

Therefore, knowing as we do that the smell and taste of real wine often does arouse the demon which has lain dormant in the reformed drunkard, I think we should follow the example of Paul, and allow nothing by which the weak brother may stumble.

For prudential reasons, and believing it to be in accordance with God's will, I will not present the cup of intoxication to my fellow-men, either at the Lord's table or elsewhere, so far as I have any control over the matter.

Yours, with respect, H. H. SHELLAND.

[9]

Poughkeepsie, N. Y., May 25, 1888.

DEAR SIR :—I have read with interest Dr. Jewett's pamphlet on "Communion Wine." You have asked my opinion. I regard the arguments presented as one-sided, viewed only from the standpoint of prejudice as much so as the views of the persons he controverts.

To a plain, common-sense person who has any knowledge of wine culture, the question at once suggested is, "Did the word *Yayin* apply to the juice of the grape when first pressed?" Cider is applied to the apple juice as soon as squeezed from the apple. If the word was so used, the proof is clear that two wines or classes of wine existed under one name. Dr. Jewett answers this question himself (p. 13): "A language rich enough in words to employ at least EIGHT for WINE, might have furnished or restricted ONE to make so important a distinction. But there is not even one adjective, or any qualifying word, employed to distinguish fermented from unfermented wine."

If this statement were true, the question would be wholly one of historical evidence as to whether wine was preserved in an unfermented state. In a review of the Bible words for wine, by Rev. Leon C. Field, in *The Methodist Quarterly Review*, April, 1882, is this statement: "And *six* Hebrew terms, and three Greek terms, NINE in all, denote some form of unfermented grape or other juice." It is needless for us to say that when a writer twists definitions to his advantage he should be taken with much caution.

In his definition of *Tirosh*, he quotes GESENIUS as far as will favor his view. He neglects to quote the same author on page 428, Lexicon, where *Tirosh* is translated "MUST, NEW WINE." As this lexicon is quoted by Dr. Jewett as the best authority, there can be but one conclusion, that the word did apply to both the MUST and the fermented wine. No living language could bear a microscopical examination of root meanings in order to show the customs of a country at any period, and surely not at all the uses of particular words at different periods. The whole essay concerning the two wines of the Bible will find a good refutation in an article by Prof. F. D. Hemenway, D.D., printed in *The Methodist Quarterly Review* of July, 1878, and which article must commend itself for great fairness of exposition.

The Communion Wine question, to my mind, is not whether the particular Hebrew and Greek words can be twisted to mean this or that, but whether in the light of modern science, modern appetites, and modern drunkenness, an element can be admitted at the Lord's table which is known to awaken passion, disgrace the Church, and destroy souls. Far better be it to put by the unfermented juice of the grape, which to all common-sense persons must comply sufficiently with the requirements of the ordinance. Yours very truly,

D. H. HANABURGH, Pastor M. E. Church, Poughkeepsie, N. Y.

[10]
Albany, N. Y., May 18, 1888.

MY DEAR SIR:—The pamphlet on Communion Wine, by Mr. Jewett, is before me. I am very little affected by linguistic quarrels of this character. Let the wise men have it out with their grammars and lexicons. I am comparatively indifferent as to whose head gets broken. I have drank two kinds of wine in wine countries, just as from a boy I have been accustomed to two kinds of cider, sweet and hard.

We are making and selling sweet wines in the streets of our own cities. All wine must be sweet before it is fermented. But I care for none of these things. I care just as little as to what kind of wine Christ and the Apostles used. It has no more to do with me than the kind of bread they ate, or the style of clothes they wore. In my short pastorate of seven years in this city, I have had two cases which necessitated a long discussion in the Session as to what could be done. One of my elders (not by any means a temperance fanatic) said to me: "I spent the whole Communion hour praying for J. B. that he might not fall through the wine."

At last, simply that the Lord's table might not prove a trap of the Devil for any soul, we have voted for unfermented wine. This whole business of Dr. Jewett's seems a feeble and profitless business. If he spent as much time for the welfare and comfort of Christ's Little Ones, I am sure his Master would be more pleased with him. Very truly yours, J. H. ECOB.

[11]

Glendale, N. Y., May 18, 1888.

DR. HOWARD CROSBY.

DEAR SIR:—Your copy of "Communion Wine" received. It should be entitled "An Attack upon Dr. Samson," for telling the *truth*.

I have read his book, and entirely agree with him, Dr. Jewett to the contrary notwithstanding. Respectfully,

GEO. H. HORNE, Pastor Wyckoff Ave. Baptist Church.

[12]

The Parsonage, Cornwall-on-Hudson, N. Y., May 18, 1888.

MY DEAR DR. CROSBY:—Thank you for Dr. Jewett's pamphlet, which I have just finished reading, with mingled profit, amusement, and indignation. As a radical of the radicals among temperance men, I have never regarded the "two-wine" theory as worth any especial fight, though I have accepted it as true, and have thought it a good explanation of some very perplexing questions that without it I find hard to solve. For instance: the unquestioned righteousness of giving an hundred gallons of wine to men already "well drunk."

I have to thank you and Dr. Jewett, therefore, for establishing my faith, and confirming me in my opinion, which I held, but was hardly willing to advocate. I am not scholar enough to judge as to the force of the verbal argument. But the assumption that it is always the use of wine that is commended and the abuse that is condemned in the Scriptures, the occasional displays of bad temper, and the frequent departures from the courtesy due from one Christian gentleman to another that these articles contain, seem to me to show both conscious weakness and the desire to make the most of a bad cause.

It was to Dr. Samson that I owed much of the impulse that led me into the Church and ministry, and I have many sacred memories of the loving and wise counsel that guided me thirty years ago. You may easily imagine, therefore, that it takes some patience to hear the words "characteristic specimen of juggling," "dishonest," "untrue," "characteristic piece of shuffling with evidence as cowardly as it is contemptible," applied to him. So much is required, indeed, that I doubt my ability to judge fairly of an argument in which they are to be found. This is hardly the sort of a reply that you expected, but if it will conduce to "the general good" for you to know that Dr. Jewett has made me a hearty believer in the "two wines," it will inform you of the fact.

Yours sincerely, GEORGE P. NOBLE.

[13]

Bainbridge, N. Y., June 22, 1888.

DEAR SIR:—On reading Dr. Jewett's pamphlet, as you requested, I was reminded of an incident said to have occurred in Dr. Joel Parker's church just previous to the late rebellion. The Doctor had made diligent search, in both the Old and the New Testaments, to prove that SLAVERY was right, and that his people were bound to return the fugitives to their lawful owners because the Bible says so, and says nothing to the contrary. As he closed his remarks and sat down, an Irishman arose in the audience and said: "The learned gintleman has been right in trying to prove from the Bible that slavery is right, but if it is, *I abhor it!*"

So, if intoxicating wine is the only kind of wine spoken of in the Bible, and we are recommended to use it temperately by our biblical guides, on scriptural grounds, then I must say with the poor son of the Emerald Isle, "I ABHOR IT!" When I know that all the misery of intemperance that curses our fair land begins in a TEMPERATE use of intoxicants, and when I know that so many who have reformed and promised before God and men to lead better lives have fallen by the presentation of the wine-cup, I can but ABHOR IT! And the wonder is, that such doctors as stand high in the Church as scholars and divines should lend their talent and influence to the encouragement of the use of intoxicating wine by the people as a healthful and harmless beverage. Eternity alone can reveal the harm they are doing by the comfort and support they are giving the liquor traffic. And, now, my dear sir, I have thought that I should like to know whether it is true, as I have heard it reported, by both the lovers of strong drink and ultra-temperance people, that you use wine as a common beverage, and that your daughters pass the wine cup to their guests. I do not wish to believe any such thing of yourself and family, and if I have something positive from you I might have a ready answer for all such. I beg pardon for writing so much and so differently from what you had reason to expect. We have a very good temperance lesson for the next Sabbath, and the Apostle asks a solemn question of all biblical scholars: "Through thy knowledge, shall the weak brother perish for whom Christ died ?"

Now, what shall I teach my class? "That the Bible sanctions the use of intoxicating wine as a beverage ?" or, "That it is good neither to eat flesh, nor TO DRINK WINE, nor anything whereby thy brother stumbleth, or is offended, or is made weak ?"

Yours for the right, GEORGE D. HORTON.

P. S.—If intoxicating wine was used at the Passover, then the question of the Irishman to the Pope, whom he offered to treat, but who instead was treated by the Pope to the best his side-board could afford, looking up with grateful emotion he exclaims: "Mister Pope, isn't it a good thing that there is no fast on the drinks ?" Then, while there were strict laws as to leaven, "there was no fast on the drinks."

[14]

Castile, N. Y., June 1, 1888.

DEAR BROTHER:—Your letter, and also the pamphlet upon the wine question, were duly received and read.

I have not time nor space to go into the *merits* or *demerits* of the article in question. I simply say, it is pretty late in this 19th Century to try to prove by all the old Hebrew and Greek lexicons that there is no difference between the "cup of the Lord and the cup of the Devil." I think you have started out on a fool's errand.

There are a great many country preachers that pity you and your pitiable classification of Jesus as a moderate wine-drinker. Such classification is simply impious and blasphemous. Don't send me any more such trash.

Yours respectfully, J. C. LONG, Pastor Presbyterian Church.

[15]

Pastorat der Deutschen Evang. Luth. Bethanien Kirche, Hicksville, L. I., June 9, 1888.

REVEREND AND DEAR SIR.—Dr. Jewett's pamphlet I have received, and carefully noted his points. It is a very fine document, with many far-fetched quotations adduced for the sake of proof, but with a view to be right.

Allow me to say that I acknowledge only one kind of wine—the wine WITHOUT "BARM," as promised in Is. xxv. 6, our German Bible, 1554—*een Gasteboth van reynem Wyne van Wyne dar nene Barme ynne is.* In Bible 1643, *ein Mahl von reinem Wein—von Wein darinnen keine Heffen ist.* In Bible (revised) called "*Probebibel*" it is the same.

How plain does God forbid our ever going into a "drink-house"—as in Jer. xvi. 8; all my Bibles call it so, and not as the English—"house of feasting."

1554—*Darümme shalten ynn nen Drinkehuss ghan by en tho Sittende, noch tho Ethende, node tho drinkende,* just so in all the others.

Why should God have called a "woe unto him that giveth his neighbor drink, etc. (Hab. ii. 15) when he wants fermented wine even in the "House of God ?"

Why, then, the "woe unto them"? (Is. v. 11 and 22). Will not verse 20 and 21 teach us to see right? What is forbidden as clear as this, we should not try to call right, try to evade on account of our taste.

To Aaron and his sons God commanded not to take wine or strong drink when ye go into the tabernacle (Lev. x. 9, 10.) How much less, then, *drink it there !*

And the "why" is answered in the 10th verse (according to our German), "that ye may discern what is holy or unholy, clean or unclean."

Certainly a man who takes from THE SAME STUFF, the same barrel, bottle etc., where the last dram of the delirium-tremens victim, dying in the gutter, came from, who: CANNOT, 1 Cor. vi. 10—"nor drunkards shall inherit the kingdom of God"—go to Heaven—is in the same way affected with the same—insanity—*and not able to discern* the holy things!

A poor drunkard does not die because taking the "last drop," but because he ever tasted the first one. If he had left it alone, never could he have cultivated a taste for it!

Lastly, why is all this necessary to speak about?

Wrong is he who doubts; the doubt itself shows him that there is a wrong. Why, then, defend with a flushed countenance a taste, desire, habits, etc.?

Ought the boy who wishes for an apple out of the grocer's barrel argue within himself about right or not right, till temptation overcomes all (conscious) scruples? He knows if he has a right to eat one, takes one and there is no occasion for dispute (1 James v. 6–8; Sirad xxii. 19; Heb. xxiii. 9).

In Prov. xvi. 2, our translation is: "To each one seem his own way clean; but the Lord alone makes our hearts sure (steadfast)."

Dear Doctor, you asked for my views, and I could not express them in a shorter way; am sorry to impose on your valuable time; remember, too, that I am a German, and therefore not a good English writer.

Our dear Saviour has so long to suffer the Christian's perversity (Matt. xvii. 17). Such questions ought not to be, but they spring out of our desire to defend against the world our weakness! Let us come "clean out" (James iv. 4). "A friend of the world is the enemy of God!"

Sincerely yours,   H. POHLMANN.

[16]

[From Rev. Wilbur F. Crafts, New York.]

1. God's Oldest Testament of Nature, as interpreted in Science, pronounces alcohol " a poison, having no place in a healthy system."

2. God's Old Testament prohibits us from even looking upon the red wine, and calls it a mocker.

3. God's Newest Testament of Modern History shows alcohol to be the Devil's prime minister in the earth.

4. Therefore, in the dispute about the meaning of Greek words I fall back on the *can nots of character*, and say that in New-Testament times the Son of God *could not have made the beverage his Father had proclaimed a "mocker" and "a poison."*

As to the claim that the word "Wine," without the adjective "new," must be understood to be prefixed by "old," I would claim, by the same logic, that where the word "man" occurs without either "good" or "bad" before it, it must mean a BAD man.

In the reference to "old bottles," a fermented and an unfermented wine are clearly contrasted.

But I rest most firmly, not in the roots of Greek words, but in the radical certainties of character. If Christ had made and used fermented wine, we should be under no obligation to follow him in either act, any more than in eating barley bread. As has been said, "The wine he made is *not* in the market to-day," and in the absence of definite information as to *its* character, I fall back on *his* character, and believe it was *not* fermented.

[17]

Southold, N. Y., June 25, 1888.

DEAR SIR :—The standard dictionaries are sufficient to teach one that unfermented wine has the same existence as unfermented yeast. Nevertheless, please accept my thanks for the pamphlet copy of the Rev. Dr. Jewett's review articles.

Yours respectfully,   EPHER WHITAKER.

[18]

Rhinebeck, N. Y., May 25, 1888.

DEAR SIR:—Your pamphlet and letter at hand. I have carefully read the pamphlet, but cannot agree with Jewett.

He has done harm to the cause if his pamphlet has come into the hands of such as do not examine for themselves. He is fully as dictatorial as he claims concerning others when he says, "One thing is very sure" (see p. 8). He mistakes the meaning of his antagonist on page 9. The power of imagination in Jewett is able to carry him over many a difficulty. The Bible is true, and though a score oppose here, as during days of slavery, the right will conquer. My views were settled before there was any party issue, and each fresh examination but deepens my conviction that the use of intoxicants as a beverage is dangerous, and with ministers, a sin, because not to the glory of God.

Yours,   C. H. TRAVER.

[19]

4 Henry Street, Utica, N. Y., June 8, 1888.

DEAR SIR:—I see nothing in Dr. Jewett's pamphlet that has not been met ·effectually over a dozen times. I would ask him to read and study Rev. William Ritchie's "Bible Wines." What I have to say in reply is fully covered by the two articles* enclosed, written in reply to Prof. Hopkins of Hamilton College. Education and habit have more to do in this question than facts, and it is not to be ·expected that men will convict themselves. I am too busy in the line of experiment to spend further time at present.

Yours truly,   J. W. WHITFIELD.

[20]

Ticonderoga, N. Y., May 25, 1888.

REV. HOWARD CROSBY, D. D.

DEAR BROTHER:—I have read carefully Dr. Jewett's pamphlet, "Communion Wine." I am not a Hebrew scholar, but have given some attention to Greek, and hence I may not be able to give ALL his arguments their full import. Whether there were two kinds of wine in early times or not I cannot tell. I do know there are two kinds now, and that the process of preserving the juice of the grape unfermented is known by every housewife that has had any experience in canning fruits.

Neither the Synoptists nor Paul mention the word οἰνος in their accounts of the Last Supper. The fact that wine was used is an inference, a strong one, however ; that the wine was fermented or unfermented, is, in either case, an inference. The Synoptists refer to γέννημα τῆς ἀμπέλου, i.e., the fruit of the vine, which is a generic term, just as βαπτίζω is. If it was ESSENTIAL that fermented wine should be used, our Lord would not have left us to guess the ESSENTIAL from a generic term. He would have given us a specific term. And I believe I am obeying the command of Christ when I use unfermented wine, for I am using "THE FRUIT OF THE VINE." Still further, I have known men who dare not commune where fermented wine is used because of early appetites. From such remove away temptations. I have not read the works that Dr. Jewett attempts to review, so I am unable to say whether his criticisms are just or not. I dislike to use at the sacred altar of God that which I know will madden the brain of my fellow-man. I believe the Church ought to cut loose from every kind of alcoholic wines under all circumstances.

Very respectfully yours,   C. E. GREEN, Pastor M. E. Church.

---

* The articles were not found enclosed. E. H. J.

[21]

Glendale, L. I., N. Y., July 7, 1888.

My Dear Sir :—Looking over Dr. Samson's "Truth as to Wines," also Dr. Jewett's pamphlet, I began to *search for myself.* In reading Clarke's "Design of the Eucharist," I came across the following, which certainly seems confirmatory of Dr. Samson's position.

"Wine is not specifically mentioned, but what is tantamount to it, viz., what our Lord terms γεννημα τῆς ἀμπέλου, 'the offspring or produce of wine.' The *yayin* of the Hebrews, the οἰνος of the Greeks, and the *vinum* of the Romans meant simply 'THE EXPRESSED JUICE OF THE GRAPE,' sometimes drunk after it was expressed, while its natural sweetness remained, and then termed MUSTUM.

"By the ancient Hebrews, it was chiefly drunk in its FIRST, or simple state, hence it was termed among them *pere haggephen, 'the fruit of the vine;'* and by our Lord in the Syriac (His vernacular language), *yaldo dagphetho, 'the young or son of the vine,'* very properly translated by the evangelist, 'the offspring or produce of the vine.' In ancient times, when only a small portion was wanted for immediate use, the JUICE was pressed by the hand out of a bunch of grapes, and immediately drank.

"After this manner, Pharaoh's butler was accustomed to squeeze out NEW WINE into the royal cup." (See Gen. xl. 11.)—*Adam Clarke's Works,* 1836, p. 59.

Comment is unnecessary!

Surely these old "fathers" knew what they were writing about?

Why, then, Jewett's labored article in favor of intoxicants upon the Lord's table? (Perhaps he drinks himself?)

Most respectfully,
GEO. H. HORNE,*
Pastor Wyckoff Ave. Baptist Church, Evergreen, L. I.

[22]

Oswego, N. Y., May 19, 1888

Dear Sir :—I have received your note of May 15th, but not the pamphlet referred to. I have not read the pamphlet, but am inclined to think Dr. Jewett mistaken. Respectfully,

J. L. BURROWS, LL.D., Rector of Church of the Evangelist.

NOTE.

In letter No. 4 of the first series, the writer states, the word תִּירֹושׁ used only in poetical language for wine, is most probably *must*, or new wine still in the press, the root of the same being (not as Jewett, according to Gesenius, thinks יָרַשׁ, 'taking possession of the brains'),'' etc. While we appreciate the writer's courtesy, and many kind words, we must beg to decline this criticism, for the following reasons :—

1. It is opposed to the uniform testimony of the ancient versions. While we admit that the word can be applied to newly-pressed *must*, like *gleukos* and *mustum* in ecclesiastical usage.* its application is extended all through the fermenting and purifying stages, until it received the name yayin—*old*, in contradistinction to *new* wine. As must commences to ferment soon after it flows into the vat,† it very soon becomes intoxicating, if partaken of too freely. Hence, the Septuagint translators rendered it in thirty-six of the thirty-eight times it occurs by *oinos* In Isaiah lxv. 8, the word *rox*, or berry of the grape, is the rendering. But the passage which determines its intoxicating quality beyond question, is Hosea iv. 11, where the rendering is *methusma*—"an intoxicating drink."—*Liddell and Scott.* The word is not found in classic usage, and is confined by the Sacred writers to the Old Testament, where it occurs seven times, and in every instance (if we include this), as the passages show, in connection with intoxication, or that which could produce it. "Drink no wine nor strong drink – *methusma.*"—" Neither let her drink wine nor strong drink ; "—" and now drink no wine nor strong drink," Judges xiii. 4, 14, 7 ;—"I have drunk neither wine nor strong drink," 1 Sam. i. 15 :—" I will prophesy unto thee of wine, and of strong drink," Micah ii. 11.—"I will fill * * * all the inhabitants of Jerusalem with drunkenness—*methusmati.*" Now, as this translation was made by Jewish scholars, living where Tirosh was as well known as bread, how shall these renderings, especially the last one, be accounted for, if it is *must*, or new wine still in the press"? Even if we accept, in opposition to Gesenius, the Arabic derivation proposed, the definition given points to *must* in a state of fermentation—"the agitating, foaming, fervescent drink."

With the Septuagint, agree the renderings of the Chaldee Targum, the Peshito Syriac, and the Vulgate Latin. The Syriac rendering, *racoyutho*, is especially strong, as we have shown (App. B, page 126), and the Vulgate and Targum are no less so. As the translators of the Chaldee and Syriac spoke a language closely allied to the Hebrew, they must have known, equally well as the translators of the Septuagint, what Tirosh was, and whether it would cause intoxication or not. And it is evident that the Syriac translators did not get their rendering through the Septuagint, as there is a marked variation in the rendering of Hosea iv 11—lit. "They love fornication ; and wine and drunkenness destroy their understanding." Jerome, in like manner, although not a native of Palestine, lived there many years, and he was too well versed in Hebrew not to know what were the nature and properties of Tirosh.

2. It is opposed to statements in the Talmud. The Gemara, as shown by Buxtorf, Lex., page 986, speaks of Tirosh as an intoxicating drink, and a source of poverty when abused. "*Quare vocatur Tirosh* תִּירֹושׁ? *quod omnis qui trahitur eo, erit pauper.*" * * * *Ergo,* "תִּירֹושׁ *dicitur, quasi* תֵּירַשׁ *eris pauper, si abutaris eo.*" Dr. Lees insists that Tirosh is "not wine at all, but the *fruit of the vine* in its natural condition." Query, How long would it take a man by eating *grapes*, or drinking *fresh must*, to become poor ?

3. It is opposed to the leading Hebrew scholarship of the present day. In the recent scholarly version of the New Testament in Hebrew by Delitzsch, *gleukos*, in Acts ii. 13, is rendered by Tirosh.‡ And this is in harmony with the Peshito rendering in that verse, where the same word in its Syriac form is given. The Syriac, moreover, stands in direct opposition to the exegesis of the *Temperance Bible Commentary* and its followers, by showing that the accusation which the Apostle repelled, was understood literally—"These have drunk Tirosh, and are drunk." *Holen meritho eshthiyu, ve raviyu.* In the latest edition of Gesenius no change has been made in the definition of Tirosh, thus showing, as one of the following writers states, "This is proof that present German scholarship has no opinion at variance with that of Gesenius when he wrote."

---

* Appendix B, page 171.　　　　　　† Ibid, page 133.

‡ מָצָא תִּירֹושׁ תְּכָה.

APPENDIX A.

Chicago, Eighteenth Day of the Session, October 26, 1886.

MESSAGE No. 72.

The House of Bishops informs the House of Deputies that it has adopted the following resolutions, which it respectfully communicates for the information of the House of Deputies:—

Resolved, That, in the judgment of the House of Bishops, the use of the unfermented juice of the grape, as the lawful and proper wine of the Holy Eucharist, is unwarranted by the example of our Lord, and an unauthorized departure from the custom of the Catholic Church.

Resolved, That the mixture of water with the Eucharistic wine is lawful, and in conformity with the usages of the Catholic Church, and that there is no objection to the use of the mixed cup, provided the mingling be not ritually introduced until it is authorized by the rubric.

W. TATLOCK, *Secretary.*

APPENDIX B.

COMMUNION WINE.

COMMUNION WINE—A CRITICAL EXAMINATION OF SCRIPTURE WORDS, AND HISTORIC TESTIMONY.

Communion Wine and Bible Temperance. By WILL-
IAM A. THAYER. National Temperance Society,
New York, 1878.

Wines : Scriptural and Ecclesiastical. By NORMAN
KERR, M.D., F.L.S. National Temperance Society,
New York, 1882.

The Divine Law as to Wines. By G. W. SAMSON,
D.D. National Temperance Society, New York,
1883.

ONE of the prominent, unsettled questions of the day
is whether it is right to use fermented wine at the
LORD's Table. For many years the matter has been under debate. Christian bodies in their ecclesiastical councils have had it in careful consideration, and have issued
formal recommendations as a guide to uneasy consciences.
But still the question is perpetually reopened. Only a
few weeks ago, the present writer received a letter from
a prominent Congregational Pastor, containing the following inquiry : " Is the wine of the LORD's Supper, as
referred to by CHRIST and Paul, *fermented* wine ? How
does the best New Testament Greek scholarship answer
this question ? Has the Episcopal Church in the United
States, in any of its higher ecclesiastical courts, made

any declaration on this question? If so, when, where, and what?"

Nor is it surprising, considering the general ignorance on the subject, that much uneasiness is felt. The demon of drunkenness is blighting and cursing his victims in all parts of the land. His debasements and cruelties rest with withering power in impoverished homes and on crushed hearts. And if wine—not to mention other liquors—in its ordinary meaning, *i.e.*, the fermented juice of the grape, is in itself an evil, discountenanced by GOD, as is strenuously maintained by a large and influential body, its use in any form must also be evil. If the results lamented flow not from excess in use, but as a natural and unavoidable consequence of participation in any way or degree, then the manufacture and sale should be prevented, if possible, by legislative enactments; and it should be the special duty of every Christian body to remove a deadly temptation from the weak when participating in the most solemn services of their holy Faith.

In addition to what has been done by individuals and Church Synods, there has been an extensive literature prepared by the National Temperance Society, designed expressly to enlighten the Christian mind, and guide the Christian conscience on this question. But all such agencies, to be a real and permanent blessing, must have their foundations firmly laid upon the rock of truth. Unwise, though well-meaning advocacies will usually do more harm in the long run to any cause, than open opposition. It is reported as a saying of one of England's greatest statesmen, "If a thing is not true, we should not lie that it may be true." Certainly GOD does not need man's lies, and the cause of our blessed REDEEMER will never be permanently advanced by unreflecting fanaticism, or misguided prejudice.

Among the more recent works having this object in view, published by that society, are those mentioned above. The first, published in 1878, was a review of an article written for the *Bibliotheca Sacra* of January, 1869. The second, published in 1882, is an expansion of a lecture delivered before the Church Homiletical Society in

the Chapter House of S. Paul's Cathedral, London, No-
vember 1, 1881, and the last, but a short time out of the
press,* is designed as an unanswerable argument in favor
of unfermented wine. According to the prospectus, " it
is a new and thoroughly scholarly book, which has been
several years in preparation, examining the entire wine
question from two thousand years before CHRIST to the
present time, and conclusively showing that the Bible
nowhere sanctions the drinking of intoxicating liquors."
    Several marked features are common to all these
works. They all adopt the same logical processes,
marked by most glaring *petitiones principii*. They all
abound in mistaken references. And in the main they
all follow the etymological guidance of the Temperance
Bible Commentary, published in 1870, by Dr. Frederick
Richard Lees, F.S.A., and the Rev. Dawson Burns, M.A.
    On the title-page of Dr. Samson's book there is a
marked instance of the fallacy mentioned. " All the
fresh unfermented wine " (*chêleb tirosh*) they shall offer
unto the LORD—MOSES' LAW AS TO OFFERINGS. The
verse quoted, *Num.* xviii. 12, is as follows : " All the
best of the oil, and all the best of the wine, and of the
wheat, the first-fruits of them which they shall offer unto
the LORD, them have I given thee." Gesenius defines
the word חֵלֶב, chêleb, "*fat, fatness* of victims." Metaph.
for the best, richest part of a thing, as *chêleb haaretz*,
the fat of the land, *i.e.*, its best fruits, richest productions. The word occurs seventy-nine times in the Hebrew original, seventy-one times of animal fat, chiefly
the fat of sacrificial victims, and eight times figuratively
of vegetable products offered as first-fruits, or as heave-
offerings. Four times only is there any reference to the
product of the vine, and then it is manifestly to the quality of the wine, offered, as of the other things mentioned,
without any allusion whatever to the question of fermentation. The word " fresh " may be applied to the
cognate châlâb, חָלָב, " new milk, and so called from its
fatness " (Gesenius) ; or " from which butter is made "

---

* The last edition published 1883.

(Fürst) ; but *"fresh,* unfermented," or " the fresh of tirosh," page 317, is language utterly foreign to the Hebrew original. The Septuagint renders the words chêleb-tirosh, ἀπαρχὴ οἴνου ; the Peshito Syriac, *shumno d'chamro,** *i.e.*, *adeps vini ;* the Vulgate, *medullam vini.*

With sublime indifference to all this, however, and with an equally sublime assurance, Dr. Lees, in his comments on this verse, after maintaining that the wine and oil denote the fruits of the earth in their solid state, tells us " This is a case in which the Jews of the Captivity seem to have lost the true and certain sense of the words *tirosh* and *yitzhar* (vine and orchard fruit), and to have narrowed their meaning down to that of a liquid prepared by man." And so reasoning by analogy [*Prelim. Dis.*], from the fact that words occasionally become obsolete, or change their meaning, as *villain, prevent,* this nineteenth-century Solomon waives aside magisterially not only the translations made by ancient scholars, with whom both languages were in great measure vernacular, but also the grand labors and decisions of modern lexicographers. For over two thousand years, he would have us believe, the whole scholarly world has been in error on this point. " The modern versions also," he adds, " all follow in the same rut." It might have occurred to Dr. Lees to examine whether " the Jews of the Captivity " (whatever that may mean) had lost the true and certain sense of other articles of daily use, as bread, butter, oil, honey, etc. Had he done so he would have found that from the earliest book in the Old Testament Canon to the latest, none of those words became obsolete, or varied in the least from their original meaning. *Lechem,* both in its generic and specific senses, was equally used by Moses, David, Isaiah, Nehemiah, and Malachi ; and equally so when used, were the others.

From the above example furnished on the title-page of Dr. Samson's book, it is easy to imagine what may be looked for in the body of the work itself. A man who

---

*

is capable of changing a Hebrew noun in the construct state, meaning etymologically and properly *fat*, or *fatness* of, into a double headed adjective, rendered "*fresh-unfermented*," is equal to any amount of linguistic legerdemain.

On page 46, it is stated that the terms in which Moses, commenting on his own record, characterises the wine with which Noah was drugged, calling it the "wine of Sodom, the poison of dragons" [*Deut.* xxxii. 32, 33], "indicates the recognition of the two classes of wine, intoxicating and unintoxicating, which he makes throughout his connected writings." Here is both a "begging of the question," and a mistaken reference, not to say anything worse of it. That there was any such recognition of "two classes of wine" by Moses, in this or in any other passage of his writings, is the merest assumption; and whatever comment he may have made on Noah's wine at some time or place not recorded, there is certainly none in the passage referred to.

On page 92, when commenting on *Hosea* iv. 11, and vii. 5, we are told, "Finally and specially noteworthy, he declares the offering of wine to JEHOVAH as displeasing to him, ix. 4, a declaration which illustrates and confirms the view of Moses' law above stated as excluding alcoholic wines." It might have been well to mention that the prophet disparaged equally the offering of sacrifices, and it would not have been uninteresting to state, that the Hebrew word *Yayin*, in that passage, is the very same word, יין, which is uniformly used by Moses when issuing the Divine command touching drink-offerings—*e.g.*, "The meat-offering thereof shall be two-tenths deals of fine flour mingled with oil, an offering made by fire unto the LORD, for a sweet savor; and the drink-offering thereof shall be of wine," יַיִן רְבִיעִת—*Yayin*, "the fourth part of a hin," *Levit.* xxiii. 13.

But to the main question. What wines were in use among the Jews, in so far as we can learn from their sacred writings, and other reliable sources? The true answer, I need scarcely say, will be found not within the sphere of imaginative sentimentalities, but in a scientific

induction of etymological and historical facts.   The word
most commonly used by the sacred writers is the one
just mentioned, *Yayin,* which is found one hundred and
forty-one times, and is rendered uniformly in the Septuagint, with one exception, Job xxxii. 19, by οἶνος.   In accordance with that law common to Semitic tongues, by
which substantives usually derive their specific meanings
from the generic conception expressed in the verbal root,
Yayin means etymologically a fermented liquor, from the
root, *Yōn,* יוֹן.   Gesenius gives the definition, " to boil
up, to be in a ferment."   The substantive itself he defines, first, " *wine,* so called from its fermenting, effervescing ;   second, Meton. of cause for effect, *wine* for
drunkenness, intoxication."   Fürst traces the word to a
supposed root now obsolete, יָיַן.   *Yavan,* meaning " to
stamp, to press."   But the best Hebrew scholarship of
the day rejects Fürst as reliable authority.   Professor
Robertson Smith, in the new edition of the *Encyclopæ-
dia Britannica,* vol. xi., p. 602, writes : " Far superior to
all other lexicons is the Thesaurus of Gesenius, completed by Rödiger [Leipsic, 1829–1858].   The Hand-
wörterbuch of Fürst [2d ed., 1863.   English translated
by S. Davidson, 1871 ; 3d ed., by Ryssel, 1876] proceeds on very faulty etymological principles, and must
be used with great caution."

The next word used with the greatest degree of fre-
quency is *Tirosh,* תִּירוֹשׁ, which occurs thirty-eight times,
and is rendered in the Septuagint by οἶνος, except in Isaiah lxv. 8, where we find the word ῥώξ, evidently in reference to the *bacca* or berry of the grape ; and Hos. iv.
11, where the rendering is μέθυσμα, *ebrietas.*   The verbal root is *Yarash,* יָרַשׁ, meaning, as defined by Gesenius,
" to take, to seize, to get possession of."   Hence the
substantive *tirosh* is defined *new wine,* so called, because it gets possession of the brain and inebriates.
Hos. iv. 11, " Whoredom, and wine, and new wine take
away the heart," *i.e.,* the understanding.

Another word in occasional use is *Chemer,* חֶמֶר, occur-
ring but twice in the Hebrew, and six times in the
Chaldee portions of Ezra and Daniel.   In every instance

the Septuagint translates by οἶνος. The verbal root, according to Gesenius, means "to boil up, to foam, to ferment, to be red, from the idea of boiling, being inflamed," etc. Hence the substantive, "*wine*," so called as being fermented. The cognate Arabic,* *chamr*, and the Syriac,† *chamro*, are used with few exceptions in the Arabic and Syriac versions in place of the Hebrew *Yayin* and *Tirosh*. Of importance also to consider is the word *Shekar*, שֵׁכָר, which is found twenty-two times, and is usually rendered in the Septuagint by σίκερα, and in English by "strong drink;" or "strong wine," as in *Numb.* xxviii. 7. Its verbal root in all the Semitic tongues means to "drink deeply, to be drunken." Gesenius defines the substantive, "strong drink, any intoxicating liquor whether *wine* or an intoxicating drink prepared from barley, honey, or dates."

In addition to the above, I will mention the word *Asis*, עָסִים, used five times, from the verbal root *Asas*, "to tread, to press," hence "what is trodden out, and so put for *new wine*, the product of the same year, like new wheat;" *Sove*, סֹבֶא, used but three times from a root meaning "*to drink to excess, to tope*;" *Shemer*, שֶׁמֶר, used, *Isai.* xxvii. 6, in the plural, of "generous old wine purified from the lees;" and *Mezeg*, מֶזֶג, found only once, *Cant.* vii. 3, referring to mixed or spiced wine.

From the above it is evident that the word *wine*, as usually understood by the Jews, referred primarily and etymologically to a fermented liquor. Certainly, in so far as anything can be gathered from the several contexts, the word *Yayin* has, in the vast majority of cases —one hundred and thirty-two times out of one hundred and forty-one—its commonly accepted signification ; or, by Meton. wine for drunkenness, as in *Gen.* ix. 24. Five times it is used figuratively, as in *Ps.* lx. 3, " wine of astonishment ;" twice proleptically of the grape itself, as the material from which wine is derived, *Jer.* xl. 10, 12 ; and twice of GOD's judgments preventing its manufacture, *Isai.* xvi. 10 ; *Jer.* xlviii. 33. It would be difficult,

---

* خمر   † ܚܡܪܐ.

in view of these facts, to find any ground upon which
to rest the theory of " two classes of wine," in so far,
at least, as *Yayin* is concerned.   One thing is very sure,
the same word is used both commendingly and disparagingly, or, rather, in the latter case, the abuse of it.   It
was *Yayin* which Melchisedec brought forth with bread
for the refreshment of Abram and his servants.   It was
Yayin in which, according to the prophecy of dying Israel, the garments of royal Judah should be washed, and
with which his eyes should be " red," as his teeth should
be " white " with milk.   It was *Yayin* which formed,
according to divine command, an integral part of the
legal sacrifices, or drink-offerings.   It was *Yayin* which
the Psalmist declares " maketh glad the heart of man,"
as oil causes the face to shine, and bread strengthens his
heart.   It was *Yayin* which Isaiah, by a figure, exhorts
the thirsty souls to buy, together with milk, without money, and without price.   On the contrary, it was *Yayin*
which Solomon tells us is a " mocker," as " strong
drink," *Shekar*, " is raging."   It was *Yayin* which he
says is the cause of woe and sorrow, through *long tarrying thereat.*   It was *Yayin* which he cautions against
looking upon " when it is red," and which " biteth like
a serpent and stingeth like an adder."

The Rev. W. M. Thayer affirms, nevertheless (page
32), " that the Bible speaks of two kinds of wine, there
can be no doubt.   It pronounces one of them a *blessing*,
and the other a *curse.*"   And in this, equally with Drs.
Kerr and Samson, he follows the guidance of Dr. Lees,
Moses Stuart, and other early agitators of the question.
President Nott innocently asks, " Can the same thing in
the same state be good and bad ; a thing to be sought
after, and a thing to be avoided ? " as though the same
might not equally be said of *fire* and *water*, and a multitude of things in daily use, which are a *blessing* or
a *curse* according as they are used.   Professor Stuart
declares, " my final conclusion is this, namely, that,
wherever the Scriptures speak of wine as a comfort, a
blessing, a libation to GOD, and rank it with such articles
as corn and oil, they mean—they can mean—only such

wine as contained no alcohol, that could have a mischievous tendency ; that wherever they denounce it, prohibit it, and connect it with drunkenness, they can mean
only alcoholic or intoxicating wine." Upon which mar-
vellous process of reasoning a writer for the CHURCH
REVIEW of 1849 wittily says : " This modern apparatus
is like that of a conjuror. You see him draw wine from
a vessel, and, when he draws wine again from the same
vessel, instead of the same wine coming out, you have
a liquor totally different. An uninitiated man reads his
Bible quietly, and thinks he knows what is meant by
wine ; but by this newly discovered legerdemain, when
he least expects it, whisk ! it is turned into a liquor totally
different from what it was just before."

The main standpoint taken by these advocates of
" two classes of wine " centres in the second word mentioned, *Tirosh*—all the others being used more or less
frequently in connection with intoxication. *Sove, Shekar*, and *Mezeg*, show etymologically their meaning as
well as *Yayin ;* and *Asis*, in two out of five instances of
its use, refers unmistakably to an intoxicating drink, *Isai.*
xlix. 26, and *Joel* i. 5. In the latter instance, the Septuagint rendering is peculiarly strong—οἶνον εἰς μέθην,
i.e., " wine unto intoxication." Of *Tirosh*, however,
the Rev. W. M. Thayer says : " All the direct endorsements of wine in the Bible are connected with the
word *Tirosh*. We affirm that in every passage claimed
to refer to the liquid product of the vine, it is spoken
of as a blessing. There is no denunciation of this
beverage, no warning against its use. This is not true
of one of the other words translated *wine* in the Old
Testament." In like spirit Dr. Samson writes [page
70] : " Modern investigations lead to the conclusion
that *Tirosh* was *Must*, or unfermented wine."

As already stated, the word occurs thirty-eight times.
Of these it is used thirty-four times in connection with
corn, or oil, or with both, as the annual products of the
land. In *Isai.* lxv. 8, the Septuagint translation is ῥώξ ;
the Peshito Syriac *Tutitho* * or *Odsho, i.e.*, the *berry ;*

* ܠܐܬܘܬܐ or ܠܐܬܝ—the MSS. differ.

and the Vulgate, *granum.* In *Judges* ix. 13, and *Isai.*
xxiv. 7, although in both instances the Greek rendering
is οἶνος, and the Latin *vinum*, the reference may be also
to the grape itself as that from which the wine is made.
Without going further, therefore, in the light of all
these facts, the untruth of the statements made by
Professor Stuart and the Rev. W. M. Thayer must be
evident.

Tirosh is *never used* in the Mosaic law of the Divinely
prescribed " drink-offerings." There, as already shown,
Yayin is the only word used. In *Deut.* xiv. 26, we find
also a striking permission to drink not only *Yayin*, but
strong drink, *Shekar.* As we learn from the context,
when the Israelites lived at a distance from the house
of GOD, they were to be permitted to sell the tithes
of their flocks, and other products of their land, and
purchase with the money such things as they required
at the end of their journey to worship at the annual
festivals. " Thou shalt bestow that money for whatsoever thy soul lusteth after, for oxen, or for sheep,
or for wine, or for strong drink ; or for whatsoever thy
soul desireth ; and thou shalt eat there before the LORD
thy GOD, and thou shalt rejoice, thou and thine household." And in that prophetic passage, *Isai.* xxv. 6, in
which the spiritual blessings of the Gospel dispensation
are portrayed under the figure of a "feast of fat things,
of wines on the lees, well refined," the word used is
Shemarim, the plural of *Shemer.*

There is one other passage, however, *Hosea* iv. 11,
which is a very difficult one for the advocates of the
two classes of wine, and the exclusive commendation
given to *Tirosh*, to manage. "Whoredom and wine—
Yayin—and new wine—*Tirosh*—take away the heart,"
i.e., the understanding. It is quite amusing to see how
Drs. Lees, Samson, and others wrestle with the difficulty. The first, true to his assumption that *Tirosh*
always means the unpressed grape, or, as he calls it,
"vine fruit," allegorises the whole verse. "By whoredom," he says, "is here to be understood illicit worship
rendered by the chosen people to heathen gods. By

Yayin, wine—the type of sensual gratification, their hearts also had been captivated. By *Tirosh*, the fruit of the vine—the type of natural, earthly good—their hearts had been taken away from GOD, as the infinite Goodness, and the fountain of spiritual joy." Dr. Samson, following here the etymological guidance of Fürst, derives the word from a secondary use of *Yarash*, which he translates "to expel, to drive out"—hence " *must* " like new cider, is an expellent. Speaking [page 180] of the word "thamrig," used by a paraphrast of *Tirosh*, he says, "it was evidently an *aperient* used *internally;* thus illustrating the effects of ' *Tirosh* ' already cited, as also of the unfermented Greek ' gleukos,' and the Roman ' *must.* '" As the Rev. Mr. Thayer informs us that "all the direct endorsements of wine in the Bible are connected with the word *Tirosh*," and that " *Tirosh* is always associated with *blessings* in the Bible," the great value and blessedness of wine would thus seem to centre around it as "an *aperient* used *internally.*" What sort of a thing " *an aperient* " used *externally* might be, we are not prepared to say.

Unfortunately for these gentlemen there is an array of testimony in opposition to their views, which can never be set aside. The Rev. Mr. Thayer indeed tells us "there are what scholars and commentators call ' epochs of exegesis.' " Luther evidently had come upon one, when he proclaimed the Epistle of S. James " *Epistola Straminea.*" Dr. Lees and others have, in their own judgment, come upon another. But it will take more than their *dictum* to convince the world, that all exegetes before their day had been incompetent to do the work they undertook—that the grand scholars of antiquity had " lost the true and certain meaning " of words which in substance were on their tongues daily. In the passage before us, the prophet seemingly rises to a climax in the use of the word *Tirosh*. *That* the ancient translators and targumists manifestly felt, and rendered the word accordingly. As the new wine *Tirosh* would naturally be more plenty than the older wine, *Yayin*, kept from former years, there would be more opportuni-

ty and temptation in it to drink to excess.   Hence the
Septuagint version has μέθυσμα, explained by Schleusner, "*potus inebrians.*"*   The Peshito Syriac has *Ra-
voyutho*, rendered by Castell, *ebrietas, vinolentia, i.e.*,
habitual drunkenness.   With this the Targum of Jonathan agrees, the same word in its Chaldee form being
used as in the Syriac.   The Vulgate rendering is *ebrietas*, drunkenness.   In the Peshito the word is especially strong, as may be seen from its use in the New
Testament, *S. Luke* xxi. 34; *Rom.* xiii. 13; *Gal.* v. 21;
S. Peter iv. 3.   In the last of these, our English rendering is, " excess of wine."   As a further confirmation, I
give the following from Gesenius, under the head of
Tirosh : "All the passages go to show that *Tirosh* is
new wine of the first year, the wine crop or vintage of
the season, and hence it is mostly coupled with corn and
oil as the products of the land.   That it was regarded as
intoxicating is shown by *Hosea* iv. 11 " [Lex., p.
1129].

  We are now ready for the inquiry, What evidence can
be found in the Old Testament Scriptures in favor of
" two classes of wine," in the sense contended for ?   Our
answer is unhesitatingly, *none*.   Wine, under every name
given, *when immoderately used*, would intoxicate.   What
was done by the Greeks and Romans in preserving
must in an unfermented state will be considered further
on.   If, however, there is even ONE *unmistakable reference* in the Word of GOD to *Tirosh*, *Yayin*, or any
other word translated wine, in the sense of *must*, preserved permanently in an unfermented state, let the
scholars of the Temperance Society produce it.   We
challenge them to do so.   In fact, the term *unfermented*
wine, in Scripture phraseology, is a misnomer and self-

_____

* It is quite possible that a traveler passing through the country at some seasons
of the year, might not see a single case of intoxication, and hastily infer that drunkenness was a total stranger in the land ; but let such a one make a tour from village
to village during the months that occur between the vintage and the beginning of
Lent, when the new wine is abundant, "and he will find intoxication in its most dis-
gusting forms.   This is the principal season for betrothals and weddings, the principal attractions of which occasions is a plentiful supply of wine."—Rev. B. LABARRE,
Jr., Missionary among the Nestorians.   Biblio. Sac., vol. xxvi., p. 180.

contradictory. Etymologically, in every Semitic tongue the word implies fermentation as much as butter implies and presupposes agitation or churning, and cheese coagulation or curding. Bread, it is true, is spoken of as both leavened and unleavened. But *two distinct words* are uniformly used, derived from verbal roots of opposite significations. The first, חָמֵץ *Chametz, i.e.*, bread soured, or leavened, from the root *Chametz*, to be sour, was used of the bread ordinarily eaten; while מַצָּה *Mat-zah, i.e.*, bread sweet, from the root *matzatz*, to be sweet, was used of the flat cakes or crackers eaten during the Passover season. In the case of wine, however, there was no such distinction made. Why this should be, it becomes the advocates of "two classes of wine" to say. A language rich enough in words to employ at least *eight* for *wine*, might have furnished, or restricted *one* to mark so important a distinction. But there is not even an adjective, or any qualifying word employed to distinguish fermented from unfermented wine. That such is the case, can be accounted for only on one supposition—*no such distinction existed!*

As a final confirmation of the position above taken, we quote the following: "The impression formed on the mind by a general review, is that both *Yayin* and *Tirosh*, in their ordinary and popular acceptation, referred to *fermented* intoxicating wine. In the condemnatory passages no exception is made in favor of any other kind of liquor, passing under the same name, but not invested with the same dangerous qualities. Nor again in these passages is there any decisive condemnation of the *substance itself*, which would enforce the conclusion that elsewhere an unfermented liquor must be understood" [*Smith's Bible Dictionary*].

The next source of authority to examine, before proceeding to the writings of the New Testament, is the literature of the Jews during the five centuries subsequent to the close of the Old Testament canon. This may be classed under the heads—1, The Apocrypha; 2, the Targums; 3, the writings of Philo and Josephus.

1. In the Apocrypha the word wine, οἰνος, occurs six-

teen times, and in each instance having its ordinary
meaning of a fermented liquor. Certainly, as in the
Canonical Scriptures, there is nothing in the several
contexts to mark any difference in the nature of the thing
itself. Rational and temperate use is commended,
while *excess* is condemned, and the evil consequences
thereof are vividly portrayed. " Wine is as good as
life to a man," affirms the Son of Sirach [*Ecclus.* xxxi.
27–29], " *if it be drunk moderately.* What life is there to
a man that is without wine ? for it was made to make
men glad. Wine moderately drunk, and in season,
bringeth gladness to the heart and cheerfulness to the
mind. But wine drunken with excess, maketh bitterness
of the mind, with brawling and quarrelling."

As a comment on this we have a characteristic specimen
of juggling from Dr. Samson. These verses, unfortunately for his purpose, stand where they will ever be
found, and of course they were very much in the way.
Something must be done, so we have a sudden change
in the *dramatis personæ* introduced. After quoting
verses 25, 26, he says, " Then follows the drinker's plea,
verses 27, 28." We need surely to be informed that this
is the " drinker's plea," for there is nothing in the narrative itself to mark any change of writer or speaker. The
narration flows steadily on without break or hinderance
such as would mark the introduction of another person.
But what the Germans call the *Einbildungskraft, i.e.,*
the power of imagination, is at times highly developed,
and if allowed free range, it will carry its possessor over
many a difficulty. Indeed, it would appear all but an
impossibility not to see that the position thus taken is
substantially that taken by Solomon, in those passages
quoted on all occasions as denunciatory of wine itself.
His instruction, to be rightly understood, must be dealt
with honestly—*taken as a whole*—and not used piece-
meal ; and it is a strange logic which would show that
because excess in any matter is denounced, all use whatever is forbidden—that *abusus tollit usum.* " Hear thou,
my son, and be wise " [*Prov.* xxiii. 19–21]. " Be not
among wine-bibbers ; among riotous eaters of flesh ; for

the drunkard and the glutton shall come to poverty !"
Now in this passage, if the injunction is against all drinking of wine, it is equally so against all eating of flesh.
But no one untrammelled by a theory would dream of
reading any such thought into the words. Thereupon
follows a warning against " the strange woman," connected almost immediately with the inquiry, " Who hath
woe ? Who hath sorrow ? " etc., together with the answer, " They that *tarry long at the wine ;* they that go
to seek mixed wine." In this connection we give a
striking passage from Pliny, who asserts that nothing is
more beneficial than wine for strengthening the body,
when moderately used ; and that nothing is more injurious when used immoderately—thus not only endorsing
the opinion of the Son of, Sirach above given, but expressing the general idea entertained on the subject by
heathen philosophers and moralists—" *Prorsus ut jure
dici possit, neque viribus corporis utilius aliud, neque
aliud voluptatibus perniciosius,* SI MODUS ABSIT." [Lib.
xiv. cap. vii.]
   The Rev. Mr. Thayer tells us, notwithstanding, " the
fallacy of the plea, It is the abuse and not the use of
intoxicating liquors which the Bible prohibits, is apparent.
As Bible temperance is the moderate use of good things,
and abstinence from evil things, any use of that which is
injurious must be an abuse of it. Besides, it is not the
abuse of wine that is called a ' mocker,' but wine itself.
Solomon does not teach us to avoid the *abuse* of wine,
or not to drink to excess, but not to look upon it." We
will leave Solomon to settle the point with each man's
own reason and conscience. But if being among " wine-
bibbers," and " riotous eaters of flesh " unto drunkenness
and gluttony, and tarrying " long at the wine," do not
imply " *abuse*," we are utterly unable to comprehend
what they do imply. One FACT, however, is very clear,
there *is not a line or a word in the Apocrypha* which
gives any support to the " two classes of wine "
theory.
   2. As regards the Targums the evidence therein given
is abundant and explicit. Although the precise time of

their formation cannot be stated, the generally received
opinion is, that the leading ones date from just before, or
about the time of our SAVIOUR. In any view of the
matter, they fall so early within the Christian era, as to
bear important witness to traditions and customs further
back than His day. As such Dr. Samson himself regards them. After commenting upon several passages,
he tells us, " the Targums, therefore, confirm, in every
respect, the view of ' *Tirosh*,' to which all the authorities compel the Bible scholar."   On page 179 he says,
" the words ' yayin ' and ' tirosh ' are usually rendered
by the common term ' chamra,' corresponding to the
Hebrew ' chemer,' which, as we have seen; is doubtless
an effervescing or light wine." By referring back to
page 65, we read: " The fourth product in order of preparation seems to be the ' chemer,' or effervescing wine,
prepared doubtless by checking the fermentation at an
early stage. . . . Hence the ' chemer ' is manifestly
a light wine." Now, all this is a mere flight of the imagination, having no authority but Dr. Samson. The
word, as previously shown, comes from a root meaning
to boil up, to foam, to be agitated, etc.; and it is the
leading word for wine in the other Semitic tongues as
"*Yayin*" is in Hebrew. What "*Yayin* " implies, therefore, in the inspired Original, that as its full equivalent
implies " *chamro*," " *chamr*," and " *chamra*," in the Peshito Syriac and Arabic translations, as well as in all the
Chaldee Targums, *e.g.*, the Syriac renders, *Gen.* ix. 21,*
" *Et bibit de vino*," "*V'ashte min chamrah;* " the
old Arabic in like manner, " *Wa shareba min 'al cham-
ri*."† And as illustrating the fixedness even of word
meanings in the " unchangeable East," we may mention
that in the new Arabic translation, made some time
since under the auspices of the American Bible Society,
the rendering is precisely the same. In the Samaritan
Pentateuch also the word is used interchangeably with
the cognate " omar." " *V'shithah man 'omrah*."‡ But

---

* ܘܐܫܬܝ ܡܢ ܚܡܪܗ *   † وشرب من الخمر ؛

‡ ࠅࠔࠕࠄ ࠌࠍ ࠀࠌࠓࠄ.‡

in the twenty-fourth verse, " Noah awoke from his wine,"
the words are " *man chamrah*."* Whether " *Chemer* "
was light or heavy, therefore, it was that with which
Noah got drunk. According to Onkelos, Noah drank,
and awoke from his " *Chamra ;* " and it is that which
Solomon, according to the Targum on the Proverbs,
affirms is the cause of woe and sorrow.

We are also informed that " Jonathan paraphrases in
the important passage, *Hosea* iv. 11, the words ' yayin '
and ' tirosh ' by 'chamra ' and ' ravyetha.' The Hebrew
verb ' ravah,' used fourteen times by writers from David
to Jeremiah, always means ' to drench,' while its adjective,
' reveh,' used three times, and its noun, ' raveyeh,' have
also the same signification. They never refer to intoxicating wine ; they are usually figurative." Now this is a
very strange passage, considering the purpose for which
it is employed. Even supposing we granted that the
words in Hebrew are usually figurative, it would be aside
from the point before us. The question is not about the
Hebrew original, but the Chaldee paraphrase, and the
confirmation thereby given to Dr. Samson's view of
Tirosh. " Yayin" in *Hosea* iv. 11 is rightly rendered by
" chamra." But what about the rendering of "tirosh "
by " ravyetha ? " Surely the author has been playing
with sharper and more dangerous tools than he was
aware of. Instead of *R'vah*—the Chaldee form of the
Hebrew *Ravah*—never referring to the effects of intoxicating wine, *that*, in both Chaldee and Syriac, is its *primary* meaning. Buxtorf, the highest authority here,
gives " Inebriari, Irrigari ; Respondet Hebræis Shekar
et Ravah." And, as the first illustration of its use, he
quotes Onkalos in *Gen.* ix. 21, *et-bibit ex vino et inebri-
atus fuit.*† The adjective "raveh " and " ravyah " he
translates *ebrius, ebriosus, temulentus*, and the noun
" ravyetha," " inebriatio." In fact, it is the same word
in its Chaldee form as that used in the Peshito Syriac
in the same verse, which, as previously shown, Castello
renders by " *ebrietas, vinolenta* "—habitual drunkenness

* אַרֲשׁ. בַּשׁ.   † וּשְׁתִי מִן הַמְרָא וּרְוִי

—and which occurs four times in the N. T. Peshito, with substantially the same meaning. To make further quotations would be useless, as the testimony throughout all the Targums is abundant and uniform; and one instance such as the above, is enough to show the absurdity of the position taken.

But what, we may ask, has either of these references, made to Targum renderings, to do with confirming Dr. Samson's view of *"Tirosh?"*   And, with one or two others, equally irrelevant, they are all he makes.   The simple truth is, the whole argument is a mere cloud of words, fit only to blind the understanding, and give an impression, to the unreflecting and unlearned, the very opposite of the truth.   The voice of the Targums, from first to last, like that of the inspired Originals, gives no uncertain sound.   But there can be no testimony found therein to two kinds of wine, *evil* and *good, per se*.   And the critic would have very sharp eyes who could find the slightest reference to *must* preserved permanently in an unfermented state.

3. The writings of the Jewish philosopher Philo demand the next consideration.   He was born at Alexandria probably a few years before the birth of CHRIST. A descendant of the priestly tribe, and occupying a position of high social and political influence, his writings, which are numerous, were greatly esteemed in his own and subsequent ages.   Philosophising, as he does at great length, on the legal system of his nation, and on peculiarities of custom, an unusual opportunity was given for noting distinctions in the nature and uses of wine. Dr. Samson therefore tells us [page 178], "Philo is full of important statements.   In his treatise on *Monarchy*, he cites, as indicating the duty of entire abstinence from wine, the prohibition to the priests, and says it was given for 'most important reasons;' that it produces hesitation, forgetfulness, drowsiness, and folly."   This is the only quotation made from Philo which has any real bearing upon the question before us; and surely, a more dishonest one was never made by any man.   That Philo adduces the legal prohibition to the priests as "indi-

cating the duty of entire abstinence from wine," is UN-TRUE. The statement made by Philo corresponds exactly with a similar one made by Josephus, given below; and neither of them had the least idea of supporting the notion thus asserted. Both refer to the fact that *during the time of their actual ministration*, the Mosaic Law forbade the priests to drink wine. But the prohibition covered only that period. At other times they were not only allowed to use wine, but, by Divine appointment, as Philo mentions in a number of instances, they received from the people, for their support, the first-fruits of *wine*, as well as of oil, flour, etc. In his treatise on " The Rewards of Priests," he writes, " GOD commanded the nation also to give them the first-fruits of their other possessions ; a portion of *wine* * out of each wine-press; and of wheat and barley from each threshing-floor." In his treatise *On Humanity*, also, he writes: " The laws command that the people should offer to the priests, first-fruits of corn, and *wine*, and oil," etc. In his " Questions and Solutions," moreover, when dwelling upon the statement made of Noah, " He drank of the wine, and was drunken," after allegorising somewhat, in his usual manner, he says, " The expression ' he was drunken ' is here to be taken simply as equivalent to ' he used the wine.' But there are two modes of getting drunk: the one is that of an intemperate sottishness which *misuses* wine, and this offence is peculiar to the depraved and wicked man ; the other is the *use* of wine, and this belongs to the wise. It is therefore in the second of these meanings that the consistent and wise Noah is here called ' drunken,' not as having *misused*, but as having *used*

---

* The word in the original is οἶνος, and not γλεῦκος—καθ᾽ ἑκάστην μὲν ληνὸν οἶνον. That the unfermented juice of the grape could have been uniformly presented to the priests, especially where the legal offerings had to be carried some distance, is impossible. " Within half an hour, in ordinary summer weather, the clearest juice of the grape begins to appear cloudy, to thicken, and to give off bubbles of gas. Fermentation has already commenced ; and within three hours a distinct yellow layer of yeast has collected on the surface, and a sensible quantity of alcohol has been formed in the body of the liquid."—JAMES F. W. JOHNSON, *Chemistry of Common Life*, Edition 1880. The supposition, therefore, that every Jew hurried with his newly pressed *must* to the priests before it had time to ferment, is equalled in absurdity only by Dr. Lees' theory, that the "vine and orchard fruit" in their " solid state," were offered, and that the priests had to press out the oil and wine for themselves !

wine." Whatever we may think of Philo's logic, it is evident that he is here speaking of an intoxicating wine, and that his condemnation is confined to its *misuse*. Among his numerous treatises there is one on *The Planting of Noah*, another on *Drunkenness*, and still another on *Sobriety*, in all of which there are abundant references to wine and its uses. On several occasions he condemns strongly, as he does in some of his other works, the free use of "unmixed wine;" but in *no instance* can it be shown that he uses the word οἶνος except in its ordinary meaning. Throughout all his writings, there is absolutely no intimation of any knowledge possessed by him of two varieties of wine, opposite in nature—one intoxicating and the other not.

By turning to the writings of Josephus, we reach the same results. Born probably about A.D. 37, and giving as he does a history of the political and social condition of the Jews from the beginning of their separate existence as a nation until his own time, as well as a brief account of the race from the time of Adam, some reference might legitimately be expected in his works bearing upon this question. Indeed, Dr. Samson would have us believe that such was actually the case. "The historian Josephus," he says, page 178, "but confirms allusions already noted in the Old Testament histories." It would have been well if Dr. Samson had been more explicit in pointing out the confirmation thus given. The careful examiner will be surprised to find how infrequently Josephus refers to the use of wine in any way. In his autobiography he mentions a piece of shrewd diplomacy to which he resorted on one occasion, in order to obtain important information from a soldier. "I perceived that he loved money, and that he was to be caught chiefly by that means, and I said to him, 'If thou wilt but drink with us, thou shalt have a drachma for every glass thou drinkest.' So he gladly embraced this proposal, and drank a great deal of wine, in order to get the more money, and was so drunk, that at last he could not keep the secret he was entrusted with." In the Eleventh Book of his Antiquities, also, he records the answer given to King Darius' question, which was the strongest, *wine*, *kings*, *women*, or *truth :* " Wine, O ye men, I find exceeds everything. It deceives the minds of those who drink it, and reduces that of the king to the same state as that of the orphan ; . . . it quenches the sorrow of those that are under calamities, and makes men forget the debts they owe to others ; . . . it takes away the remembrance of their friends and companions, for it arms men even against those that are dearest to them ; . . . and when they are become sober, and have slept out their wine in the night, they arise without knowing anything they have done in their cups." Now in both these instances, there can be no doubt either as to the *kind* of οἶνος used, or the *manner* of its use. In a few instances, he connects wine with oil and flour, or wheat, in the sense of provisions, as the canonical Scriptures and Philo do. He mentions that the Nazarites use no wine—that the priests are not allowed to drink wine during the time of their service in the Temple, "lest otherwise they should transgress some rules of their ministration "—and that in the Divinely appointed sacrifice, " they bring the same quantity of oil which they do of wine, and they pour the wine about the altar." But in cases where a good opportunity was given to speak in condemnation of wine, or of some special kind of wine, he says nothing whatever. He does not mention the drunkenness of Noah, or of Lot ; or moralise upon the wisdom of Solomon's injunctions about wine as a " mocker." The simple truth is, we have in the above assertion both a *suppressio veri* and a *suggestio falsi*. Josephus " confirms " no " allusions " whatever, such as the unwary reader would naturally be led to suppose. From first to last his references to wine are merely incidental ; and he gives not a line, or even a hint, to distinguish *good* wine from *evil* wine—fermented from unfermented—one variety in itself a blessing, and the other a curse.

One main argument used in discussions on this subject is, that the Greeks and Romans preserved *must*, unfermented, for at least a year. The fact being undisputed, it is an easy step to the assumption that the same customs obtained among the Jews. Drs. Stuart and Nott used this argument with great zeal. "Facts show," says the former, "that the ancients not only preserved wine unfermented, but regarded it as of a higher flavor and finer quality than fermented wine." "That unintoxicating wines existed from remote antiquity," declares the latter, "and were held in high estimation by the wise and good, there can be no reasonable doubt."

That *must* was thus preserved is, of course, well known. Cato, Columella, and Pliny not only refer to the custom, but describe the methods used for that purpose. But that these preparations were regarded as *wine*, in the proper sense of the term, is mere assumption; and that they were ever spoken of as *unfermented wine*, is untrue. Such a conception would never be formed in the mind of a native of any wine-producing country. "To me," said the distinguished Father Gavazzi, "as an Italian the expression (unfermented wine) imports downright nonsense. In fact, wine is only wine by fermentation, and to speak of unfermented wine is to speak of dry water, of nightly sun, of unelectric lightning" [*Belfast Witness*, May 14, 1875].* Still, innumerable changes are rung upon the term, and even the words of the Latin writers above mentioned are pressed into giving a testimony which their authors never dreamed of, *e.g.*, Pliny, lib. xiv., ii., describing a method of preserving MUST, which the Greeks called *Aigleucos—always must*—says : *Medium inter-dulcia vinumque est, quod Graeci aigleucos vocant, hoc est, semper mustum. Id evenit cura, quoniam fervere prohibetur ; sic appellant musti in vina transitum. Ergo mergunt e lacu protinus in aqua cados, donec bruma transeat, et consuetudo fiat algendi.* Dr. Lees translates the first clause thus: "There is an intermediate (article) between dulcia (sweets) and (what is technically) wine," etc. The last clause in the brackets is Dr. Lees' own *gloss*, and it stands in manifest opposition to

---

* Presbyterian Review, January, 1881.

Pliny's thought and language. In classic Greek, *gleucos* is the equivalent of *mustum*, and therefore, as distinct from anything which could properly be called *wine*, this preparation was called *aigleucos, semper*, or ALWAYS MUSTUM. And the reason why it was thus called, he states, *quoniam fervere prohibetur"*—" since it is kept from fermenting." That fermentation was necessary to its becoming wine he then proceeds to show, *" sic appellant musti in vina transitum*—thus they call (*i.e.*, that is the common expression for) the passing of *must* into wines." Even here Dr. Lees cannot suffer what is the simplest possible Latin to pass without a gloss. He renders, "so they call the passage of *musts* into [common] wines." Now if anything is, or can be clear and certain, it is that Pliny here marks the difference between *must* and *wine*. Before the *transitus* it was *must*, subsequently it was wine. When the *transitus* was prevented, as in this case, it remained what it was—SEMPER MUSTUM, AIGLEUCOS.

Another instance equally marked. Mr. Thayer, as a " proof of the existence of unfermented wine in ancient times," quoting from Dr. Lees' work, *Wines Ancient and Modern*, says : " The original is in Columella, ' *De re Rustica* ' [xii., c. 27], *vinum dulce sic facere oportet. Uvas legito, in sole per triduum expandito, quarto die meridiano tempore calidas uvas proculcato, mustum lixivium, hoc est, antequam praelo pressum sit, quod in lacum musti fluxerit, tollito cum deferbuerit in sextarios quinquaginta iridem bene pinsitam nec plus uncia pondere addito, vinum a fecibus eliquatum diffundito. Hoc vinum erit suave, firmum, corpori salubre*—Gather the grapes in the bunches—spread them out in the sunshine for three days ; on the fourth day at the noontide hour, *proculcato* tread out the grapes, *calidas*, while they are hot (by several hours' exposure to the sun's rays) ; take the *mustum lixivium*, that is, such as should flow into the lake of *must* before it (the mass of grapes) should be pressed by the beam ; *cum deferbuerit*, when it shall have cooled down (the grapes having been trodden while hot), add to every fifty sextarii (of must) not exceeding an ounce of iris well pounded, rack off the wine by pouring it from the dregs (this being a more careful operation than straining). This wine will be sweet (or smooth), sound-bodied, and wholesome to the body." The brackets here are made to do splendid service. But what about the rendering of "*cum deferbuerit*, when it shall have cooled down (the grapes having been trodden while hot) ?" We can well imagine what a hearty laugh Columella would have had at such a twisting of his words. But this is not enough for Dr. Lees. He further explains : " He here bids you spread out the grapes to the heat of the sun long enough to thicken the juice *to the degree known to prevent fermentation.*" Unfortunately for Mr. Thayer and his preceptor, Dr. Lees, with their unfermented wine (which, in this case, was certainly fermented, as the expression "*cum deferbuerit*" honestly rendered shows),* no such exposure to the heat of the sun would prevent fermentation. "Grapes were anciently trodden after being exposed on a level floor to the action of the solar rays for TEN days and were then placed in the shade for five days more, in order to mature the saccharine matter. . . . *The fermentation* is facilitated greatly by this process" [Redding, *On Wines,* p. 55]. Not even boiling *must* for a time will prevent fermentation, although Mr. Thayer, with his customary garbling, after quoting Dr. Eli Smith's statement, " The juice of the grape is boiled down before fermentation," says, " It was boiled to *prevent* fermentation." Dr. Eli Smith's own statement, given in his description of the various methods of making wine in Syria, is this : " (b.) The *must* is boiled down from four to five per cent., *and then fermented.* (c.) The grapes are dried in the sun

---

* Since writing the above, we have discovered the following reference to this " *Vinum Dulce* " of Columella, in the article on "Wine" in Smith's Dictionary of Greek and Roman Antiquities, in which the same view of " *cum deferbuerit* " is evidently taken—" for the *Vinum Dulce* of Columella (xii., 27) the grapes were to be dried in the sun for three days after they were gathered, and trodden on the fourth day during the full power of the mid-day heat. The *mustum lixivium* alone was to be used, and after the fermentation was finished an ounce of well-kneaded iris-root was added to each fifty sextarii ; the wine was racked off from the lees, and was found to be sweet, sound, and wholesome " (p. 1203).

from five to ten days, they are then pressed, and *must*, skins, stems, and all are put into open jars to ferment about a month " [*Biblio. Sac.*, January, 1869]. Without adducing further instances, therefore, we hesitate not to affirm, that in the writings of no classic author is the distinction between *mustum* and *vinum* disregarded. Both in Greek and Latin, there is an occasional use of the latter, as in the Scriptures, by Metonym, or proleptically ; but, in ordinary usage, the discrimination between the juice of the grape before, and after fermentation, is always made. *Unfermented* wine, in fact, would have been as much " downright nonsense," to Cato, Columella, and Pliny, as " dry water," or " unelectric lightning."

Granting all, however, that can be demanded with regard to these Greek and Roman customs of preserving *must*, the point legitimately to be determined is, how far they were known to, and practised by the Jews ? That abundant opportunity was given to acquire the knowledge, especially after the Macedonian conquest, is certain. And it might be impossible to prove, that in some instances and localities, the knowledge was not practically applied. But, on the other hand, it is impossible that the practice could have been general, without leaving some trace in the language and literature of the nation. Even if the Aramean tongues were too sterile to furnish native words for these artificial productions (Pliny, speaking of them, says, "*ingenii, non naturæ opus est*"), the Greek or Roman names could, and would have been introduced. This was done, as we well know, in other cases. That it was not done in this, however, is certain. Neither in the Apocrypha nor in the Targums, in the writings of Philo or of Josephus, can one word or sentence be found to prove that the customs were either known or practised in Judea.* Indeed on this point the artillery of the Temperance Society scholars can be turned against themselves. Dr.

* In what abhorrence all Gentile wines were held by the Jews, may be seen in No. LIV. of Dr. McCaul's *Old Paths*.

Lees tells us in his article on wine, in Kitto's *Bib. Cyclop.*, p. 956 (which article was dropped from the later revised edition by Dr. W. Lindsay Alexander), that "the Jews carefully eschewed the wines of the Gentiles," and as a reason therefor, he states, " The prohibition had reference chiefly to the Roman practice of fumigating them with sulphur, the vapor of which absorbed the oxygen and thus arrested the fermentation." Now, if the Jews were thus careful to avoid unnatural or artificial productions, which resulted from an interference with a simple natural law, when offered by the Gentiles, what reason have we to suppose that they would make equally *unnatural* ones for themselves ? The *onus probandi* at least lies with those who maintain that such was done ; for certainly no evidence has yet been produced from any Jewish source to make the matter even probable. In short, the juice of the grape, kept permanently unfermented, was, in so far as anything can be shown to the contrary, as unknown anciently in Bible lands as in the Bible record itself.

That such is the case now, and has been during all the intervening centuries is equally certain. The testimony of missionaries and others, whose interest and prejudices in some instances might have influenced them to at least a withholding of the truth, is very full and explicit. Dr. C. V. A. Van Dyke, after a residence of more than a quarter of a century in Syria, writes : " In reply to your question about wine for Communion, there is not, and so far as I can find out, never was (in Syria) anything like what has been called unfermented wine. The thing is not known in the East. . . . In Syria, and as far as I can learn in all the East, there is no wine preserved unfermented. . . . The native churches— Evangelical, Maronite, Greek, Coptic, and Armenian— all use fermented wine at the Communion. They have no other, and have no idea of any other " [*Biblio Sac.*, vol. xxvi., p. 167]. To this testimony may also be added that of the Rev. Eli Smith, twenty years missionary in Syria. " Unintoxicating wines," he says, " I have not been able to hear of. All will intoxicate more or less.

So in regard to fermentation. When inquiring if there exists any such thing as unfermented wine, I have uniformly been met with a stare of surprise. The very idea seems to be regarded as an absurdity. The name for wine in Arabic, *chamr*, the same as the Hebrew chemer, is derived from the word which means to ferment. I have not been able to learn even that any process is adopted for arresting the vinous fermentation before it is completed " [*Biblio. Sac.*, vol. iii., p. 388].

With regard to the testimony thus given by the latter of these writers, we have another characteristic piece of shuffling with evidence from Dr. Samson as cowardly as it is contemptible. Instead of *denying* and *disproving* Mr. Smith's statements, if that were possible, he intimates that he was an ignoramus, unqualified to give reliable testimony. "He was," we are told, page 248, "when he accompanied Dr. Robinson, an observer but not a scholar." . . . "His lack of logical reasoning is seen in the report of the second witness called to confirm the conclusions sought. In an article on *Produce of Vineyards in the East*, Rev. Henry Homes, missionary at Constantinople, reports no less than *twelve* artificial products of the grape." After referring to several of them, he concludes thus : " All unconsciously Mr. Homes' statements are in entire harmony with all history." But why, we ask, did not Dr. Samson report this witness fully and honestly ? Why did he pass over, without one word of comment or allusion, the confirmation given in that same article to the reports of Dr. Van Dyke, Mr. Smith, and many others ? Mr. Homes asserts distinctly, " In the present use of language an unfermented wine is an impossibility. All that which is now called wine in the East is as truly wine as that which is called wine in France. Whether boiled or not, whether sweet or sour, all the known wines are intoxicating. The boiling which the people of certain districts give to their *must* for the purpose of securing a wine that will keep better, should not be confounded with the boiling of the same *must*, for the purpose of making sugar and molasses " [*Biblio. Sac.*, vol. v., p. 292].

In like manner an effort is made to extract the sting from the following statement:

"We, the undersigned, missionaries and residents in Syria, having been repeatedly requested to make a distinct statement on the subject, hereby declare that during the whole time of our residence and travelling in Syria and the Holy Land, we have never seen or heard of an unfermented wine; nor have we found among Jews, Christians, or Mohammedans, any tradition of such a wine having ever existed in the country. Rev. W. M. Thomson, D.D.; Rev. S. H. Calhoun; C. V. A. Van Dyke, D.D.; Rev. James Robertson; Rev. H. H. Jessup; Rev. John Wortabet, M.D.; James Black, Esq.; Michael Meshaka, doctor; Rev. John Crawford; R. W. Brigstocke, M.D., F.R.C.S.; Rev. Wm. Wright, B.A.   May, 1875."

Utterly disregarding the high character of the signers of this important document, Dr. Samson says: "It was a prejudged and formulated statement, prepared in Scotland by interested parties, and sent to Syria for *ex-parte* testimony."   Are we to understand by this that those "missionaries and residents in Syria" subscribed an array of falsehoods?   Or were they like Mr. Smith, "observers but not scholars"?   A straightforward and manly course would have been to rebut these statements, if it could be done, by others equally well indorsed of an opposite character.   *Why has it not been done?*   An honest man will not have far to go to find the answer. There is more, however, than an implication against the honor of those gentlemen in Dr. Samson's assertion. The assertion itself is UNTRUE.   As we learn from a very able article, in the *Presbyterian Review* of January, 1881, by the Rev. Dr. Moore, the Rev. W. Wright, a former missionary at Damascus, drew up the document, and in reply to Dr. Moore's inquiries states the following: "I deeply regret to observe that so good a cause should be advocated by the ignoble use of misrepresentation. It is not a fact that the paper which I submitted to the General Assembly was 'prepared in Scotland by interested parties, and sent to Syria for *ex-parte* testimony.' The paper was prepared by me, and submitted to the men most competent in the whole world to speak on the subject. The document was not the result of any suggestion from home. London, September 6, 1880."

Alas for the claims of truth and righteousness when men have hobbies to ride! We turn back to and admire with fresh zest the noble maxim, "If a thing is not true, we should not lie that it may be true."

EDWARD H. JEWETT.

COMMUNION WINE.

SECOND ARTICLE.

IN continuing this subject, entered upon in our previous article, we find, as we had anticipated, a perfect agreement between the language and teaching of the Old and New Testaments. Like every other creature of GOD's bounty, wine is regarded as good in itself, and is looked upon as harmful only when misused. While in some respects there is not as much prominence given to it as in the writings of the Old Testament, its legitimate use is clearly marked, even in the teachings and example of our LORD Himself; and the HOLY SPIRIT in the writings of the Apostles warns against, and denounces all excesses therein. As an element of food and social enjoyment, it was partaken of by CHRIST, as his own words declare (*S. Luke* vii. 34), and His first recorded exercise of omnipotent power was its miraculous creation for the enjoyment of wedding guests. On the contrary, the drunkard, equally with the glutton, is regarded as a misuser of GOD's bounties, and in company with murderers, fornicators, and evil-livers in other respects, is denounced as resting under GOD's wrath, and the evil to come.

The word uniformly used for wine, οἶνος, with one exception noted below, is found 33 times, and is manifestly equivalent, to the *Yayin*, *Tirosh*, etc., of the Old Testament. In scope and meaning it is the same

in Hellenistic as in classic Greek, *i.e.*, the fermented
juice of the grape. By some classic writers it is occasionally used of the fermented juice of other fruits, and
even of fermented decoctions of grain. In a few instances it occurs in poetry, where it is applied by prolepsis to the grape itself. Through a singular mistake,
Dr. Lees adduces a metaphorical expression of Pindar,
ἀμπέλου παῖς—" child of the vine," as one of these instances, and says it is one of the " passages in which
wine is spoken of as produced within the grape and the
cluster." The reference is not given, but we have found
it in the *Ninth Nemean Ode*, line 126; and viewing it
in connection with what immediately precedes, it is difficult to believe that he had ever read the Ode. In
classic Greek, as in Hellenistic, the word παῖς is used
of a descendant, male or female, without any reference to
age; *e.g.*, Herodotus [i. 27] represents Crœsus expressing a wish that his enemies the Cicilians would attack
the "sons of the Lydians with cavalry"—ἐλθεῖν ἐπὶ
Λυδῶν παῖδας σὺν ἵπποισι. Homer also [*Iliad* ix. 494]
describes the aged Phœnix addressing Achilles as his
adopted son: "Thee I made, Achilles, rival of the gods,
my son"—ἀλλὰ σὲ παῖδα θεοῖς, etc. Achilles at that
time was certainly anything but an unweaned, undevel-
oped baby; and just as little was Pindar's *ampelou pais*,
the unpressed or unfermented juice of the grape. We
give the preceding lines in Wheelwright's translation:

> Where'er the festal cup is shown
> The voice assumes a bolder tone.
> Let this by any mingled be,
> Sweet harbinger of revelry!
> Let him in silver goblets pour
> The *potent* offspring of the vine.

Nonnos, indeed, in one of his *Bacchanal Songs* [xii.
42] refers to the grape bunch as οἰνοτόχον, " the wine-
bearer; " and Anacreon in his 52d Ode describes the
treaders as "letting loose the wine."

> μόνον ἄρσενες πατοῦσι
> σταφυλὴν λύοντες οἶνον.

This instance is adduced by Dr. Kerr in connection with a similar one from Ovid [*Trist. liv.* iv. ch. 6] :

Vixque merum capiunt grana quod intus habent,

and one also from Goethe:

Lastende Traube
Stürzt ins Behalter
Drängender Kelter,
Stürzen in Bächen
Schäumende Weine.
—*Faust.*

No one in his senses, however, unless he had some theory to support, could mistake the meaning in these and similar instances. And yet, in company with Dr. Kerr, all the leading colaborers in the same cause seize exultingly upon them, imagining that therein lies an immovable foundation for their theory that οἶνος is a generic term, and may be legitimately used of grape-juice while unfermented. Professor Stuart labored hard on this point in his day, and Dr. Lees asserts, quite magisterially, that "Wine primarily expressed the *relation* of 'liquid offspring of the vine cluster;' but it does not, never did, nor, in the nature of things, ever can mark out the later, and for thousands of years obscure, relationship of fermentation" [*Prelim. Dis.*]. If Dr. Lees had given some instances from Orpheus or Musæus, or even from Homer and Hesiod of this attested "primarily expressed relation," his argument might have had some weight. As the truth stands, however, the *earliest* references to οἶνος in Greek literature are manifestly to a *fermented liquor.* The first reference to it in the *Iliad* [i. 462] describes it as αἴθοπα οἶνον, "ruddy or sparkling, wine;" and the second [iii. 246], οἶνον εὔφρονα, "cheering or merry-making wine." What the intoxicating, yea, even maddening, properties of Homer's οἶνος were, when too freely indulged in, may be seen in the *Odyssey* [xviii. 330, 390]. Homer's heroes also are represented as drinking their wine mixed with water, which is an unmistakable evidence that it was fermented, and which the concurrent testimony of antiquity affirms to have been a most ancient custom, and a sign of civilisation. To drink wine ἄκρατος, or unmixed, was to "drink like a Scythian," *i.e.*, like a barbarian. "The custom of diluting wine can be traced up to the earliest periods, and its origin is referred to Amphictyon, who learned it from Bacchus" [Becker's *Charicles*, p. 334].

Where the "obscure relationship" mentioned exists it would moreover be difficult to point out, except in the imagination of Dr. Lees. Every standard Greek lexicon which we have been able to consult* defines οἶνος as the product of fermentation, primarily and mainly of the juice of the grape, and *in no instance otherwise*, except as already mentioned. Γλεῦκος was the word used by the Greeks for *must*, or unfermented grape juice, and as synonymous or interchangeable with it οἶνος was never used. In every Semitic tongue, moreover, as already shown, the leading words for wine point etymologically to the work and product of fermentation.

Of the 33 times of its use in the New Testament οἶνος occurs six times figuratively, as in *Rev.* xvi. 19, "The cup of the wine of Divine wrath," and once possibly [*Rev.* vi. 6] it is used in connection with oil by prolepsis of the maturing products of the year. In every other instance, in so far as anything can be discovered to the contrary from the several contexts, the word has its simple and ordinary meaning. The Peshito Syriac follows the Greek closely in using the word *Chamro*, the Vetus Latina the word *Vinum*, and the Coptic the word *Hêrp*. In the Gospels it is classed with "strong drink," σίκερα, as forbidden to be used by John the Baptist, where the reference is manifestly to it as an intoxicating liquor; and in the Epistles there is no mistaking the meaning of the assertion, "It is good not to drink wine whereby thy brother stumbleth," or the injunction not to "be drunk with wine, wherein is excess."

---

* *Wein*, Ausgepresster und gegohrener Traubensaft—pressed out, and fermented grape juice (Passow).
Wine, the fermented juice of the grape. 2. Also the fermented juice of apples, pears, etc. (Liddell and Scott).
Wine, also a kind of beer made from wheat; also the name was given to liquors made from the juices of several fruits, as cider (Donnegan).

The advocates of the two classes of wine theory, however, adopt the same logical processes in dealing with
the New as with the Old Testament writings. Thus
in speaking of the miracle at Cana, after stating that
wine is nothing else than water having in solution the
sugar, spice, and gluten which form grape-juice—*i.e.*,
simply *must*, Dr. Samson says, " The wine made was
manifestly the simplest product of the grape, as is indi-
cated by the exclamation of the governor of the feast on
tasting it, ' Every man at the beginning doth set forth
good wine, and when men have well drunk, then that
which is worse ; but thou has kept the good wine until
now.' " In other words, we are to understand from the
whole tenor of Dr. Samson's reasoning that οἶνος was not
οἶνος at all in that instance, although called so by the
Evangelist, but γλεῦκος—" the simplest product of the
grape." As a matter of fact, however, it was in no sense
a product of the grape, any more than our first father
Adam was a product or descendant of a previous human
ancestor. It was a *distinct* and *separate* creation—a
work of omnipotence, wrought in attestation of CHRIST's
Divinity, and as a means of " setting forth His glory."
That it differed from ordinary wine, however, except
in its excellence of quality, is mere assumption, and
directly in the face of the governor's commendation
honestly understood. Certainly, unless we are to believe that our LORD played a trick, and that all were deceived, we must believe that it was WINE, good WINE, the
BEST which up to that time had been drunk at that wedding feast.

Dr. Lees states in this connection, " The process of
fermentation is one of decay, and it is not probable that
it would have been imitated, or its results realised by
the fiat of the SAVIOUR. In all fermentative action vital
growth is arrested, organised matter is disintegrated,
and a retrogression ensues. It is a passage from more
complex to more elementary form—in fact, from diet to
dirt." . . . " It is against the principle of scriptural
and moral analogy to suppose that the SAVIOUR exerted
His supernatural energy in bringing into being a kind

of wine which had been condemned by Solomon and the prophets as a 'mocker' and defrauder, and which the HOLY SPIRIT had selected as an emblem of the wrath of the Almighty," But what if our LORD previous to the Incarnation, as the I AM, the head of GOD's covenant flock under the old dispensation, prescribed in sacrificial offerings the use of the very same *oïros* or *Yayin* of which Solomon speaks disparagingly—that is, when it becomes a means of dissipation, through long tarrying thereat? The proof that such was the case has been abundantly given, and it lies, and ever will lie, clear and distinct on the sacred page for anyone who is competent and cares to examine it. The passage of *gleukos* into *oinos* may be, in Dr. Lees' judgment, "a passage from diet to dirt," and its use thereafter "against the principle of scriptural and moral analogy," but it never HAS BEEN, and it NEVER CAN BE PROVED, that two kinds of wine, opposite in nature and character, were used by the Jews under the one name of *Yayin*. The logic, therefore, of the argument is worthless, and the underlying assumptions are derogatory reflections upon the wisdom of GOD in His dealings with His ancient covenant people.

In treating of our LORD's assertion touching the superior excellence of old wine, Drs. Lees and Samson allegorise the passage with its context as they do that troublesome verse, Hosea iv. 11. The latter says, "Luke records [v. 39] an added illustration of CHRIST's principle: 'No man having drunk old'—the word wine being understood—'straightway desireth new;' the idea being that neither the Jewish Pharisees, nor even the disciples of John, accustomed to the Old Testament dispensation, were prepared at once, 'straightway' to appreciate fully the principle of the New Testament." And as illustrating the lengths to which hobby-riding will carry men sometimes, we give the following: "Luke's mention [vii. 33, 34] of John's abstinence from wine, and especially of abandoned women as the 'sinners' who were sometimes at the table where He feasted [vii. 37] shows, as the best interpreters have agreed, that the charge that CHRIST drank intoxicating wine was as unfounded as the charge that He was sensual and lascivious. To argue that JESUS must have drunk intoxicating wine, because He was at a table where wine was drunk, compels also the admission that He yielded also to gluttony and lust." Now this is a dreadful sentence, and the dictates of charity compel us to hope that the author did not weigh his thoughts, or realise what he was writing. When, and where is it ever stated that " abandoned women " were " sometimes at the table where He feasted " ? Which one of the Evangelists has even alluded to His presence at a Bacchanalian entertainment ? Turning to the reference given, we find that on one occasion, when eating in a Pharisee's house, a poor, sin-weary penitent, loathing her sin with its degradation, and learning of His presence there, came and "stood at His feet, behind Him, weeping, and began to wash His feet with tears, and did wipe them with the hairs of her head." And yet, if Dr. Samson's language means anything, it means that this " abandoned woman " was equally with Himself a guest at the Pharisee's table !

But who are "the best interpreters" that have "agreed" in maintaining the horrible inference and *non sequitur* suggested ? The real truth is, that right here lies one main weakness in the whole theory advocated by these gentlemen, and one of the most unanswerable arguments against it, viz., that its origin is comparatively but of yesterday. No recognised scholar and interpreter of GOD's Word, patristic, mediæval, or modern, in any branch of the Catholic Church, has ever advocated the views contended for. The same is equally true of the ablest writers among the different Protestant bodies ; and when Dr. Samson states, as he does [p. 235], that " Luther was as earnest as any modern advocate for abstinence as for temperance," and that he saw " unfermented wine in the cup of both the ancient Jewish and the Primitive Church," he states what is unqualifiedly false. Indeed, this " epoch of exegesis," with its " two classes of wine " theory, commenced only in the earlier half of the present century, and the decades of its active advocacy can be counted on the fingers of one hand.

The crucial point of the whole argument, however, turns upon the question, " What was the ' fruit of the vine ' which our Lord used in instituting the Sacrament?" Now, if it could be shown that two kinds of grape-juice, fermented and unfermented, were in use among the Jews, then it might perhaps be legitimately argued that He would use the kind which would be the least liable to be abused. Or, if it could be proved that the Mosaic legislation included the fermented juice of fruits in the prohibition of things leavened, then the question might be regarded as settled beyond the need of controversy. But as regards the former of these suppositions, we have already abundantly shown that not a particle of evidence has come down to us in Jewish literature, sacred or profane, that there was any such preparation of grape-juice known, or in use, as unfermented wine. With regard to the latter supposition, notwithstanding a large amount of special pleading to the contrary, the evidence is abundant to show that the juice of the grape, in any condition, formed no part of the Mosaic prohibition.

Dr. Lees asserts, however [p. 28] : " The prohibition against the presence of ferment, and the use of all fermented articles, is very severe. . . . No plea that would exempt fermented liquors from the sweep of this prohibition can be sustained without ignorantly assuming a difference that does not exist, and ascribing the same ignorance to the lawgiver of Israel." Again [p. 280] : " Obedience to the Mosaic law required the absence of all fermented articles from the Passover feast. The law forbade *scor*—yeast, ferment, whatever could excite fermentation. . . . Fermented grape-juice must, therefore, by the necessity of the case, have been equally interdicted with fermented bread. . . . We here reach the last pinch of the argument, Did the Saviour understand the law, or did He not? Did He observe the law, or break it? If He used fermented liquor, He must either ignorantly or intentionally have broken it. And reverence for their Master ought surely to lead Christians to the conclusion that the cup He blessed and gave to His disciples contained nothing which the law of Moses had interdicted."

A careful examination of the original words used by Moses will enable us to judge how correct these assertions are. The leading word is חָמֵץ, *chamêtz, sour*, or *soured bread*, and it is found 11 times in the canonical Scriptures, 10 times in the writings of Moses in connection with the Passover, and once [*Amos* iv. 5] where the reference is manifestly to ordinary sour or leavened bread. *In every instance*, as the contexts show,* the reference is to bread, and to nothing else. From this root also comes the word מַחְמֶצֶת, *mechmetzeth*, a Hiph. part., used in two instances [*Ex.* xii. 19, 20] and translated "leavened." Another word, שְׂאֹר, *seor*, is also used, which occurs five times, and *in every instance*, as the subjoined passages show, synonymously with *chamêtz*. " Seven days shall ye eat unleavened bread (מַצּוֹת, *matzoth, i.e.*, sweet cakes or wafers made from flour and water), even the first day ye shall put away leaven, *seor*, out of your houses : for whosoever eateth leavened bread from the first day until the seventh day, that soul shall be cut off from Israel" [*Ex.* xii. 15]. " Seven days shall there be no leaven, *seor*, found in your houses : for whosoever eateth that which is leavened," etc. [*Ex.* xii. 19]. " Unleavened bread shall be eaten seven days ; and there shall be no leavened bread, *chamêtz*, be seen with thee, neither shall there be leaven, *seor*, seen with thee in all thy quarters" [*Ex.* xiii. 7]. " When any will offer a meat-offering unto the Lord, his offering shall be of fine flour." . . . " No meat-offering which ye shall bring unto the Lord shall be made with leaven, *chamêtz*, for ye shall burn no leaven, *seor*, nor any honey in any offering of the LORD made by fire" [*Levit.* ii. 1, 11]. " And there shall be no leavened bread, *seor*, seen with thee in all thy courts

---

* It is not necessary to be a Greek or Latin scholar in order to be able to test the truth of the assertion here made. With the help of a concordance or a good reference Bible every instance where the words "leaven" and "leavened" occur can readily be found. For the convenience of those who have no concordance we give the places : Ex. xii. 15 ; xiii. 3, 7 ; xxiii. 18 ; xxxiv. 25 ; Levit. ii. 11 ; vi. 10 ; vii. 13 ; xxiii. 17 ; Deut. xvi. 3 ; Amos iv. 5.

seven days " [*Deut.* xvi. 4]. These passages, with those
referred to above, are all the instances in which the
words *chamêtz* and *seor* are found, and nothing but a
perverted ingenuity could discover a reference to wine
or any other liquor in any of them.

In the face of it all, however, Dr. Less has the
effrontery to use the all but blasphemous language
above quoted, and also to say in addition : " It might
seem superfluous to raise the question whether *khamatz*
includes liquids as well as solids, since it is equivalent to
asking whether fermentation is itself or something else."
It might have been well if Dr. Lees, in the first place,
had learned to spell the word correctly ; and had then
given some instances of its use in connection with the fermentation of liquors. This, however, he has not done,
and could not do for two reasons—no such instance
exists ; and, as will hereafter be shown, the words
which describe the fermentation of liquors differ etymologically from those used for the leavening of bread.

At the original institution of the Passover, as recorded
by Moses, there is no allusion to drinking whatever.
The prohibition, as already shown, was confined exclusively to the eating of soured or leavened bread.
And the reason for the ordinance lies upon the face of
the narrative. The urgency of Israel's departure from
bondage necessitated the use of *matzoth*, or unleavened
cakes. As we read [*Ex.* xii. 39] : " And they baked unleavened cakes of the dough which they brought forth
out of Egypt, for it was not leavened : because they
were thrust out of Egypt, and could not tarry, neither
had they prepared for themselves any victual." This
necessity, with the attendant circumstances, became the
occasion for the institution of a memorial ordinance ; but
it was an ordinance referring purely to the manifested
power, mercy, and goodness of Jehovah. Of the truth
of this we may find sufficient proof in the direction
given by Moses for the perpetuation of the service after
the people had become established in the promised
land : " Unleavened bread shall be eaten seven days,"
etc. " And thou shalt show thy son in that day, saying,

This is done because of that which the LORD did unto me when I came forth out of Egypt. And it shall be for a sign unto thee upon thy hand, and a memorial between thine eyes, that the LORD's law may be in thy mouth : for with a strong hand hath the LORD brought thee out of Egypt. Thou shalt, therefore, keep this ordinance in his season from year to year " [*Ex.* xii. 7–10].

But might not the use of wine have been included in the prohibition, even though not expressed ? Professor Stuart reasons : " As the word eating is in cases without number employed to include a partaking of all refreshments at a meal, that is, of the drinks as well as the food, the Rabbins, it would seem, interpreted the command just cited as extending to the wine as well as to the bread of the Passover " [*Biblio. Sac.,* 1843, p. 507]. If the " cases without number " here mentioned have reference to a loose way of speaking in social intercourse generally, the point may be granted. But if the reference is to the ordinary *modus loquendi* of the Scriptures, the assertion is incorrect. " To eat bread " at an ordinary meal might, of course, imply a partaking of such food, both solid and liquid, as was provided on such occasions, as in *Gen.* xliii. 25. When the act of " eating," however, is described, the thing eaten is mentioned, as in *Gen.* ii. 16 ; *Ex.* xii. 4 ; *Judg.* xiv. 9. Or if liquids in any form are partaken of, the fact is also stated, as in *Ruth* iii. 3 ; *Job* i. 4, 13, 18 ; *Isai.* xxii. 13. The Passover solemnity, strictly speaking, however, was not a social meal, but a religious ordinance of strict obligation, with ritual ceremonies minutely prescribed. All the substances specified were such as could be partaken of only by eating : a lamb, bitter herbs, and unleavened cakes. The lamb was to be a yearling male, without blemish. It must be roasted whole, and eaten without the breaking of a bone, etc. Had the drinking or non-drinking of wine been in any way contemplated, it is very strange, to say the least, that it is in no way alluded to. Indeed, Professor Stuart himself admits, a few lines below the passage quoted, " I am disposed to believe that the original precept of Moses had reference only to the bread of the Passover, and not to any drink that might be used. In fact, not one word is said about any drink on that occasion when it was first instituted."

The whole confusion, in fact, arises from the assumption that the leavening of bread, *per se*, being, as is maintained, a process of corruption—" rotting albumen "—and hence symbolical of evil, underlay and furnished the main reason for the establishment of this ordinance. Indeed Dr. Lees asserts [page 29], " The principal reason must be sought in that association of ideas by which ferment and fermented things are regarded as symbolical of moral corruption and disorder." But at that time there is not a particle of evidence to show that any " such association of ideas " existed. It is true that subsequently the word חָמֵץ, *chamétz*, as the verbal root, furnished certain derivative forms which were used metaphorically in that way. In *Ps.* lxxi. 4, the word חוֹמֵץ, *chōmétz*, a participial derivative is used of a " cruel man ; " and in *Isaiah* i. 17, the cognate word חָמוֹץ, *chamōtz*, is used passively of one "oppressed." That there was any such metaphorical reference intended, however, in the institution of the Passover, is pure assumption. Neither directly nor indirectly can any such reference be found there, and the fact that both our LORD and S. Paul used the word "leaven " thus figuratively, rightly considered, in no way fastens such a reference upon the original institution. Moses has stated the real reason as above given. It is clear, rational, and sufficient. To add others from " association of ideas " to which there is no allusion whatever on the sacred page for centuries afterward,* is to allow imagination and prejudice to play a trick upon the understanding, and to compromise the cause of truth.

---

* The fact that leaven was forbidden in the meat-offerings, in no way militates against the position here taken. Honey was also forbidden to be offered, and evidently for the same reason. And many fanciful explanations have been given, both by Jewish and Christian writers. Philo says, with regard to the honey, it was forbidden, " perhaps, because the bee which collects it is not a clean animal, inasmuch as it derives its birth, as the story goes, from the putrefaction and corruption of dead oxen, just as wasps spring from the bodies of horses." " But Maimonides seems to

Another point of considerable moment should also be taken into consideration in connection with this subject, viz., the lack of accurate scientific knowledge on the part of Old Testament writers. The assumption that the leavening of bread was known then, as now, to be chemically identical with the fermentation of liquors, is absurd. Chemistry as a science, in most of its higher departments, dates comparatively from yesterday. As evidence, however, on this point, we may call attention to the root-meaning of the words used, all being based, in accordance with the genius of Semitic tongues, upon phenomenal or sensible peculiarities, *e.g.*, *chamêtz* etymologically means "*to be acid*," hence *acidity*, something *pungent* to the taste, *sourness*. From this root-meaning comes also the word חֹמֶץ, *chŏmetz*, vinegar, that which has become sour. *Seor*, in like manner, is derived from an obsolete root, which Gesenius regards as identical in origin with our own word *sour*. "In Western languages," he says, "we find from the same stock, Germ. in Ottfr., *saur ;* Anglo-Saxon, *sur ;* German, *sauer ;* English, *sour.* Hence, שְׂאֹר, *seor*, leaven." Taken in connection with its cognate, שָׂאַר, *shaar*, "to become full and turgid, to swell up or out," we get the idea of inflation, puffing up, as in the rising or swelling of leavening. But these characteristics are found united in many kinds of leavened bread. The common black bread of Germany is made sour designedly. As an illustration of our LORD's parable of the leaven hid in the meal, it is customary to use, for the purpose of leavening, a piece of the *sauerteig*, or sour dough from the previous baking. This, under the arranged conditions, raises the bread, and secures also the presence of *seor*, sourness. In fact, in all lands, as every good housekeeper is aware, if the heating, swelling process is continued too long, even when ordinary yeast is used, the result will be a batch of sour bread.

---

me to have given the best account of this in his *More Nevochim* [par. iii., cap. 46], where he saith, GOD prohibited this to root out the idolatrous customs of those days, as he found in the books of the Zabii, who 'offered to their gods no bread but leavened.'" And, "there was scarce any god among the heathen to whom honey was not offered" [Bp. Patrick, *Levit.* ii. 11].

The fermentation of wine, however, phenomenally considered, occupied in the Semitic mind a somewhat different plane. Both the leading words *Yayin* and *Chemer* are derived from the boiling, bubbling appearance of the grape-juice while undergoing fermentation—the immediate result of which was NOT SEOR. Chemically considered, the leavening of bread and the fermentation of wine may be identical ; but it would be antedating scientific investigations and discoveries to ascribe to a Jew in the time of Moses or of David a knowledge that both processes came from " rotting albumen " ! The probabilities as suggested by these etymological considerations are, that the ordinary leavened bread of the Hebrews, like that of the Germans at the present time, was sour. *But their wine was not.* The wines of Judea, like those of all warm countries, were sweet and palatable, " making glad the heart of man." Before such wine could become *seor*—soured or "sick wine," *chömetz*—it must pass through another fermentation, the acetous, whereby a further chemical change is effected.

Maintaining then, as we certainly may, that the use of wine formed no part of the Divine prohibition in connection with the Passover solemnities, it must have come from later ecclesiastical legislation, if any such prohibition existed. Was this the case ? Professor Stuart in the same article says :

When the Jewish custom began of excluding fermented wine from the Passover feast, is not known. That the custom is very ancient ; that it is even now almost universal ; and that it has been so for time whereof the memory of man runneth not to the contrary, I take to be facts that cannot be fairly controverted. . . . I cannot doubt that חָמֵץ in its widest sense was excluded from the Jewish Passover, when the Lord's Supper was first instituted ; for I am not able to find evidence to make me doubt that the custom among the Jews of excluding fermented wine, as well as bread, is older than the Christian era.

From this it is evident Professor Stuart believed that at one time, although subsequent to the original institu-

tion of the Passover, the drinking of wine was introduced, and became thereafter the national custom, until
the further change which he mentions took place. That
the drinking of wine was introduced and sanctioned by
ecclesiastical authority we learn from the post-biblical
writings of the Jews, in which also the reason for the
custom is stated. But as regards the subsequent change
in the nature of wine used, nothing whatever is adduced
by him from ancient authorities in its support. Nor is
it to be wondered at, when it is considered that there is
absolutely nothing worth one moment's consideration to
adduce ; while the statement may be both controverted
and denied that the Rabbins with any uniformity interpreted the prohibition as " extending to the wine as well
as to the bread of the Passover ; and that the custom
" even now is (or ever has been) almost universal."
This point is one of great moment, and we propose to
examine it carefully and thoroughly. The Jews as a religious people, since before the Christian era, *have*, or
they *have not* discarded the use of fermented wine at the
time of their Passover solemnities. What are the facts
in the case ?

In the *Talmud*, as Dr. Lightfoot very clearly showed
two centuries ago, the drinking of wine at the Passover,
although not viewed as of Divine appointment, was regarded as being in perfect accordance with the general
spirit of the Mosaic legislation, especially in *Dcut.* xiv. 6.
" The eating of unleavened bread at this time," he says,
" was enjoined by special and express command [*E.v.*
xii. 18] ; but the drinking of wine they added on the
general principle that a man should cheer up his wife and
children, and cause them to rejoice at that festival. And
with what do they cheer them up ? With wine. And
so strenuous are they in this matter that the poorest man
was required to drink on the Passover evening four
cups of wine, even though he lived on charity. Nay.
moreover, if he had no other resources for obtaining so
much wine he must sell or pawn his tunic, or hire himself out, and thus make sure of the four cups." *Diserto
mandato tenebantur ad comestionem panis azymi hoc*

tempore [*Ex.* xii. 18]; *sed potum vini adjecerunt generali principo nixi : Quia oportebat virum lauté excipere uxorem et liberos, ut in hoc convivio hilares essent. Qua autem re eos exhilarabat? Vino. Atque adeo erant in hoc negotio severi, ut vel pauperrimus Israëlis tenerétur bibere quatuor calices vini hoc nocte, etiamsi eleemosynis victitaret : ac si non posset aliter tantum vini sibi comparare, vel si eleemosynarum non acciperet ad habendos quatuor calices, oportebat eum vendere vel oppignorare tunicam suam, aut operam suam elocare pro quatuor vini calicibus* [Edit. Frankfort., A.D. 1699, p. 735].

What the nature of the wine thus referred to was, is no less certain than the fact that its use has been from the time "when the memory of man runneth not to the contrary." From the same source we also learn :

(*a*) That the •wine used at the Passover was mixed with water, and for the reason given it was too strong, חָזֵק מְאֹד, and hence unfit, without dilution, to be drunk in so large a quantity. Also, when mixed with water it was considered to be more wholesome, and gave less occasion for intoxication. "*Vinum eorum strenuum erat admodum, ad potationem non idoneum absque immixta aqua. . . . Immistio aqua uniquique poculo contulit ad salubritatem, atque ad fugam ebrietatis*" [Vol. ii., p. 380]. It was, moreover, forbidden that grace should be said over the cup of blessing until it had been mixed with water. "*Gemaristæ paulo post. Suffragantur. . . . Non benedicendum esse super poculum benedictionis donec immisceatur ei aqua.*" And as showing that the law of the mixed cup was general, he states that in the rubrics of the festival services, where there was mention made of wine, the word *mázagu*—"they mix"—was always inserted. "*Vulgo aquam immiscuerunt : hinc in Rubrica festorum, cum mentio fit de vino, semper adhibent vocem* מזגו, *miscent ei poculum.*"

(*b*) The permission was granted to drink additional wine, if desired, between the second and third cups, but not between the third and the fourth. As the Paschal eating terminated before the ceremonial drinking of the third cup, and as no limit appears to have been set to time or social intercourse, if anyone needed or desired more drink while still eating he was allowed to have it. Lightfoot cites from the Jerusalem *Gemera* the reason for this practice, which, he says, was "to prevent their being drunk." He cites, also, the explanation given for the seeming inconsistency. "What prevention could this be?" they ask, and give a poor answer, "Because wine at meat maketh not a man drunk, but wine after meat does."

(*c*) In the Jerusalem *Talmud* it is ordered that the Passover Service should be celebrated with *red wine*—יַיִן אָדוֹם. And as though to prevent any mistake, or the use of anything else, it is also ordered that it is necessary that it should look and taste like wine, עָרִיךְ שֶׁיְּהֵא בּוֹ טַעַם וּמַרְאֶה, upon which order the gloss, by way of explanation, states that it should be *red*, שֶׁיְּהֵא אָדוֹם, *ut sit rubidus*. From this fact alone it is evident that the wine used was a fermented liquor; for the color of the wine comes only from the coloring matter contained in the grape skin, which is extracted *during the process of fermentation.**

By turning to the Passover Service as still in use among the Jews, we may derive some additional facts : 1, That only leavened bread is ordered to be searched for and removed ; and, 2, That both *yayin* and *chōmetz* —*vinegar*—are used by rubrical direction. On the first page, among the directions for the arrangement of the feast, we find the following:

On the evening preceding the fourteenth day of the month Nissan, it is requisite for the master of every family to search after leavened bread in every place where it is usually kept, gathering all leaven lying in his way. The pieces of leaven which have been gathered being carefully secured, are burnt the following morning about ten o'clock.

Then, after the formalities to be observed in removing

---

* The color of the wine is dependent on the mode in which the fermentation is effected. Red grapes may be made to yield a white wine if the husks of the grapes be removed before fermentation begins, as in the preparation of champagne and sherry ; but if the skins be left in the fermenting mass, the alcohol, as it is formed, dissolves the coloring matter, producing the different shades of red wine [Miller's *Organic Chemistry*, Part III. pp. 187, 188.

the leaven, we have the direction for preparing the Passover table as follows :

The table-cloth being laid as usual, three plates are placed there-
on ; in one put three cakes (generally called *mizvos*) ; in another
the shank-bone of the shoulder of lamb and an egg, both roasted
on coals ; in a third some lettuce and celery, or chervil and parsley,
and a cup of vinegar or salt water ; likewise a compound formed
of apples, almonds, etc., worked up to the consistency of mortar.

The table being thus formed, every one at table has a glass or
cup of wine placed before him ; for on these nights every person at table is obliged to drink four glasses of wine, called
ארבע כוסות. The four cups which are in commemoration of the
four different expressions made use of at our redemption from
Egypt, viz.,* והצאתי, והעלתי,
וגאלתי, ולקחתי.

Thereupon follows a ceremonial washing of hands
and the drinking of the first cup or glass of wine, called
the " wine of sanctification." Then the master of the
house " takes some parsley or chervil, and dips it into
vinegar or salt water ; and having distributed some to
everyone at table, they all say the following grace before they eat it : " Blessed art Thou, O LORD our GOD,"
etc. After this follow a number of ceremonies and historical recitations, or reminiscences of the national origin,
and subsequent experiences, with comments and explanations of leading rabbies, closing with the following
statement of reasons for the ordinance itself, and the
symbolical meaning attached to the various articles of
food taken :

Rabban Gamliel saith that whosoever doth not make mention of
the three things used on the Passover, hath not done his duty ; and
these are they : *the Paschal lamb, the unleavened cake, and bitter herb.*

The *Paschal lamb*, which our ancestors ate during the existence
of the holy temple, what did it denote ? It denoted that the Most
Holy, blessed be He, passed over our fathers' houses in Egypt ; as
is said : And ye shall say, It is the LORD's Passover, because He
passed over the houses of the children of Israel in Egypt, when He
smote the Egyptians, and delivered our houses.

These *unleavened cakes*, wherefore do we eat them ? Because there
was not sufficient time for the dough of our ancestors to leaven,
before the Holy Supreme King of kings, blessed is He, appeared

---

* And I will bring forth, and I will deliver, and I will redeem, and I will take.

unto them, and redeemed them ; as is said : And they baked unleavened cakes of the dough, which they brought out of Egypt ;
for it was not leavened, because they were thrust out of Egypt, and
could not tarry, etc.

This *bitter herb*, wherefore do we eat it ? Because the Egyptians
embittered the lives of our ancestors in Egypt ; as is said : And
they embittered their lives with cruel bondage, in mortar and
brick, and in all manner of labor in the field ; all their labor was
imposed upon them with rigor.

Then follows the rubrical direction—take the cup or
glass of wine in the hand and say:

We therefore are in duty bound to thank, praise, adore, glorify,
extol, honor, bless, exalt, and reverence Him, Who wrought all the
miracles for our ancestors and us : for He brought us forth from
bondage to freedom ; from sorrow to joy ; from mourning into
holy days ; from darkness to great light ; and from servitude to redemption : and therefore let us chant unto Him a new song, Halle-
lujah !

Now here be it observed, there is no mention of any
commemorative signification in this drinking of wine, as
in the case of eating the lamb, etc., thus proving that it
formed no part of the original institution.   The language
shows that it was designed as a special act of rejoicing,
with thanksgiving and praise for the mercies granted,
and the miracles performed in Israel's behalf.   And be
it also observed, that the reason given for the eating of
unleavened cakes, is simply that already stated, and derived from the express words of Moses.   Jewish scholars
in this particular have manifestly not come as yet upon
an " epoch of exegesis," in which they have made the
discovery, that the " principal reason " for the establishment of the ordinance, lies in that " association of ideas
by which ferment and fermented things are regarded as
symbolical of moral corruption."

After this recitation of reasons, with additional thanks-
givings, they proceed to break and eat the cakes and
the bitter herbs.   The direction for the latter is as follows :

The master of the house then takes some bitter herbs, and dips
them into the חֲרוֹסֶת, *charoseth*, and says, Blessed art Thou, O
LORD our GOD, etc.

What, then, is this *charoseth* ? It is the compound
formed of " apples, almonds, etc., worked up to the con-
sistence of mortar," already mentioned, one important
ingredient of which was *chŏmetz*, or sour wine. In
proof, we transcribe the recipe for making it as given
by Buxtorf [*Lex.*, p. 831]. After stating that the compound was made in consistency like mortar, and eaten
with the bitter herbs in commemoration of the hard
service endured in Egypt, he says, *Sumebant dactylos
aut ficus arefactos, vel uvas passulas, et similia, et con-
culcabant ea*, ACETOQUE *perfundebant, et condimentis con-
diebant vel permiscebant instar cæmenti, et sic vespera
paschatis mensa apponebant.* Whatever may be imagined therefore with regard to the nature of the wine used,
there can be no doubt as to the fact that the *acetum*
mentioned was wine-vinegar, made from the *fermented*
juice of the grape, or some species of fruit, as vinegar
made from all kinds of grain was rigorously excluded.
Nor will it help matters to say that the acetous fermentation takes away the *curse* from the vinous ; for, if the
latter be a " process of corruption," a change " from
diet to dirt," the former is even more so, being a further
change, not in the line of elevation but of deterioration,
only one remove from the fermentation of putrefaction !
    We are now ready with the answer to the question,
" What was ' the fruit of the vine,' which our LORD
used in instituting the Sacrament ? " It was, we unhesitatingly assert, the ordinary fermented juice of the
grape, mixed with water, which, in accordance with the
uniform ecclesiastical usage of the Jews, was drunk at
the Passover. Nor does the peculiar phraseology furnish any argument, as is claimed, in favor of an unfermented liquor. Dr. Samson tells us, notwithstanding,
" The care with which all these writers [*Matt.* xxvi. 29 ;
Mark xiv. 25 ; and *Luke* xxii. 18] have used the expression ' fruit,' or product of the vine, must be supposed to have arisen from an emphasis put upon it by
CHRIST. The word ' gennema,' both in classic Greek
and also in the Greek Old and New Testament Scriptures, is applied without exception to the *natural* prod-

uct, as it is gathered and stored." Had Dr. Samson
with all his learning gone a little further, he might have
made the discovery that in using that form of expression our LORD merely quoted the language of the Passover Service, which in all its essential features was the
same then as now. That service, as any one upon ex·
amination can see, abounds in periphrastic expressions,
e.g., " Blessed art Thou, O Eternal, our GOD ! King of
the Universe, Creator of the radiance of the fire "—
בּוֹרֵא מְאוֹרֵי הָאֵשׁ;—" Blessed art Thou, O LORD, our GOD !
King of the Universe, Creator of the fruit of the earth "
בּוֹרֵא פְּרִי הָאֲדָמָה—. Precisely analogous with this, we find
the blessing as used over the cup at least *four times*—
" Blessed art Thou, O Eternal, our GOD ! King of the
Universe, Creator of the fruit of the vine."

בָּרוּךְ אַתָּה יְיָ אֱלֹהֵינוּ מֶלֶךְ
הָעוֹלָם בּוֹרֵא פְּרִי הַגָּפֶן.

If we must accept the theory that the fruit of the vine
was literally the " *natural* product as it is gathered and
stored," by parity of reasoning we must maintain that
the Passover bread was simply the grain as it is reaped
and brought in from the field. Such argumentation, I
need scarcely say, always defeats its own ends. The Pass·
over occurred six months after the time of grape harvest.
Wine then used must have been, from the nature of the
case, as the above extracts prove that it was, a FER·
MENTED LIQUOR. That grapes were kept and freshly
pressed, especially for use at that time, or that heathen
methods of preserving *must* unfermented were resorted
to, is a " fond imagination," having no ground of proof
whatever to rest upon, and standing in direct opposition
to abundant and incontrovertible evidence to the contrary.

And so matters stand in Jewish practice to-day, notwithstanding the assertion of Professor Stuart, and the
persistent endeavors on the part of later writers to prejudice the cause of truth in this matter. Lack of space
forbids much to be said here. And it is not needed.

The following extracts from Dr. Moore's able article [*Presbyterian Review*, January, 1882], who collected abundant evidence on this point, will suffice. The extracts were called out in answer to letters of inquiry made by him. Dr. F. Delitzsch, of Leipzig, a Hebrew scholar of world-wide reputation, and thoroughly versed in Jewish literature and customs, ancient and modern, writes :

What Moses Stuart affirms in the *Bib. Sac.*, 1843, p. 508, is incorrect. The wine of the Passover has at all times been fermented wine, which, according to the prevalent custom, was mixed with water.

Professor C. W. Palotta, of Vienna, an Israelite by birth, and competent in every respect to give testimony, writes :

To my knowledge the question of the lawfulness of fermented wine at Easter has never been started by any Jewish doctor. No strict Jew drinks any other than wine שֶׁל פֶּסַח (pesach) at the Passover ; but this simply means that the wine has been manufactured under Jewish supervision. Among the many thousands of bottles of Passover wine sold at Vienna every year, there has never been one of unfermented juice.

The Rev. D. Edward, of Breslau, another competent witness and scholar, writes :

In all my intercourse and negotiations with Jews for nearly forty years, and in all my acquaintance with their literature, I have never met an allusion to any such practice as the use of unfermented wine at their feasts or in the temple libations. The one rule they insist upon since the Captivity is, that the Jews beware of *nesekh* (נֶסֶךְ), wine prepared by Christians. Their wine must be gathered and prepared by Jews, and have a certificate as ceremonially clean. If there had been any rule about the use of unfermented wine, there would have been as much *pilpul* (rabbinic disputation) about it as would have filled volumes.

In addition to the above, the same writer sent the following declaration form the Rabbis of the Jewish Theological Seminary of Breslau, who are regarded as the most learned Jews in Germany :

Ungegohrener Wein (Must) wird nicht als Wein betrachtet, und würde der Pflicht Wein am Pesach-abende zu trinken nicht genügen— Unfermented wine (Must) is not regarded as wine, and would not suffice for the fulfilment of the duty to drink wine on the Passover eve.

The Rev. J. H. Bruehl, Superintendent of the Jewish Operative Institution, London, writes :

So far as can be seen from the Talmud, the Jews of our SAVIOUR's time had no hesitation whatever about fermented wine at the Passover. Not *vinous*, but *farinaceous* fermentation was prohibited. I do not know of any unfermented real wine. In countries which do not produce wine the stricter Jews, especially those of the poorer classes, use both for the Sabbath and the Passover raisin- wine.

To these testimonies from abroad may be added the following from two of the best known Israelites and scholars in the United States—Dr. Isaac M. Wise, of Cincinnati, editor of the *American Israelite and Deborah*, and Dr. G. Gottheil, Rabbi of Emmanuel Temple, New York. The former states :

All Jews at all times have used at the Passover, not only wine and cider, but also vinegar made of wine or of *fruit*. In all Jewish ceremonies, as marriages, circumcisions, the beginning and close of the Sabbath, the feast of Passover, wine—fermented wine and not *must*—has been, as it is still, in use.

Dr. Gottheil writes :

It is proper to use *fermented* wine at the Passover. That is the rule. Unfermented is permitted in case the former cannot be obtained, or is forbidden from sanitary reasons. So it is with mead, raisin wine, and spiced wine. Where these are not obtainable, any other beverage which takes the place of wine in the customs of the country may be used. These are concessions made to the force of circumstances. *The law treats invariably of wine in the ordinary sense of the word;* and that it is supposed to possess the intoxicating property is clear from the precept that the celebrants of the Passover are forbidden to drink of the wine between the prescribed cups at certain portions of the ritual, lest their minds should get clouded and thereby unfit to perform the ceremonies and recite the prayers with proper devotion. . . . Paschal wine is fermented grape juice which has been carefully kept from contact with leaven. I was reared in strictly orthodox surroundings, and have had, besides, ample opportunities of observing the customs

of my brethren in many lands ; yet, I never heard it so much as
questioned that fermented wines are lawful for use, and I am quite
at a loss to account for the positive assertions to the contrary by
M. Noah and the late Professor M. Stuart. It was by Christians,
and not by Jews, that this discussion was started. The Rabbis did
not fear that the use of the cup under religious sanction would
turn the faithful into drunkards, and experience has proved that
they were not mistaken.

With this has been the concurrent opinion and practice of the Church under the New Dispensation from
the beginning; although Dr. Samson, with his usual
acumen in perverting the truth, asserts [p. 171]: "The
early Christian interpreters, studying CHRIST's meaning
in the land where He spoke, and while the Greek of His
day was still its language, mention, as if no one then
thought otherwise, that JESUS used this expression (fruit
of the vine) because the consecrated cup at the Supper
contained the fresh juice of the grape, as distinct from
the wine, its artificial product." We scarcely know how
to understand a man who can make such an assertion,
or restrain indignation at such an unblushing perversion
of truth. His whole argument from the testimony of the
early Church, in fact, furnishes a sad comment upon
human perversity, in making the worse appear the better
reason in order to bolster up a favorite theory at any
cost.

That the wine used by the Corinthian Church was intoxicating is manifest. So clear a case indeed is it, that
Dr. Lees makes every effort to show that μεϑύω in this
place does not mean to be intoxicated, but to be *gorged*.
He translates thus, "καὶ ὃς μὲν πεινᾷ, ὃς δὲ μεϑύει—and
one indeed is hungry, but another is overfed = gorged."
This explanation he also tells us " has been adopted by
the whole body of expositors, ancient and modern."
Query, What could our translators of 1611 have been
about if such is the case? And we find that the revisers
of 1881, notwithstanding their well-known *cacoëthes
mutandi*, have repeated the same blunder, for once at
least (for the sake of variety perhaps) using the very
same words, " one is hungry, and another is drunken."
Yea, all the leading translators, both ancient and modern,

have done the same thing. The Vulgate renders the word by *ebrius, drunken*. The Peshito Syriac by ܪܘܐ =as already seen in its root form to the Hebrew רָוָה, the meaning of which, according to Gesenius, is "*to drink to the full, to be sated with drink, drenched*, as שָׂבַע, to be sated with food." The Coptic in like manner renders by the word ⲡⲉⲧⲑⲓⲕ̅ⲓ, *petthikhi*, which is translated uniformly in Wilkin's version by *ebrius*. Wycliffe translates, "And sothely anothir is hungrie, another foresoth is drunkyn;" Tyndale, "And one is hongrye, and another is dronken;" Cranmer, "And one is hongry, and another is droncken;" The Geneva version precisely the same; the Rheims version, "And one certes is an hungred, and an other is drunke;" Beza, "*Hic quidem esurit, ille vero ebrius est;*" Luther, "Und einer ist hungrig, der andere ist trunken." The lexicographers also have some claim to be heard, and their testimony is clear and consentient. "Μεθύω, to be drunken with wine, to be drenched, or soaked with, steeped in any liquid. II. Metaph. to be drunken or intoxicated with passion, pride, etc. Like Lat. inebriari." [*Liddell & Scott.*] In the Septuagint, "μεθύω, *ebrius sum, irriguus sum*. Cognate, μεθύσκω, *inebrio, inebrior*, =רָוָה." *Schleusner*. In the New Testament, "μεθύω, to be drunk, to get drunk, to carouse." *Robinson*. To adduce all this evidence on this point, may appear to some to be needless—*actum agere;* but we desire to show how utterly these temperance writers set all evidence and truth at defiance. What the real testimony of the "whole body of (reliable) expositors, ancient and modern" is, can easily be imagined.

That it was wine in its ordinary sense also which S. Paul advised Timothy to drink a little of for his stomach's sake, is equally certain. Had the Apostle desired to have him use unfermented grape juice, why did he not take the word which would have expressed his desire, without any possibility of misunderstanding? Why use a word which for over a thousand years had described uniformly a fermented liquor? After suggesting that the passage may be spurious, Dr. Lees says, "Nothing is plainer about this advice than that it was meant for Timothy alone and for reasons personal to him. . . . He " would use a little wine," and as seldom as need be, not for gratification, but for medicinal service." Indeed ! but no matter *how little at a time*, or *how infrequent the use*, the " cursed drink " is here conceded to have been recommended by an apostle, for the use of his disciple and fellow-laborer in the Gospel, as a *means of good*—of health and strength !

The Materia Medica of that day has also some important testimony to give on this point. Indeed the general sentiment of antiquity with regard to the relative values and uses of oinos and gleukos, is too well known to be disputed. By the Jews, not only was wine valued according to its age ("a new friend is as new wine : when it is old thou shalt drink it with pleasure" [*Ecclus.* ix. 10 ; *S. Luke* v. 39]), but in its unfermented state its use was supposed to aggravate, if not to cause the *affectio cardiaca*. Thus, Buxtorf, quoting the *Talmud, Gittin. cap.* 7, translates in answer to the question, Quid est cardiacus ? "Is quem mordet sive pungit vinum novum torcularis." Doubtless Dr. Samson had come across this fact, hence his assertion that gleukos, like new cider, is " an aperient used internally." By the Greeks also the same views were entertained, as we learn from Hippocrates and others. The statements of Pliny, which bear on both sides of the question, show that corresponding views were held likewise by the Romans. In Lib. xxiii., chap. 18, after speaking of the different kinds and qualities of *must*, he states, as a general rule, it may be said that it is useless to the stomach—*Mustum omne stomacho inutile.* Shortly after he states also that it causes pains in the head, and is useless for throat troubles— *Capitis dolores facit, et gutturi inutile.* In *chap.* 22 he proceeds to speak of the different uses of wines with the attendant benefits and evils. By wine, he says, the natural powers, the blood and the complexion are nourished—*Vino aluntur vires, sanguis, colosque hominum ;* by moderate use the nerves are benefited, but taken in large quantities they are injured ; in like manner also the eyes—*Vino modico nervi juvantur, copiosiore læduntur ; sic et oculi ;* the stomach also is reinvigorated, appetite for food is incited, sadness and care are blunted, and sleep is secured—*Stomachus recreatur, appetentia ciborum invitatur : tristitia et cura hebetatur ; somnus conciliatur.*

Passing then to caps. 24 and 25, he treats of the uses of wines in sickness, and in the opening of the latter chapter he asserts that for this *affectio cardiaca*, or trouble in and about the stomach, wine is the sovereign remedy—*Cardiacorum morbo unicam spem in vino esse certum est.* A few lines further on he also says that for weakness of the stomach, and for indigestion, wine should be given—*Si dissolutio sit stomachi, dandum ; et si cibus non descendat.* To this custom of prescribing wine for cardiac trouble Seneca alludes in his *Epis.* xv. — *Bibere et sudare, vita cardiaci est* — frequent draughts being given to induce perspiration ; and by Juvenal, also, [*Sat.* v. 32] *Cardiaco cyathum numquam mixturus amico.* Celsus, iii. 19, likewise gives corresponding testimony, and in cases of weakness of the stomach and indigestion, he advises that when the stomach refuses to retain food to drink a cup of wine, and after the lapse of an hour a second cup—*Si ne id quidem manserit, sorbera vini cyathum, interpositaque hora, sumere alterum.* With these facts before us, and the no less important fact of the apostle's undoubted knowledge with regard to these generally recognised medicinal uses of wine, to suppose him to have meant that Timothy should drink for his stomach trouble a little unfermented grape juice, is sublimely ridiculous !

We find, moreover, an unassailable argument in the fact that the primitive Church uniformly used the mixed cup at the Holy Supper, as the Jews did at the Passover. In the middle of the second century, Justin Martyr, in his account of Christian worship at that time, says : " To each of those who are present, a portion of the Eucharistic bread, and wine, and water are given"—*τοῦ εὐχαριστηθέντος ἄρτου, καὶ οἴνου, καὶ ὕδατος*

[*Apol.* ii. p. 162]. Irenæus, also, near the close of the second century, and Clement of Alexandria (not to mention others), bear corresponding testimony. Indeed, the tradition was universal in the early centuries that our LORD Himself had instituted the Sacrament in that manner. Cyprian [*Epis.* 73 *ad Cæcilium*] writes, *Admonitos nos scias, ut in calice offerendo Dominica traditio servetur, neque aliud fiat a nobis, quam quod pro nobis Dominus prior fecerit—ut calix, qui in commemorationem ejus offertur, mixtus vino offeratur.* To this, were it necessary, a mountain of evidence might be added from the early liturgies, canons of provincial councils, etc.

And there is absolutely nothing which, rightly considered, militates against all this. During the period of the six accepted General Councils, A. D. 325, to A.D. 680, there is no proof whatever that the question of fermented *vs.* unfermented wine was ever dreamt of, as had been equally the case in the previous centuries. In none of the synodal Epistles or Canons of those Councils, is the subject alluded to. That there could have been such absolute silence as there is, supposing the question to have been an open one, is impossible. In Can. XXIV. of the Third Council of Carthage, bearing upon the Eucharistic elements, there is a reference to the traditional custom of the mixed chalice—*Ut in sacramentis corporis et sanguinis Domini nihil amplius offeratur, quam ipse Dominus traditit, hoc est panis et vinum aqua mixtum.* But whence came this tradition? And why the universal prevalence of this custom, if unfermented Eucharistic wine was in existence? Some of the Fathers, it is true, give several fanciful reasons therefor, but the real reason obviously rests upon the preceding Jewish custom at the Paschal feast. And why the mixed cup was then used has already been shown. A Jewish family-head would have found diluted grape juice unfermented, rather a weak material with which " to cheer up his wife and children " at that annual festival !

In *case of necessity*, it has, in some instances, been regarded as lawful to use the fresh juice of the grape. On the Festival of the Transfiguration, also, it was customary in some places, from a somewhat fanciful reason, to press out the grape-juice into the chalice, and use it in the Sacrament. To this use of fresh grape-juice, in *case of necessity*, we find a reference in a note on page 285 of the *Temperance Bible Commentary*, where the attempt is made to show that Thomas Aquinas, as a representative of the Roman Church, sanctioned the use of *must* in the Eucharist. In a quotation of the answer to the question, " Whether wine of the vine is a proper material for use in the Sacrament ? " we read, *Mustum autem jam habet speciem vini*—grape juice has the specific nature of wine ; and he decides [Aquinas], *Ideo de musto potest confici hoc sacramentum*—therefore this sacrament can be kept with grape juice." But why were the intervening words omitted, in which sweetness or pleasant flavor is cited as proving it to be no longer crude *must—Nam ejus dulcedo attestatur digestioni, quæ est completio a naturali calore*. It would not have answered the author's purpose in the text to which this note is appended, to have the legitimate inference drawn, that *mustum* here, like *gleukos* in Acts ii. 13, was new wine, freshly fermented. That gleukos, in Hellenistic Greek has such meaning is proved from that passage. Hence, Robinson [*Lex. New Testament,*] renders the word, " In New Testament *sweet wine* fermented and intoxicating [*Acts* ii. 13 "]. That mustum in ecclesiastical Latin has also occasionally the same meaning, is shown in this passage omitted in the quotation, by the words " *a naturali calore,*" which can refer only to the result of fermentation. Scudamore likewise [p. 771] gives the same meaning to the word. " In the *Manipulus Curatorum* " he says, " we are also told that the ' Celebration may be in *mustum,*' by which was understood (probably) the fermented juice before it was refined." Similarly, Jacobus a Viatrico, a century before: " The Sacrament may be made of *mustum,* though it be sweet, for it is wine ; but it cannot be made of sour juice of the grape, because it is not yet wine."

It will be a hopeless task for any one to cite the
authority of Aquinas in support of the unfermented-wine
theory. His whole argument shows that under ordinary
circumstances grape wine—*vinum vitis*—is the proper,
and the only proper material to be mixed in the eucharistic chalice. After making several general statements
with regard to wine, he asserts that whole grapes pressed
are not to be used, and that fresh *must* is equally forbidden because of its impurity. *Non tamen debent uvæ in-*
tegræ huic Sacramento misceri, quia jam esset ibi ali-
quid præter vinum. Prohibetur etiam ne mustum statim
expressum de uva in calice offeratur, quia hoc est in-
decens, propter impuritatem musti. He then makes
the statement that in case of necessity freshly pressed
must may be used, and cites in support a somewhat
doubtful decree of Pope Julius I.: *Potest tamen in ne-*
cessitate fieri : dicitur enim eodem Julio Papa [loc. cit.
in Arg.] " *Si necesse fuerit, botrus in calice comprima-*
tur" [*Quæst. lxxiv., Art.* v., Ed. Neapoli, 1766]. Whatever views and practices may have obtained in the earlier
and middle centuries, the more modern legislation of the
Roman Church is far more stringent. In the list of
things which vitiate wholly or in part the matter of the
Eucharist, it is stated that the Sacrament cannot be
celebrated with wine that has become vinegar, or corrupted, or that was not made from ripe grapes. *Si*
vinum sit factum penitus acetum, vel penitus putridum,
vel de uvis acerbis, seu non maturis expressum, etc. Non
conficitur Sacramentum. Also, if the Celebration is
with wine that has begun to sour, or be corrupted, or
with *must freshly pressed*, or not mixed with water, the
Sacrament is administered, but the consecrator is guilty
of a grave sin—*Si vinum cæperit acescere, vel cor-*
rumpi, . . . *vel mustum de uvis tunc expressum vel*
non fuerit admixta aqua, . . . *conficitur Sacra-*
mentum, sed conficiens graviter peccat [*De Defect.,*
tit. v., § 1, 2, *Missale Romanum*, Ed. Rome, 1826].

That there were bodies of Christians in the early
centuries who refused to use wine in the Sacrament is,
of course, well known. As early as the middle of the

second century, Tatian and his followers used water instead of wine. Manichean in principle, they rejected flesh food and marriage, equally with wine, as inventions of the devil. And in this fact there is negative, but important evidence that at that time the Eucharist was not celebrated with unfermented wine. Had such an article been in existence, there was no good reason why those Encratites or Aquiarii, as they were called, should not have used it, inasmuch as the reason given by them for rejecting wine in the Sacrament was its intoxicating properties—*temperantiæ prætextu vinum refugiebant.* They did not, however, reject grapes, hence we find S. Augustine exclaiming with reference to the same views and practices in his day, " What perverseness is this, to feel no scruple as to grapes, and yet to call wine the gall of the prince of darkness ! . . . They regard it as a sacrilege to touch wine, as if it were a creature of the evil one, and, therefore, an impure thing, although they willingly eat the fruit of the vine " [*De Hæres.*, viii. 51].

These and similar notions, however, were held only by those who, for other reasons, were regarded as heretics, and cut off from the communion of the Church. In short, it was to prevent the introduction of such views and practices within the Church itself, that the 51 and the 53 of the Apostolic Canons, so called, were framed. " If any Bishop, Presbyter, or Deacon, or any at all of the Sacerdotal List, shall abstain from marriage, or flesh, or wine (οἴνου), not for discipline, but because he abhors them ; forgetting that all things are very good ; let him amend, or be deposed and cast out of the Church. Likewise a layman" [*Can.* 51]. " If any Bishop, Presbyter, or Deacon will not partake of flesh and wine on festival days, because he abhors them, and not on account of discipline, let him be deposed as a man who has seared his own conscience, and who is a cause of offence to many " [*Can.* 53].

In closing this discussion, which has extended far beyond our original intention, we wish to say, that with the questions of partial or total abstinence from fermented liquors as a rule of daily life, and of the duty of self-denial under certain circumstances, for weak brethren's sake, our argument has had no connection. They are highly important questions in themselves, and are worthy of frequent and serious consideration. That intemperance abounds in high places and in low, with the debasement and woe thereby occasioned, we are painfully aware ; and we fully realise the duty of placing ourselves second to none in the earnest desire and endeavor, that all men should live soberly, righteously, and godly in this present world. But we deprecate all attempts at being wise above what is written, and of professing to adopt a standard of moral conformity loftier than that observed by Him whose disciples we claim to be. His omniscient eye must have taken in all possible contingencies in each age and generation, until his final advent in judgment; and to suppose that He neglected any necessary safeguard, either in His sacramental appointments, or in the example of His daily life, is to make an arrogant and impious reflection upon His boundless wisdom, mercy, and beneficence. Certainly, all attempts to press the oracles of revealed truth into the support of theories utterly antagonistic to truth can never receive His sanction or blessing. A temporary triumph for some particular notion or hobby may be obtained, but the ultimate and permanent result can be only disaster.

EDWARD H. JEWETT.

APPENDIX C.

[LETTERS RECEIVED AFTER ELECTROTYPING OF CORRESPONDENCE.]

[1]

138 West 6th Street, Oswego, July 27, 1888.

REV. HOWARD CROSBY, D.D.

DEAR BROTHER :—So far as I have been able to get the time, I have examined the pamphlet on "the two wines" with great satisfaction, and entirely approve of the positions taken therein, so far as I have been able to read it.

I have no patience with the attempt made by some of the ministers of our own Church to palm off on the Communion table some vile composition, which is not fit to be drunk *anywhere;* certainly not to commemorate the blood of our Lord Jesus Christ.

Not long ago I was called on to administer the Sacrament in a Congregational church, where the "stuff" designed to represent wine was so abominable I could hardly swallow it.

I do wish that those who profess and call themselves *Christians* would be controlled in this matter, not by their own fanatical *notions,* but by the plain teachings of our Saviour, as well as by the example of the early Church.

Yours fraternally,   W. B. PARMELEE.

[2]

Grace Church Rectory, Waterville, N. Y., July 27, 1888.

REVEREND AND DEAR SIR :—I received from you, some time ago, a copy of Dr. Jewett's pamphlet, with a request for my "opinion as to its merits on the question of two wines." It seems to me so show conclusively that the question is not concerning "two wines," but as to whether we should use wine or something else in the celebration of the Eucharist. Our Lord chose and appointed the symbols to be used, and it is not for us either to question his wisdom or to break his commandment, even though we think it to be "one of the least." I think it was Coleridge who said, "It is the man that makes the motives, not the motives the man;" and it is evident enough, in the case of these perverse disputers about wine, that it is the conclusion that makes the reasons, not the reasons the conclusion. The miscalled "temperance" agitation is a notable instance of the way in which men seek to substitute the being righteous overmuch in one point for the keeping of the whole Law.

Respectfully yours,   J. W. HYDE.

[3]

60 King Street, New York, July 31, 1888.

MY DEAR DOCTOR :—Several years ago I had occasion to study the "two-wine" question, for a debate. At that time I examined every word, in the Hebrew and in the Greek, pertaining to the subject; my opponent, who had the "two-wine" side, was routed, "horse, foot, and dragoons," and he admitted to me, at the close of the debate, that he had no case. The reading of the pamphlet of Dr. Jewett only serves to confirm and strengthen the opinion formed at that time.

Cordially,   A. W. HALSEY.

[4]

Yonkers, July 23, 1888.

MY DEAR DR. CROSBY :—I write to place upon paper what I said to you by word of mouth—that I quite agree with you that there is no evidence (at least, I know of none) of a non-intoxicating wine in the S. S. The wine used by our Lord was the same substance against whose abuse the Bible contains so many warnings.

Yours cordially,   HENRY M. BAIRD.

[5]

Mount Vernon, N. Y., July 25, 1888.

DEAR SIR:—Some time since I received a pamphlet entitled "Communion Wine," by Edward Jewett, S.T.D., also a circular over your signature, asking for such a criticism of the views taken by the author as my judgment approved. I have also carefully examined the literature of the other side of the question. In such an array of opposing scholarship I am bewildered. It is astonishing that these old Greek and Hebrew roots are so prolific. But supposing God's book does speak in tolerating terms of these ancient customs of wine drinking. So it does of polygamy and slavery, which the light of a better civilization has steadily driven back into outer darkness. I find it difficult to make myself believe that Christ turned good water into intoxicating wine, and our scholarly oracles severally hear the old languages say that he did and he didn't. But I am inclined to the faith that if in the twilight of the Christian morning he did so, were he to come again to a modern wedding, his miracle of holy expediency would be to turn the wine into water.

Very respectfully and truly,   I. SIMMONS,

Pastor of the M. E. Church, Mount Vernon, N. Y.

www.ingramcontent.com/pod-product-compliance
Lightning Source LLC
Chambersburg PA
CBHW030846270326
41928CB00007B/1238